SMALL MEDIUM AND LARGE SCALE CHEMICAL INDUSTRIES

The unique book on Chemicals & Allied manufacturing industries containing the formulations and manufacturing processes of 27 lucrative chemicals & allied industries alongwith the addresses of plant, machinery and raw material suppliers with the valuable addresses of All India Trade & Industry Organisation and Financial Institutions in India for the aggrassive entrepreneurs & industrialists.

By:
EIRI Technocrats
&
Sudhir Gupta
Recipient of Udyog Rattan Award

PUBLICATION DIVISION
ENGINEERS INDIA RESEARCH INSTITUTE
4449, Nai Sarak, Main Road, New Delhi - 110 006 (INDIA)
Phones : 291 8117, 291 6431, 292 0361 ◆ Fax : 91-11-291 6431

Printed & Published by

ENGINEERS INDIA RESEARCH INSTITUTE

Regd. Office : 4449, Nai Sarak, Main Road, New Delhi - 110 006 (INDIA)
Phones : 291 8117, 291 6431, 292 0361 ✱ Fax : 91-11-291 6431

Distributed by

SMALL INDUSTRY RESEARCH INSTITUTE

New Delhi (INDIA)

ISBN : 81-86732-06-3

Printed in New Delhi (India)

Rs. 375

Printed & Published by **Sudhir Gupta** for **'Engineers India Research Institute** and Laser Type Set by Amarjeet Singh at Engineers India Research Institute, and Printed at 'Kumar Offset Press', 251/8, Padam Nagar, New Delhi - 110 007

PREFACE

The development of chemical industry in the last couple of decades has added a new dimension to the industrial world. Though most of the industrially significant chemicals are being manufactured in the country to-day, yet there exists a gap between demand and supply. The statistics of production capital in chemical industries employment, gross output etc., exhibit an ever increasing trend and its allocation in our plans has enhanced multifold.

However, apart from the big chemical units, the small scale chemical industries play a vital role in the country's economy. Moreover, traditional consumer goods no longer catch the market.

This book deals with the chemical structure/formula of the product, raw materials used with quantities required, for the production, used of the product, manufacturing process details, with flow diagrams, type of equipment required for setting up the small unit etc.

The book deals with preparation of agriculture chemicals, textile ausiliaries & chemicals, dye & intermediates, chemicals used in fire works, photographic chemicals, electroplating chemicals, paints, pigments, varnishes, dries, etc., pharmaceutical chemicals, rubber chemicals, greases & lubricants, in organic adhesives, cosmetics and perfumes, lab chemicals & reagents, etc.

For the preparation of chemically pure substances, their standardisation, preparation of extra chemicals, analytical reagents, dressing materials for surgical use, antiseptics, certain drugs, etc., involve such processing as repeated crystallization to attain high rate of purity, distillation or repeated washing to remove impurities, etc., it will be observed that a good number of industries can be started on small scale economically.

The book concluded with adresses of machineries manufacturers National and State level institutions providing industrial finance etc.

Director
ENGINEERS INDIA RESEARCH INSTITUTE
Nai Sarak, New Delhi.

CONTENTS

S.No.	Particulars	Pages
1.	Acetylene Gas Oxygen Gas (Integrated Unit)	1
2.	Activated Carbon From Coconut Shell	13
3.	Automobile Polish	20
4.	Bleaching Powder (Stable)	28
5.	Barium Carbonate	34
6.	Calcium Carbonate (Precipitated & Activated)	40
7.	Chemicals From Prawn Fish Head	46
8.	Detergent Cake & Powder	51
9.	Dry Distemper	58
10.	Dead Burnt Dolomite	66
11.	Gas Filling of L.P.G. Cylinder	71
12.	Hydorchloric Acid (HCL)	77
13.	Hydrogenation of Non-Edible Oils	82
14.	H-Acid	87
15.	Hydrogen Gas Plant	92
16.	Indian Made Foreign Liquor (IMFL)	94
17.	Integrated Complex of Esters and Allied Products	105
18.	Mini Sugar Plant	116
19.	Menthol Crystals From Menthol Oil	122
20.	Organic Manure	128
21.	Potassium Iodate	135
22.	PVC Stabilizers	143
23.	Phenyl (Black & White)	148
24.	Sodium Meta Silicate	153
25.	Silicone Emulsion	159
26.	Textile Auxilliaries	164
27.	Unsaturated Polyster Resin	173
28.	Manufacturers and Suppliers of Plant & Machinery	179
29.	Financal Institutions in India	184
30.	All India Trade & Industry Organisation	185

Chapter-1

ACETYLENE GAS AND OXYGEN GAS (INTEGRATED UNIT)

INTRODUCTION

A: Acetylene:

Acetylene is a colourless inflammable gas obtained by the action of water on calcium carbide:

$$CaC_2+2H_2O \longrightarrow C_2H_2+Ca(OH)_2+30.4kg.\text{-}cal.$$

When pure, it has a slightly ethereal odour, but when produced from commercial calcium carbide, it has a distinct unpleasant odour due to the presence of traces of phosphene, etc. In small quantities the gas is non-poisonous, but when present in concentrations of more than 40 per cent., it may produce asphyxiation. Acetylene dissolves in an equal volume of water. It is more soluble in organic solvents, especially in acetone. At ordinary pressure and 15° acetone absorbs 25 times its volume of acetylene. At 12 atm., it takes up 300 volumes and at 15 atm. nearly 375 vol. This property is made use of for the storage of acetylene in the dissolved state.

Acetylene is an endothermic compound, its heat of formation being nearly 50kg.-cal. g. mol. Both the gas (tc, 370; Pc, 62 atm.) and the liquid (b.p.,83.6o) are highly explosive, particularly under pressure. The gas forms explosive mixtures with air. DIt burns with sufficient air, it gives a clear white light. Its molecular heat of combustion at standard pressure is 320 kg.-cal.g. mol. Its cal. val. is ca. 1500 B. Th. U./c.ft. compared with 500 in the case of coal gas. The large amount of heat thus evolved is made use of in the oxy-acetylene flame.

B. Oxygen Gas:

The great importance of the industrial gas, oxygen is due to the usefulness of the acetylene torch for steel welding and steel cutting, and for the welding of other metals, to lesser degree to the oxyhydrogen flame. Oxygen gas in the breathing apparatus for a visitors at high altitudes and for oxygentents in hospitals is a high altitudes and for oxygentents in hospitals is a more recent development. An extension of of the use of oxygen lies in the increased intensity and speed of reactions brought about by oxygen enriched air instead of ordinary air; the reduction of the cycle time so achieved in chemical or metallurgical process permits a greater yield per volume of equipment, and brings about lower costs. Oxygen as a raw material for synthesizing chemical compounds is in daily use (ethylene oxide, sodium peroxide). Liquid oxygen mixed with carbon black may yet become an important and cheap explosive.

PROPERTIES

A. Acetylene

Colorless, flammable gas, odourless when pure, but ordinarily has a garlic-like odour because of impurities.

Mol. wt.	26.04	F.P.	-81.8°C
Sp. gr.	0.613(-80oC) Liquid	B.P	-83.6°C

One pound of acetylene is equivalent to 14.5 cu ft. Soluble in acetone (2500 cc gas per 100 g, 30000 cc gas per 100 g at 12 atm), alcohol (600 cc per 100 g), water (100 cc per 100 g), and liquid ammonia at room temperature.

Flash point		Gas
Ignition temperature		635°F
Vapor density (air = 1)		0.91
Explosive limits (% by volume in air)	Lower	2.3
	Upper	80

Grades. Technical (97 to 99 per cent).

B. Oxygen

Oxygen is a diatomic gas at ordinary temperatures. It condenses to a pale blue liquid at -182.97o which rapid evaporation or by cooling in liquid hydrogen forms a bluish white solid, m.p. - 218.8oC. Oxygen is moderately soluble in water (30.8 ml gas/litre of water at 25oC and at atmosphere. Many metals particularly silver and palladium physically absorb large volumes of oxygen, a property which is taken advantages of in catalytic reactions.

Molecular oxygen dissociates into atomic oxygen at high temperatures the dissociation being complete at 5000oC. Atomic oxygen is unstable and highly reactive. It polymerizes to ozone.

Oxygen combines directly with practically all chemical elements except insert gases. Most elements form oxides when heated in an atmosphere containing oxygen, many of them, eg. iron, lead chromium sulphur and Nitrogen, form more than oxide. Some metals, eg.sodium and potassium ignite spontaneously in oxygen and alkaline earth metals ignite easily. Metals like iron copper oxidise slowly at ordinary temperatures but rapidly when heated. sulphur burns in oxygen with a lavender blue flame forming sulfur dioxide. Phosphorous burns in oxygen forming a white could of phosphorous pentoxide.

PHYSICAL PROPERTIES OF OXYGEN

PROPERTY	VALUE
Triple point temperature, K	54.359 ± 0.002
Pressure, Pa (mm Hg)	146.4 (1.098)
Density, g/L (lb/ft3)	
gas	0.0108 (0.000674)
liquid	1306.5 (81.56)
solid	1300 (81.2)
Boiling point	
temperature, K	90.188
pressure, kPa (psi)	101.325 (14.696)
density, g/L(lb/ft3)	
gas	4.470 (0.27886)
liquid	1141.1 (71.212)
Critical point	
Temperature, K	154.581
pressure, MPa (atm)	5.043 (50.14 atm)
density, g/L (lb/ft3)	436.1 (26.63)
Gas, at 101.3 kPa (1 atm)	
Density, g/L (lb/ft3)	
at 0oC	1.42908 (0.0892121)
at 21oC	1.327 (0.08281)
heat capacity, J/(mol.K) Btu/mol.oF))	
Cp, at 25oC	29.40 (0.1549)
Cp/Cv, at 26oC	1.396
dielectric constant at 20oC	1.0004947
n°D 1.0002639	
viscosity at 25oC, μPa.s (lb/ft.s)	20.639 (13.869 x 10-6)
thermal conductivity at 0oC, mW/(m.K) (Btu/(h.ft.oF))	2.448 (14.2 x 10-3)
sound velocity at 0oC, m/s (ft/s)	317.3 (1041)
Liquid	
heat capacity, salt liq, J/(mol.K) (Btu/(mol.oF))	54.317 (2.862 x 10-2)
heat of vaporization, J/mol (Btu/(mol))	6820 (6.468)
viscosity, μPa.s (lb/(ft.s))	189.4 (127.3 x 10-6)
thermal conductivity, m@/(m.W) (Btu/h.ft.oF)	149.87 (86.65 x 10-3)
sound velocity at 87 K, m/s (ft/s)	904.6 (2968)
surface tension at 87 K, N/m (lbf/ft)	13.85 x 10-7(9.490 x 10-4

PROPERTY	VALUE
Volume ratio, gas at 21°C to liq at bp	859.9
Solid	
heat of sublimation, J/(g.mol) (Btu/mol)	8204.1 (7.7838)
heat capacity, J/g.mol.K) Btu/(mol.oF))	46.40 (2.4458 x 10-2)
heat of fusion, J/(g.mol) (Btu/mol)	444.5 (0.4217)
Solubility, mL O_2 at STP per mL H_2O	
0°C	0.0489
5°C	0.0429
10°C	0.0380
15°C	0.0342
20°C	0.0310
25°C	0.0283
30°C	0.0261
40°C	0.0231
50°C	0.0209
60°C	0.0195
70°C	0.0183
80°C	0.0176
90°C	0.0172
100°C	0.0170

PHYSICAL PROPERTIES

Oxygen is colorless, odorless, and tasteless. When cooled to 90.188 K it becomes a pale-blue liquid, slightly more dense than water. On further cooling, it becomes as blue solid. The blue color is probably due to a small equilibrium concentration of associated oxygen molecules since the liquid becomes colorless when passed through a bed of carefully activated silica gel, presumably because the associated molecules are removed. The color returns after some hours of standing. Oxygen is moderately sobluble in water.

CHEMICAL PROPERTIES

Oxygen reacts with all other elements except the light rare gases helium, neon, and argon. The reactants usually must be activated by heat before the reaction proceeds, and if the final union releases more than enough energy to activate subsequent portions of both reactants, the overall process may be self-sustaining. The process is known as combustion when light and heat are evolved. For certain elements process is known as combustion when light and heat are evolved. For certain elements such as the alkali metals rubidium and cesium, activation energy provided by the heat of room temperature is sufficient, and reaction becomes spontaneous upon contact. Other metals such as finely powdered iron and nickel may be pyrophoric by careful preparation and reduction of surface oxides. They then ignite spontaneously upon contact with air and continue to react with the evolution of light and heat.

Most materials must be heated to some particular temperature (ignition temperature) to initiate combustion. However, in the presence of moisture, combination with oxygen frequently occurs slowly even at ordinary temperatures. The most important examples of this phenomenon are found in the respiration of organisms, the rusting and corrosion of metals, decay of wood, or hardening of linseed oil. On the other hand extreme temperatures can be reached, for example, by burning acetylene with oxygen. The process of cutting iron has been reached by heating with the torch

When fuels such as petroleum oils, natural gas, or coal burn with an excess of oxygen (air or O2), the products are heat, carbon dioxide, and water plus the residues of air (nitrogen, oxygen, etc). However, if the amount of oxygen is limited, carbon monoxide and hydrogen are formed. This reaction produces the gas mixture that reduces iron ore to pig iron in a blast furnace. It provides a gas mixture from which methanol may be synthesized, or which may be further processed to provide hydrogen for ammonia synthesis. At lower temperatures, frequently in the presence of catalysts, oxygen reacts with organic chemicals to give oxygenated hydrocarbons.

USES AND APPLICATIONS

A. Acetylene Gas

Acetylene is also the starting material for the production of the synthetic rubber, known as chloroprene or neoprene, and vinyl resins and plastic. When heated acetylene is polymerized to benzene, and under the influence of heat and pressure it yields a complicated mixture of tars, oils and resins.

The first commercial use to which acetylene was put as an illuminant. Though superseded to a large extent by electricity, acetylene is still widely used as an illuminant for marine and aeronautical purposes in buoys, light-houses, signaling lamps, etc. Large cylinders holding, in some cases, 500 c.ft. of dissolved acetylene and provided with automatic control and lighting devices are fitted to buoys.

At present the most important use of acetylene is in the welding and cutting industry. Nearly all metals can be welded by the oxy-acetylene flame which reaches a temperature of nearly 35000o. The equipment consists of oxygen and acetylene cylinders, fitted with pressure reducing valves and regulators and a welding blowpipe. Blowpipes are available, suitable for welding the thinnest gauge of mild steel and also for welding steel up to I" in thickness. Blowpipes have also been especially designed for the welding of lead sheet used in the construction of storage batteries. According to the type of blowpipe and the size of nozzle or welding tip, gas consumption may vary between 0.2 and 90 c.ft. per hour. Equal quantities of oxygen and acetylene are usually consumed during normal Welding. But in special cases, it is possible to use a slight excess of acetylene. It is widely used for the welding of non-ferrous metals, particularly aluminium in aircraft and automobile industries, and for welding copper in chemical industry.

When welding non-ferrous metals, it is usually necessary to employ a flux, the composition of which depends upon the nature of the material being welded. Oxy-acetylene welding finds its greatest scope in light engineering industry, and in the resurfacing of worn parts.

Acetylene is also used very extensively as a fuel gas for the oxygen cutting process. Its high calorific value, ready portability and ease of manipulation, particularly in the dissolved state, make it superior to most other fuel gases. It is also employed in blowpipes called pistols to melt wires used in metal-spraying.

OXYGEN:

Oxygen is used in industry for fusion, welding of metals, metal cutting and other purposes, Oxyacetylene (oxygen acetylene) flame is used for welding steel. As a cutting medium, oxygen is used for scrap cutting and shaping, of steel plates, slabs upto several feet thick can be out into desired sized and shapes, under water cutting of plates can be effected by using an oxyhdrogen flame shrouded by compressed air.

Cleaning of steel structure by oxyacetylene flame removes rust and scale. A clean surface ready is obtained. Oxygen is used also for flame plating, a mixture of oxygen, acetylene and the coating powder (i.e.tungsten dioxide) is explosed in a gun, the force of explosion causing the powder to adhere to the metal surface.

Chemicals

Oxygen is used for partial oxidation of synthesis gas and production of synthesis gas, acetylene, and propylene. It is employed also for coal gasification by lurgi or their process for producing synthesis gas.

Explosives

Oxygen is used in the production of liquid oxygen explosive (L.O.X.) employed in blasting operations.L.O.X. is prepared by impregnating a cellulose base cartridge consisting of combustible ingredients enclosed in a paper cover, with liquid oxygen.

PROCESS OF MANUFACTURE OF ACETYLENE

Reaction

$$CaC_2 + 2H_2O \xrightarrow[93\text{-}95\%]{} CH - CH + Ca(OH)_2$$

RAW MATERIAL REQUIREMENTS

BASIS	1 M^3	ACETYLENE
CALCIUM CARBIDE		3.498 KGS.
WATER		28.885 KGS.

PROCESS DESCRIPTION

There are two standard methods for the production of acetylene from calcium carbide and water.

a) The wet process.
b) The dry process.

Wet Process

The wet process consists of adding the carbide to a relatively large quantity of water releasing acetylene gas while the calcium hydrate residue is discharged in the form of a lime slurry containing approximately 90% water.

Dry Process

In order to eliminate the waste of calcium hydrate the dry process was originated where a limited amount of water (1to 1 by weight) is added to calcium carbide in a generator. The heat of reaction (166 btu per cu ft acetylene generated) is employed to vaporize the excess water over the chemical equivalent, leaving a substantially dry calcium hydrate suitable for reuse as a lime source. The temperature must be carefully controlled, since acetylene polymerizes to form benzene at 600oC and violently decomposes at 780oC, and air mixtures may explode at 480oC. Generators of both types are usually designed to operate below 300oF and 15 psi.

The crude gas (containing traces of hydrogen sulfide, ammonia, and phosphine) from the generator is either scrubbed with water and caustic soda solution or led to a purifier, where the impurities are absorbed by the use of iron oxide or active chlorine compounds. The dry gas is fed to cylinders or manufacturing units.

PROCESS OF MANUFACTURE OF OXYGEN GAS

Air is drawn through a filter before being compressed upto a maximum pressure of 200 kg/cm2 required for initial start up and approximately 85 kg/ c m2 pressure for normal operation.

Air at the outlet of the compressor is cooled in the heat exchanger with water nitrogen and oxygen. The condensed water is separated in a separator. Air then passes through a combined drying and carbon dioxide removal unit.

Dry and purified air Passes through a Freon Evaporator and Cold Exchanger where it is further cooled by heat exchange with waste nitrogen and evaporating liquid oxygen. The cold air stream is then expanded into the medium pressure column.

In the column the rising vapour stream becomes poorer in oxygen and liquefies at the top of the column producing a "Liquid" with high nitrogen content. The reflex liquid flowing down becomes rich in oxygen and produces a liquid fraction called " Rich Liquid" containing less than 40% oxygen.

A vaporiser supplies the medium pressure column with the cold required at its upper section to condense nitrogen by heat exchange with boiling liquid oxygen at the base of the low pressure column. The vaporised oxygen provides the Vapour load required for rectification in the low pressure column.

The Nitrogen is used as refluex streamed is the medium pressure coloum conduced at the upper section of the medium pressure column - Reflux stream after passing through sub cooler item and expansion to the top of low pressure column.

The rich liquid available at the bottom of the medium pressure column is passed through the rich liquid Filter oum acetylene absorbers and after expansion an expansion value delivered to the middle section of the low pressure column Cooling of the lean liquid in sub-cooler reduces vaporization during expansion and increases the relax in the low pressure column.

At the low pressure column, the vapour rising from the vaporiser (E 61) becomes progressively poorer in oxygen as it passes up the column. Reflex liquid streams coming down the column becomes richer in oxygen. The outgoing oxygen stream at the bottom of low pressure column contain 99.5% oxygen.

MANUFACTURE

Most of the oxygen producing plants in India work on the H.P. system employing the Heylandt cycle A few plants of India oxygen Ltd and the Asiatic oxygen and Acetylene Co. Ltd., operate on nozzle expansion.

DISTRIBUTIONS

For general engineering uses, oxygen is compressed into cylinders and distributed by road or rail. Specially designed compressors are used. Soft water or distilled water, not oil, is used as lubricant in order to avoid contamination. Interestage coolers are provided and after the final stage, the gas is passed through a separator to remove water and the water blower out at intervals through a valve.

From the separator the gas passes to the filling deok. In the pit filling method the filler stands in a pit for convenience of connecting and disconnecting cylinders from manifolds on either side of the pit. Cylinders are raled into position and by manipulating the valves. both or either of the manifolds can be connected while others are being filled. The method of stalk filling is adopted when large quantities of gas are to be handled. A stack of empty cylinders is built in individual bags on a deck and filling is done by connecting the cylinders to filling points on a trolley which can be moved around as required. The trolley in turn being connected to the main oxygen supply line means of flexible pipes. Special pumps are used for pumping liquid oxygen. Direct to cylinders the liquid being gassified in the process.

CYLINDERS

The capacities of cylinders in common use are 2000,385,236,185,175,165,150,100,80,40, cu.ft. Oxygen cylinders must be of rigid construction and must conform to stringent specification. According to the British Standard Specification N.400-1931. The cylinder should be made of carbon still containing, 0.15-0.25%, Sulphur less than 0.045%, phosphorus 0.045% mn less than 0.045-0.75 and silicon less than 0.3 %. It should satisfy the following mechanical tests, 15 Ton sq.in, Elongation on gauge length 15% (min), maximum work stress 8 Tips/sq inch, Hydraulic Test, 3000 lbs/sq. inch and working pressure 120 atm. The cylinder should conform to a weight test and carry a hydraulic test certificate it must be numbered, stamped and registered and each cylinder should carry a test history.

PLANT & MACHINERY SUPPLIERS

A. FORACETYLENE

M/s. Indian Oxygen Limited,
Oxygen House, P-34,
Taratola Road,
Calcutta -700 053.

M/s. Industrial Gases Limited,
15, Ganesh Chander Avenue,
Calcutta - 700 013.

Factory :

40, Factory Area,
Fazal Ganj, P.B. No. 373,
Kanpur (U.P)

B. FOROXYGEN

M/s. Industrial Gases Ltd.,
130, Canning Street,
Calcutta-700 001.

M/s. Power Gas Ltd.,
254-D, Dr.A.B.Road,
Worli,
Mumbai-400 025.

SUPPLIERS OF COMPLETE PLANT

M/s. Sanghi Oxygen,
Mahakali Caves Road,
Andheri (East),
Mumbai-400 093.

PLANT ECONOMICS

Rated Plant capacity = 1. 480 CUM/DAY, ACETYLENE GAS
2. 480 CUM/mDAY, OXYGEN GAS

LAND & BUILDING COST Rs. 1,18,00,000.00
(Land 2 acres)

PLANT & MACHINERY

1. **A. *FOR ACETYLENE GAS:***
   Acetylene gas generator M.S.
2. Water flushing tank M.S
3. Feeding system conveyor feed
4. Syphon Drain sustain M.S.
5. Gas Holdu M.S.
6. Purifiers with filling bed
7. L.P. Driers
8. H. P. oil purger
9. Compressor
10. H. P. Drier with filled bed M.S.
11. Flush Back arrestors
12. Non-return valves
13. Charging mani fold system
14. Spinkler system
15. Water recirculation system
16. Water Tank M.S.
17. Reactivator
18. Limit Switches
19. Cylinder Testing equipments
20. Filling station auxillaries & accessories
21. **B: *OXYGEN GAS*:** Containing multistage compressor, purifiers,refrigerator & liquid Oxygen pump with parts.
22. Water softening plant
23. D. G. Set
24. Lab. Testing equipments
25. Instrumentation & process control
26. Miscellaneous equipments, valves,
    pipe fittings & spairs, etc.

FIXED CAPITAL

1.	LAND & BUILDING	Rs. 1,18,00,000.00
2.	PLANT & MACHINERY	Rs. 98,87,500.00
3.	OTHER FIXED ASSETS	Rs. 2,71,50,000.00
	TOTAL	Rs. 4,88,37,500.00

WORKING CAPITAL REQUIREMENT/MONTH

RAW MATERIALS

1. **A. *FOR ACETYLENE GAS:***
   Calcium Carbide
2. Acetone
3. Calcium Chloride
4. Misc. Chemicals
5. **B: *OXYGEN GAS:***
   Caustic soda
6. Lubricating Oil
7. Miscellaneous

TOTAL WORKING CAPITAL/MONTH

1. RAW MATERIAL	Rs.	6,98,000.00
2. SALARY & WAGES	Rs.	1,92,000.00
3. UTILITIES & OVERHEADS	Rs.	1,30,000.00
TOTAL	Rs.	10,20,000.00

TOTAL CAPITAL INVESTMENT

TOTAL FIXED CAPITAL	Rs.	4,88,37,500.00
TOTAL WORKING CAPITAL FOR 3 MONTHS	Rs.	30,60,000.00
TOTAL	Rs.	5,18,97,500.00

TURN OVER/ANNUM

1. 1,44,000 cu m Acetylene gas (dissolved in acetone) (dissolved acetylene)
2. 1,44,000 cu m Oxygen gas

TOTAL Rs. 3,88,80,000.00

PROFIT = RECEIPTS - COST OF PRODUCTION

= 3,88,80,000.00 - 2,48,47,925.00

= 1,40,32,075.00

PROFIT SALES RATIO = Profit / Sales x 100 *= 36.09 %*

RATE OF RETURN = Operating profit / T.C.I x 100 *= 27.04 %*

BREAK EVEN POINT (B.E.P) = 50.22 %

Chapter-2

ACTIVATED CARBON FROM COCONUT SHELL

INTRODUCTION

Activated carbon is any form of carbon shows high absorptivity for gases, vapours and colloidal solids in either the gasion or liquid phase. It is available in many form such as pellets, granules and in powder form. Activated cabon is very important chemical has wide application and employed by numerous industries which require absorption of certain gases and vapours in purification, in catalytic chemical reactions, decolorisation of vegetable oil and sugar soloution. Activated carbons have a large surface area, liquid phase activated carbons are light in weight, fluffy powder while gas phase activated carbons are hard and are in the form of pellets.

The term Activated carbon, active carbon, or active charcoal is usually applied to amorphous carbons possessing higher absorption capacities than wood or animal charcoal. Many processing were developed during world war for the production of effective adsorbents for use in gasmasks. Industrial activated carbons in the forms of pellets, granules or fine powders, and with many industrial applications, are now on the market under different trade-names.

Commercial adsorbent carbons may be grouped into decolorizing, gas adsorbent, metal adsorbent, and medicinal carbons according to their physical structure, properties, and applications. No one type of carbons can be used for all purposes. A large variety of raw materials are available for the manufacture of these products, Coal, petroleum coke, and wood charcoal are activated by gas activation. Industrial waste e.g. raw dust, bagasse, molasses, straw, tanbark waste, coconut pericarp and shell, corn cobs, paddy and ground nut husk, cocoa been shell, distillery slop, waste Mahua flowers, waste wood pulp liquor, and filter press mud from sugar factories have been utilized for the production of active carbons by chemical activation.

USES AND APPLICATIONS

For Purification of liquids, the powdered form of activated carbon is added to the liquid to be purified and the mixture is agitated and finally filtered.

Granulated activated carbons are used for purification of gases or liquids and are used in a vertical carbon packed column.

PROPERTIES

The most important chemical properties of activated carbon are the ash content ash composition, and pH of the carbon. Discrepancies between the expected performance of an activated carbon, based upon surface area and pure size distribution data, and actual adsorptive capacity can offen be explained by oxygen containing groups on the surfaces of the carbon. The pH & pka of the carbon as a measure of surface acidity or basicity of the oxygen containing groups, assists in predicting hydrophilicity and anionic or cationic adsorptive preferences of the carbon.

DIFFERENT TYPES OF ACTIVATED CARBON

Activated carbon can be divided into two main classes, those for adsorption of gases and vapours for which a grannular material is generally employed and those used in purification of liquid from which a powdered material is desired.

MANUFACTURING PROCESS OF ACTIVATED CARBON FROM COCONUT SHELL

Activated carbons are highly specific in character and are prepared for a particular end use. The use depends on the source of material is activated. Activated carbon is made by the phenomenous of activation which ios a physical change where is the surface of the carbon is tremendously done by high temp. oxidation or lower temperature chemical dehydration or chemical reaction. Activation involves pyrolysis of pyrolysis of the source material and necessarily involving controlled oxidation.

There are three method for the production of activated carbon.

1. Gas Activation
2. Chemical Activation
3. Deposition of carbon on a porous inorganic basis.

The chemical activation involves the following operations & process.

1. Preparation of Raw Materials.
2. Making the raw materials with chemical impregnating agent to form paste.
3. Extruding the mass.
4. Drying the extruded mass.
5. Calcination of the dried mass.
6. Cooling the mass obtained after calcination.
7. Washing with water and hydrocloric acid to remove inorganic residues.
8. Drying the washed mass.
9. Pulverization & Screening.
10. Pacakaging.

The raw material like saw dust, or rice husk or coconut shell is first grounded in the form of powder by use of pulveriser.

The powders raw material are taken into a mechanical mixer. Now the solution of 50% Zinc Chloride is prepared and incorporated into the mechanical mixer. The mixing is done by use of slower and heated so that, thick paste of raw materials powder and zinc chloride takes place.

This thick paste is then passed through an extruder of having an extrusion plate with 1/84 size perforation. The paste is extruded under pressure into the form of granulated mass.

The graulated mass is then dried by blowing hot air and taken into the Rotary kiln. The kiln is heated to the temperature of 850° to 1000°C by means of furnace flue gas.

The hot activated carbon thus produced is then cooled in an iron box in absence of air.

The cooled product is then taken into a washing tank where the water hydrochloric acid are sprayed on the activated carbon to remove the inorganic chemicals like zinc compound and the residual acid.

Now, washed activated carbon is dried in the air stream heated kiln at the temperature of 275° to 300°C. The activated carbon is then pulverised and screened as per the requirement and then packed in polythene laminate jute bags.

SUPPLIERS OF RAW MATERIALS

ZINC CHLORIDE

M/s. A.B.S Chemicals Pvt. Ltd.,
5, Fancy Lane,
Calcutta - 700 001.

HYDROCHLORIC ACID

M/s. Alfa Texdyes Industries,
Kalupur, Panohpiple,
Near Tadni Sheri,
Ahmedabad.

POLYETHYLENE PIPES AND FITTINGS

M/s Garware Plastic & Polyester Pvt Ltd.,
P.B. No 6853,
50-A, Swami Nityanand Marg,
Vile Parle (E),
Western Highway,
Mumbai- 400 057.

SUPPLIERS OF PLANT AND MACHINERY OF ACTIVATED CARBON

CONVEYORS AND BUCKET ELEVATORS

M/s Ahmedabad Victoria Iron Works Company Pvt. Ltd.,
Dudheshwar Road,
Ahmedabad - 380 001.

M/s Alfa Enginnering Company Limited,
Station Road,
Bhandup,
Mumbai.

CONVEYORS MACHINERY

M/s. Andhra Pradesh Heavy Machinery & Engineering Ltd.
Kondapalli - 521288,
Andhra Pradesh.

SIEVING MACHINE

M/s. Atlas Engineering Works,
8, Diwan Hall,
Chandni Chowk,
Delhi - 110006

FILTER PRESS

M/s. Arvnoday Engineering Works,
Near Somnath Temple,
Bilimora, Gujarat..

KILNS

M/s. Macnally Bird Engineering Company Limited.,
Chartered Bank Building,
Calcutta - 700 001.

PULVERIZER

M/s. Chemcon International Chemical Engg. Consultants,
B-10, South Extension,
Part II,
New Delhi-110 049.

PALLETIZER

1. **M/s. Associated Cement Company Limited,**
Engineering Division,
121 Queens Road,
Mumbai - 400 020.

COMPLETE PLANT AND MACHINERY

1. **M/s. A.P.V. Engineering Company,**
No-2, Jessore Road,
Dum Dum,
Calcutta.

PLANT ECONOMICS

Rated Plant capacity = 1.00 TON/day
ACTIVATED CARBON FROM COCONUT SHELL

LAND & BUILDING COST	Rs.	12,75,000.00

(Land Area required, 1000 sq. mts.)

PLANT & MACHINERY

1. **ACTIVATED CARBON SECTION:** Kiln for drying coconut shell.
2. Briquettes making machine
3. Drying chamber continuous type
4. Automatic filling, Sealing and Packaging Machine.
5. Quality testing and process control equipments & instrumentations
6. Bucket Elevator.
7. Pipes and fittings, pumps, valves and other tanks, Motors etc.
8. Jaw Crusher
9. Boiler
10. Pulveriser
11. Mixing machine
12. Conveyor belt
13. Activation chamber
14. Cooling chamber
15. Washing tank
16. Drying chamber
17. Vibrating screens
18. Pulverising Machine.

FIXED CAPITAL

1. LAND & BUILDING	Rs.	12,75,000.00
2. PLANT & MACHINERY	Rs.	35,70,000.00
3. OTHER FIXED ASSETS	Rs.	7,50,000.00
TOTAL	Rs.	55,95,000.00

WORKING CAPITAL REQUIREMENT/MONTH

RAW MATERIALS

1. Coconut Shell
2. Zinc Chloride
3. Hydrochloric Acid
4. Packaging materials
5. Miscellaneous

TOTAL WORKING CAPITAL/MONTH

1. RAW MATERIAL	Rs.	1,94,500.00
2. SALARY & WAGES	Rs.	68,000.00
3. UTILITIES & OVERHEADS	Rs.	1,37,000.00
TOTAL	Rs.	3,99,500.00

TOTAL CAPITAL INVESTMENT

TOTAL FIXED CAPITAL	Rs.	55,95,000.00
TOTAL WORKING CAPITAL FOR 3 MONTHS	Rs.	11,98,500.00
TOTAL	Rs.	67,93,500.00

TURN OVER/ANNUM

1. By sale of Activated Carbon,
   300 Tons.

TOTAL	Rs.	1,05,00,000.00

PROFIT = RECEIPTS - COST OF PRODUCTION

= 1,05,00,000.00 - 72,60,945.00

= 32,39,055.00

PROFIT SALES RATIO = Profit / Sales x 100 = 30.85 %

RATE OF RETURN = Operating profit / T.C.I x 100 = 47.68 %

BREAK EVEN POINT (B.E.P) = 51.58 %

Chapter-3
AUTOMOBILE POLISH

INTRODUCTION

Automobile polishes are designed to remove road dust and oxidised paint and to lay down a continuous glossy film, which resists removal by water and car wash detergents. The kind of dirt and soil encountered in the open and on the roads is different. The kind of dirt and soil encountered in the open and on the roads is different from met inside the home. Hence a polish suitable for a car finish would in many instances be too harsh for use on furniture. Abrasives, for example are important constituents of auto body polishes. Similarly polishes that serve efficiently on floors would find tough going when exposed to wind, rain and sun. Although there are certain common features, autombobile polishes may be divided into four main classes.

a) Emulsion polishes
b) Cleaner Polishes
c) Pre waxing compounds
d) Wax Polishes

With exceptions of a few products, particularly some in the last group, most modern automobile polishes are produced as emulsions. Hence they combine the benifits of water soluble or water miscible cleaning agents with the polsihing effects of oils and waxes.

PROPERTIES

Properties of different types of waxes used for Automobile polishes.

Shellax Wax: Melting point 74-80°C. It has qualities similar to carnauba wax and is cheaper and inigeneously available.

Carnauba Wax Yellow: Melting point 78-80°C. This type of wax is used in comibination with other waes in order waxes in order to raise the melting point of the polish. Increase its lustre and harness and reduce stickness. It is a costly wax.

Sugar Cane Wax: Melting point 66-67°C. Sugar cane wa is not much used for boot polish manufacture.

Microcrystalline Wax: Melting point 75-85°C. This type of wax is extracted from heavy lubricating and cylinder oil stocks. It is lustrous with a capacity for even filming.

Mountain Wax: Melting point 66-67°C. Mountain wax is extracted from lignite and is lustrous and hard. It used to reduce cost and toincrease fexibility.

Hard Paraffin Wax: Melting point 54-57°C. Hard Paraffin wax is less lustrous than shellac. Carnauba or microcyataline waxes.

Bees Wax: Melting point 60-72°. Bees wax is generally mixed with adulternats to bring down the cost of production. In unadult erated from it possesses a high plasticity moderate gloss and gives a tough film.

USES AND APPLICATIONS

Motor car polishes are now almost as universal as shoe, floor and furniture polishes and it is an indication of present trends that the labels of most motor car polish containers recommended that the contents can also be used with advantage for floors, leather, furniture and paint work, which is indeed quite a reversal from the times when the tin of paste floor polish was practically the sole source of motor car polishing materials. The practically the sole source of motor car polich is in the general trend in the development of motor car polish is in the field of liquid emulsion type polishes. Car wash/polish products combining detergents and polish ingredients have been developed.

B.I.S. SPECIFICATIONS

The following Indian Standards have been prescribed by the B.I.S.

I S : 5480 - 1983 Automobile Polish, Paste (first revision)
I S : 7982 - 1976 Automobile Polish liquid (with Amendment No.1)

Above Specifications may be obtained from

Bureau of Indian Standards,
9, B.S. Zafar Marg,
New Delhi - 110 002.

MARKET POTENTIAL

Metal surface generaly get tarnished on exposure to air atmosphere. By the application of metal polish, which contain finer grades of abrasives, the metal surface regains its shine or lusture. Metal polish is being used for polishing the metal surface i.e. for increasing its shine. Although in a liquid form it does not necessaril follow that a iquid-polish is less economical than pastes, because the efficiency of both is dependent upon the efficiency of both is dependent upon the amount of oleic acid they contain and liquid polish is reich with respect to paste, especially those containing much waxy and earthy material. Thus it is fact that an ounce of fluid polish may posses more polishing potency than equal weight of the paste.

Now-a-days, the liquid metal polish is taking the place of paste with the respect of case in handling high polishingpotency, economical.

FORMULATION AND MANUFACTURING PROCESS

FORMULATION

The following formulation gives an auto polishing powder:

Parts By Wt.

Oleic Acid	2
White Mineral Oil	12
Carnuba Wax	2.5
Yellow Bees Wax	2
Wase	28
Triethanoloamine	13
Infusorial Earth	100
Powdered Gum Gragacanth	4

PROCESS DESCRIPTION

The first four ingredients are melted together with gentle heating. In a separate vessel, the solution of triethanolamine and water is heated to near boiling. The oil-wax mixture is added to the aqueous solution in a slow stream with constant stirring and maintained and below boiling temperature until a smooth emulsion is formed. The heating is cut off and stirring coninuted until cold and then infusorial earth is added. Mixing is continued and the mixture is allowed to dry until al the water is evaporated. Finally tragaceanth powder is added and miing and sfting is done thoroughly. An acceptable auto polish can be obtained by mixing thoroughly 0.5 to 0.75 kg. of this powder to 10 litres of water.

FORMULATION

The following is a best quality wax formulation for automobiles.

	Kgs.
Paraffin Wax	13.3
Carnauba Wax No.1	15.3
Mineral Spirit	15
Carbon Black	1
Nigrosine Dye, Oil Soluble	0.25

U.S. Patent 30,71,479(1663) provides a wax paste composition in which silicone oil causes particles of the abrasive, pigment and grime to be more easily removed from the wax film and makes possible the buffing of the film to a higher gloss. Silicone oil causes reduction in viscosity and impros the spreading properties.

RAW MATERIAL SUPPLIERS

MICROCRYSTALLINE WAX

M/s. Prestige Chemicals,
D-134, Sector-7,
Noida - 201 301 (U.P).
Ph.: 555382

MONTAX WAX

M/s. Mukesh Trading Corporation,
Homby Building 2nd Floor,
172/74, Dr. D.N. Road,
Post Box No.52,
Mumbai - 400 001.

ALIMINIUM SILICATE

M/s. Aunkur Chemical Works,
4007, Ajmeri Gate,
Delhi - 110 006.

M/s. Bee Chems,
E-5, Panki Industrial Area,
Udyog Nagar,
Kanpur - 208 002.

SILICONE EMULSIONS

M/s. Ashok Chemical Industries,
106, Mayur S.U.P. Road,
Borivli,
Mumbai - 400 092.

M/s. Dadia Chemical Industries,
9-Laxmi Palace,
5th Floor, R.B. Mehta Marg,
Chatkopar,
Mumbai - 400 077.

SPIRIT DENATURED

M/s. India Chemical Industries,
53, Mittal Court,
B-Wing, 5th floor,
226, Nariman Point,
Mumbai - 400 021.

SPIRIT WHITE

M/s. P.K. Industries,
Sodal Road,
Jalandhar City,
Punjab.

OLEIC ACID

M/s. Gandhi Parekh Investment Corporation,
Marker Bhavan No.2,
18, New Marine Lines,
Mumbai - 400 020.

MORPHOLIXI

M/s. Amines & Plasticizers Ltd.,
Building,
Shiv Sugar Estate,
Dr. Annie Besant Road,
Worli,
Mumbai - 400 018.

SOLVENT NAPTHA

M/s. Hindustan Petroleium Corporation Ltd.,
Marketing Division,
Hindustan Bhawan,
S.V. Marg,
Mumbai - 400 038.

PLANT AND MACHINERY SUPPLIERS

CHEMICAL PLANT & EQUIPMENT

M/s. ATV Projects India,
D-8, Street No.16,
Marol, Andheri (E),
Mumbai - 400 093.

M/s. D.K. Corporation,
384 - M, Kalbadevi Road,
4th Floor,
Mumbai.

MIXERS

M/s. Alankar Industries,
P.B. No. 27371,
Andheri (West),
Mumbai - 400 058.

M/s. Mac Neill & Major Limited,
Kilburn Division,
2-Faurlie Place,
Calcutta.

TANKS

M/s. Annu Rashyan Udyog,
184, D.S.I.D.C Sheds,
Okhla Industrial Area-1,
New Delhi - 110 020.
Ph.: 6813624

M/s. Chemi Tex Engineering Enterprises,
Plot No.277,
GIDC Industrial Estate,
Opp. L-1, Shed,
Behind IBP Petrol Pump,
Odhav,
Ahmedabad - 382 415.

M/s. Flowlink Industries Private Limited,
D-15, Commercial Complex,
Prashant Vihar,
Delhi-110 085.
Ph.: 7267006/7267007
Fax: 91-11-7267007

AUTOMATIC FILLING MACHINES

M/s. Premier Engineering Corporation,
B-19, DSIDC,
Industrial Complex,
Rohtak Road,
Nangloi,
Delhi - 110 041.

PLANT ECONOMICS

Rated Plant capacity = 300.00 KGS/day
AUTOMOBILE POLISH

LAND & BUILDING COST Rs 8,72,500.00
(Land 500 Sq.mts)

PLANT & MACHINERY

1. S.S. Jacketted vessel with sterrir, cap. 500 kgs alongwith electric heater all accessories No.1
2. S.S.Tank with mixer complete with all accessories cap 100 kgs
3. Misc. equip. such as mild steel pans, aluminum vessels solvent storage tanks, weighting scale etc.
4. Automatic Filling Machine Cap.
5. Kgs/hrs - 1 Nos.
5. Pumps & Blowers
6. Piping & Instrumentation
7. Lab Testing Equipment

FIXED CAPITAL

1.	LAND & BUILDING	Rs	8,72,500.00
2.	PLANT & MACHINERY	Rs	1,50,000.00
3.	OTHER FIXED ASSETS	Rs	1,15,000.00
	TOTAL	Rs	11,37,500.00

WORKING CAPITAL REQUIREMENT/MONTH

RAW MATERIALS

1. Montax Wax
2. Microcrystalline Wax
3. High Viscosity silicone
4. Low viscosity silicone
5. Tin container (Printed)
6. Aliphatic Hydrocarbons kerosene & mineral spirits
7. Alumminium silicate abrasins
8. Water
9. Emulsifier

TOTAL WORKING CAPITAL/MONTH

1.	RAW MATERIAL	Rs	1,52,620.00
2.	SALARY & WAGES	Rs	53,125.00
3.	UTILITIES & OVERHEADS	Rs	34,500.00
	TOTAL	Rs	2,40,245.00

TOTAL CAPITAL INVESTMENT

TOTAL FIXED CAPITAL	Rs	11,37,500.00
TOTAL WORKING CAPITAL FOR 3 MONTHS	Rs	7,20,735.00
TOTAL	Rs	18,58,235.00

TURN OVER/ANNUM

1.	Receipts from sale of 90,000 kgs. of Automobile Polish (in 100 gm. pack 98)	Rs	45,00,000.00

PROFIT = RECEIPTS - COST OF PRODUCTION

= 45,00,000.00 - 33,88,814.20

= 11,11,185.80

PROFIT SALES RATIO = Profit / Sales x 100 = 24.69 %

RATE OF RETURN = Operating profit / T.C.I x 100 = 59.80 %

BREAK EVEN POINT (B.E.P) = 45.47 %

Chapter-4

BLEACHING POWDER (STABLE)

INTRODUCTION

Bleaching process are those which remove colour from natural or artificial products. In early times bleaching was done by mechanical means and bleached goods were available only to rich. Today the bleaching to textile, paper and other materials constructed from natural fibres is done largely by the chemical agents and bleached articles are available to all.

Although most bleaching is attached by oxidizing agents on important class of agents bleaches by reduction action.

True bleached should be distinguished from optional bleached whose effects is a whitening by the addition of agents that convert a portion of invisible ultraviolet radiation into blue or blued green light. This changes the shade of articles that have light yellow or brown tone to neutral gray. In the last decade optical bleaches have become quite popular in the textile fields.

Bleaching was not generally practiced during the Dark Ages, although knowledge of the art persited. Following the renaissance there was a strong demand for the bleached cloth which until this time was luxury item and seldom work by the masses. By 1700 the bleaching of cloth had become a major industry however land requirements for the so called bleachingoperations imposed a severed strain on the economy of the more progressive countries as the land was needed to provide food for the expanding population. Until the 1700's bleaching method has not changed much from Roman times. In 1750 Home Published theory showing that a dilute solution of sulfuric and was as effective and more convenient to work with. Textile bleaching with chlorine was developed by Bathlot in 1786. Tenant passed chlorine into milk of lime to prepare bleach liquor. By 1799 Tenant developed bleaching powder by passing dilute moist chlorine gas over slaked lime.

PROPERTIES

Bleaching powder is a white amorphous powder which should contain no lumps if pure line has been used in its preparation accompanied by complete chlorination it is almost entirely soluble in water. If chlorination was incomeplete, free calcium hydroxide will be present. Which settles down as an insoluble sludge or precipitate when the powder is extracted with water. The use of a low grade lime also increases samples contain from 35-38% of chlorine which can be used for bleaching, or available chlorine as it is generally termed.

USE OF BLEACHING POWDER IN BLEACHING

Animal fibres can not be bleached by means of chlorine or bleaching powder. Proteins or amino compounds, such as wool and silk are rapidly converted into chloramines, and if excess of bleaching powder or chlorine is or dissolved. Vegetable fibres, such as cotton are nearly always bleached by means of a solution of bleaching powder and if the operator is carried out under suitable conditions the fibre is not damaged.

But unsuitable conditions, such as excess of the bleaching agent, too high a temperature or the presence of catalytic agents such as metallic oxides cause the cellulose of the cotton to become partly or entirely changed into oxycellulose. A clear solution of the powder issued, obtained by stirring it with water and allowing the sludge to settle. Such a solution has, however comparatively little bleaching action. The bleaching action becomes marked only under conditions which ensure that either nascent chlorine, or free hypochlorous acid or both are present. With a weak acid there is less chlorine and more hypochlorous acid, the ratio of these depending upon the hydrogen ion concentration of the acid used. Both the cheapest and best acid to employ is the carbon dioxide of the atmosphere. This is always done in bleaching and the bleacher obtains it by aeration of either the goods or the bleaching liquor. The action may be explained in the following way:-

1. When the bleaching powder is treated with water a solution of calcium hypochlorite and calcium chloride is obtained, together with some calcium hydroxide.

2. The calcium hypochlorite becomes hydrolysed into hypochlorous acid and calcium hydroxide till the concentration of the latter establishes a position of equilibrium.

3. At the same time some nascent chlorine is produced.

4. Both the hypochlorous acid and the nascent chlorine bleach the colouring matter of the cotton, but more of them is required than can be present by this mechanism.

5. Atmospheric carbon dioxide however neutralizes some of the calcium hydroxide in the solution. This destroys the equibrium of the equation.

$$Ca(Ocl)2 + 2H2O \longleftrightarrow 2Hocl + Ca(OH)2$$

And cause more hypochlorous acid to be liberated by hydrolysis or traylor's views are accepted, the liberation of chlorine. This process continues as long as carbon di- oxide is present. Thus, bleaching powder owes its bleaching powder owes its bleaching effect to the action of atmospheric carbon di- oxide.

STABLE BLEACHING POWDER MANUFACTURE

Chlorine Containing Bleaching Compounds

Classes of chlorine containing compounds are used as bleaching agents:

Chlorine, hypochlorites and N chloro compounds two classes termed as available chlorine compounds produce hypo chlorous acid and hypochlorite alnion in bleaching baths.

Calcium HYPO Chlorine (Stable Bleaching Powder)

Theoritically conversion of chlorine to hypochlorite may be expressed by the reactions.

$$2Ca(OH)2 + 2Cl2 \longrightarrow Ca(Ocl)2 + Cacl2 + 2H2O$$

$$2NaoH + Cl2 \longrightarrow NaOcl + Nacl + H2O$$

It is well known that the chemical instability of ordinery lime bleach. Previously it was discovered that stable dry bleach (essentially calcium hypochlorite) could be made according to the reaction.

$$Cacl2 + 2NaOcl \longrightarrow Ca(Ocl)2 + 2Nacl$$

In which unstable NaOcl in reaction (2) and the detrimental Cacls from reaction (1) are converted into harmless Nacl and stable Ca(Ocl)2.

The reaction mechanism are are as follows:

$$2NaOH + Cl2 \longrightarrow NaOcl + Nacl + H_2O$$

$$2\ Ca(OH)_2 + 2Cl_2 \longrightarrow 4Cl_2 + CaCl_2 + 2H_2O$$

$$2Ca(OH)_2 + 4NaOH + 4Cl_2 \longrightarrow Ca(Ocl)_2 + CaCl_2 + 2NaCl + 2Nacl + 2NaOCl + 4\ H_2O$$

So, the final reaction is :

$$2(Ca(Ocl)_2 + NaOCl + Nacl + Ca(Ocl)_2 + Cacl_2 + 2H_2O \longrightarrow 4Ca(Ocl)_2 + 2H_2O + 4NaCl$$

MANUFACTURING PROCESS

Lime stone of higher lime concentration is taken and crushed into small lumps by the help of Jaw crusher. The small lumps of lime stone is mixed with coal and charged into the kilns for 24 hours. The lime stone will be calcined completely into slaked lime. The charge is cooled and again crushed and pulverised to fine powder. The powder is now fed into the tank for making milk of lime by mixing with sufficient quantity of water. The mass is stirred completely and filtered through a stainer to remove the bigger lumps.

Now the milk of lime is fed into the chlorinator and temperature is raised to 105°F. The chlorine gas from the bottom is injected into the chlorinator till the reaction is complete. The bleaching liquid is passed through centrifuge to remove the excess water. The slurry is now fed to the rotary vacuum drum dryer and mass is allowed to dry completely. The dryed mass is pulverised into fine paprticles and packed in the polyethene bags by automatic packing machine. The product is now ready for storage and despatch.

SUPPLIERS OF PLANT AND MACHINERY

CRUSHING, GRINDING AND PULVERIZING MACHINE

M/s. Patna Machinery Private Limited,
Plot A - 160, Main Road,
Wagle Industrial Estate,
Thane - 400 604.

M/s. Singh Engineering Works,
B-22/47, MIDC Industrial Estate,
Satpur, Nasik - 422 007.

STORAGE TANKS

M/s. P.J. Surotia & Company,
Near Chakudia Mahadev,
Rakhial, Ahmedabad - 380023.

M/s. Naresh Fabricators,
Bawana Road, Samaipur,
Delhi - 110 042.

SUPPLIERS OF RAW MATERIALS

LIQUID CHLORINE GAS

M/s. Dhrangadhra Chemical Works,
Nirmal, Nariman Point,
Mumbai-400 021.

LIME

M/s. Om Shivam Buildmats Chem.
F 14, M.I.D.C. Kulgaon,
Badlapur, Dist Thane.

PLANT ECONOMICS

Rated Plant capacity = 50.00 TON/day
STABLE BLEACHING POWDER

LAND & BUILDING COST	Rs.	1,41,50,000.00

(Total land required 10 Acres)

PLANT & MACHINERY

1. Jaw crusher
2. Distintegrator
3. Pulveriser
4. Belt conveyor
5. Vibrating screen
6. MS FRP lined overhead storage bin
7. Chlorine reaction system
8. Bucket Elevator (M.S. bucket)
9. Water storage tank (PVC syntex type)
10. Chlorine gas holders
11. Instrumentation and process control equipments.
12. Laboratory testing equipments.
13. Pollution control equipments.
14. Fire fighting and safety equipments
15. Pipe, Pumps, valve, fittings, tanks and misc. equipments.

FIXED CAPITAL

1.	LAND & BUILDING	Rs.	1,41,50,000.00
2.	PLANT & MACHINERY	Rs.	1,16,25,000.00
3.	OTHER FIXED ASSETS	Rs.	68,00,000.00
	TOTAL	Rs.	3,25,75,000.00

RAW MATERIALS

1. Hydrated Lime
2. Liquid chlorine gas cylinder
3. Packaging material plastics bags

TOTAL WORKING CAPITAL/MONTH

1.	RAW MATERIAL	Rs.	45,05,000.00
2.	SALARY & WAGES	Rs.	4,46,875.00
3.	UTILITIES & OVERHEADS	Rs.	12,42,500.00
	TOTAL	Rs.	61,94,375.00

TOTAL CAPITAL INVESTMENT

TOTAL FIXED CAPITAL	Rs.	3,25,75,000.00
TOTAL WORKING CAPITAL FOR 3 MONTHS	Rs.	1,85,83,125.00
TOTAL	Rs.	5,11,58,125.00

TURN OVER/ANNUM

1. By sales of 15000 MT bleaching Powder Rs. 12,75,00,000.00

PROFIT = RECEIPTS - COST OF PRODUCTION

= 12,75,00,000.00 - 8,77,03,543.75

= 3,97,96,456.25

PROFIT SALES RATIO = Profit / Sales x 100 = *31.21 %*

RATE OF RETURN = Operating profit / T.C.I x 100 = *77.79 %*

BREAK EVEN POINT (B.E.P) = 35.05 %

Chapter- 5

BARIUM CARBONATE

INTRODUCTION

Natural barium carbonate, was formerly mined com merially in England. Precipitated barium car bonate is the most widely used barium chemical with the exception of natural barite. It is a fine white powder with an absolute density of 4.25 and bulk density varying from 0.80 to 2.16 g/em3 (50-135 lb/ft3). depending on the grade. The commercial material assays 99% $BaCO_3$. 0.06-0.12% total sulfur as S.Particle size varies with the grade. Ranging from 0.1 to 10 gm with considerable agglomeration. The index of refraction is low 1.6. and hardness is 30-3.75 on Mohs scale.

In contrast to calcium and strontium carbonates barium carbonate is thermally stable. Conversion to barium oxide is effected by heating with carbon.

PROPERTIES, GRADES & REGULATIONS

1. White Crystalline powder
2. Molecular wt - 197.37
3. Specific gravity - 4.29
4. Melting point - 811°C (tr to L- from) 982°C (tr to B-form)
5. Boiling point - 1450°C (decomposes). Barium Carbonate is insoluble in water , soluble in most acids, expect sulfuric Acid, where extremely insoluble barium sulphate is formed.

Grades:-

Natural (witherete), precipitated (98 to 99%), sulfur free, C.P. & Technical.

Containers & Regulation:-

Bags (50,80,100 lb) drums, barrels. No (I.C.C.) shipping level required.

USES & APPLICATION

Barium carbonate is the most important and widely used barium compound,. expect for natural barium sulfate. It used in the brick ceramic, oil-well drilling, photograph, glass and chemical manufacturing industries.

The greatest tonnage of barium carbonate is used in bricks industry. Brick making clay frequently contains appreciable quantities of calcium and magnesium sulfates and related compounds more or less soluble in water.

During drying water these dissolved salts migrates to the surface and evaporates, depositing the calcium sulfate and other salts as an irregular whitish undesirable discoloration known as scum. Barium carbonate, when mixed with the wet clay, immobilizes the soluble salts in the interior of the brick by forming barium sulfate and calcium carbonate, resulting in the production of uniform red bricks.

Another major is in the manufacture of other barium salts by treatment with acids stronger than carbonic acid. Relatively pure salts are obtained after evaporation or crystallization.

In the oil-well drilling industry the barite suspension used as drilling as drilling mud can be destabilized by the presence of soluble materials such asgypsum. Addition of barium carbonate renders the gypsum insoluble, inhibits the coagulation and thus permits the mud to retain the desired consistency and dispersion.

Barium carbonate is used in the manufacture of photographic paper to generate barium sulfate, to impart a flat white appearance.

In the glass industry, formulas containing various percentages of barium oxide are used for several purposes. The barium is commonly added as barium carbonate, although in some cases it is added to the glass furnace in the form of barium sulfate.

MANUFACTURE OF BARIUM CARBONATE

Ore size reduction is generally accomplished by a jaw crusher followed by a hammer mill. Because conversion of $BaSO_4$ to BaS decreases with increasing silica content in the low grade ores must be beneficiated by floation of the ground barite. Untreated ores or floation concentrates of 85 to 95% $BaSO_4$ are generally acceptable. Nearly all barite ores contain varying amounts of silica, iron aluminium, calcite, gypsum, and dolomite. Calcium and magnesium appear to cause no deleterious side reactions during the reduction step, but silica, iron, and aluminum all react with barium to form water-insoluble products. Silica is by far the most common impurity in barite and it generally ties up barium in the form of the metasilicate ($BaSiO_3$) or Ba_2SiO_4. Since Ba_2SiO_4 decomposes in water to give $BaSio_3$ plus $Ba(OH)_2$, only barium metasilicate is of concern. The advantage of a grade ore or concentrate is readily apparent.

The overall reduction which takes place in the kin is $BaSo_4+4CO=BaS+4CO_2$. Carbon is added to the feed to provide a source of carbon monoxide in the bed. Coke is usually used but coal, oil,gas, and other fuels have been proposed [5]. The reaction is diffusion controlled and the ore must be ground below 20 mesh for reasonably fast reaction rates. Dustlosses from the kiln and grinding can be recycled with or without pelletizing.

Coke reactivity and sizing are important considerations. Sizing must be controlled to provided adequate coke surface for reaction. At the same time, size must be large enough to burn throughout the length of the reaction zone to shield the product from oxidation. High CO_2 reactivity of the coker is desirable to provide CO for the reduction reaction and to climinate CO_2 from the reaction zone CO_2 reacts slowly with barium sulfide to form barium carbonate which in turn reacts with silica present to form barium metasilicate. Ore to coke ratio between 2 to 1 and 4 to common.

Temperatures normally range between 1100 and 1200°C. At higher temperatures the reaction to form barin silicate proceeds more rapidly. At high temperatures, barium sulfate combines directly with silica to form barium silicate. At lower temperatures the reduction rate is slower and longer retention times are necessary. With these increased retention times the side reactions to form barium silicate again increase.

As mentioned earlier, the reaction of barium sulfate with carbon monoxide to form barium sulfide is diffusion controlled. In general it can be stated that retention times should be sort with rapid heating to the desired reaction temperature to avoid side reactions. This means that the rotary kiln need not be long and that a high rotation rate shallow bed are most desirable.

The off-gases from the kiln must be cleaned to avoid an air pollution problem. The formation of brain silicate in the kiln produces sulfur dioxide. This combined with sulfur dioxide from the sulfur in the coke fuel, can produce sulfur dioxide concentrations up to 1o or greater in the fuel gases. Further oxidation can produce SO_3. Sulfuric acid mist can also be formed. Hydrocarbons are distilled from the volatile matter in the coke. A certain amount dioxide scrubbing are required. While expensive, pollution control for the black ash process can achieved effectively using todays's technology.

Requirement for 1 Ton of Barium Carbonate
Black Ash (65% Bas) - 1.18 MT
Barites
Soda Ash ($NazCo_3$) 588 Kg
[58% Na_2o]

SUPPLIERS OF RAW MATERIAL

SODA ASH

M/s. Tata Chemicals Limited,
Bombay House,
24, Bruce Street, Fort,
Mumbai - 400 001.

M/s. Saurashtra Chemicals,
Bilanagar,
Gwalior.

BARITES (BLACK ASH)

M/s. Reckitt & Colman of India Ltd.,
41, Chowringhee Road,
Calcutta - 700 016.

SUPPLIERS OF PLANT & MACHINERY

FILTER PRESS

M/s. Udayraj & Sons,
158, Lohar Chawal,
Mumbai-400 002.

M/s. Indian Sugar & General Engg. Corportaion,
Yamuna Nagar,
Ambala (Haryana).

STORAGE TANKS

M/s. Flowlink Industries Private Limited,
D-15, Commercial Complex,
Prashant Vihar,
Delhi-110 085.
Ph.: 7267006/7267007
Fax: 91-11-7267007

M/s. Annu Rashyan Udyog,
184, D.S.I.D.C Sheds,
Okhla Industrial Area-1,
New Delhi - 110 020.
Ph.: 6813624

PLANT ECONOMICS

Rated Plant capacity = 1.00 MT/day
BARIUM CARBONATE

LAND & BUILDING COST	Rs.	6,90,000.00
(Land 1500 sq.mt)		

PLANT & MACHINERY

1. Jaw crusher
2. Ball mill
3. Tray Drier
4. Storage tank
5. Crystallier
6. Grinder
7. Vibrating screen
8. Evaporator
9. Vibrating screen
10. Coal Fired Furnace/Kiln
11. Storage tank for cooling
3. Flotation cell (screw conveys type)
7. Leaching tank made of M.S.
8. Storage tank (washing purpose)
9. Rotary drum filter (vaccum type)
10. Continuous stirred tank reactor
17. Weighing cum packing machine
18. Pipe line, valves, pumps, conveys systems, material handling system with motor etc.

FIXED CAPITAL

1. LAND & BUILDING	Rs.	6,90,000.00
2. PLANT & MACHINERY	Rs.	8,12,000.00
3. OTHER FIXED ASSETS	Rs.	1,35,000.00
TOTAL	Rs.	16,37,000.00

WORKING CAPITAL REQUIREMENT/MONTH

RAW MATERIALS

1. Black Ash (65% Barium Sulphide)
2. Coal 9 MT
3. Soda Ash (Na_2CO_3) 12.3 MT

TOTAL WORKING CAPITAL/MONTH

1.	RAW MATERIAL	Rs.	2,82,000.00
2.	SALARY & WAGES	Rs.	61,740.00
3.	UTILITIES & OVERHEADS	Rs.	39,000.00
	TOTAL	Rs.	3,82,740.00

TOTAL CAPITAL INVESTMENT

TOTAL FIXED CAPITAL	Rs.	16,37,000.00
TOTAL WORKING CAPITAL FOR 3 MONTHS	Rs.	11,48,220.00
TOTAL	Rs.	27,85,220.00

TURN OVER/ANNUM

1. Reciept after sale of 300 MT of Barium Carbonate commercial grade
2. Receipt after sale of 176.4 MT of Na_2s sodium sulphite

TOTAL Rs. 68,64,000.00

PROFIT = RECEIPTS - COST OF PRODUCTION

= 68,64,000.00 - 52,95,541.30

= 15,68,458.70

PROFIT SALES RATIO = Profit / Sales x 100 = *22.85 %*

RATE OF RETURN = Operating profit / T.C.I x 100 = *56.31 %*

BREAK EVEN POINT (B.E.P) = 43.06 %

Chapter- 6

CALCIUM CARBONATE (PRECIPITATED AND ACTIVATED)

INTRODUCTION

CALCIUM CARBONATE

Calcium carbonate, $CaCO_3$ forms a major constituent of the earths crust and occurs as massive beds of limestone, chalk and marble. It is found as dolomite in which a part of the calcium is replaced by magnesium.

PRECIPITATED CALCIUM CARBONATE

The term precipitated Calcium Carbonate applies to the commercial type of compound obtained by chemical means and distinguishes it from the material produced by mechanical treatment of natural varieties of Calcium carbonate such as calcite, marble, limestone and sea shells. Precipitated calcium carbonate is produced in a number of different grades which range in particle size from 9.03 to 15 micron I.P. grade precipitated calcium carbonate is used indentificers, foods, cosmetics, pharmaccuticals, and antibiotics. Technical grades are used as in ingredients in the manufacture of ceramics, putty, polishes, insecticides, inks, shoe dressings and as a filler in the production of adhesives, matches, linoleum and welding rods.

USES AND APPLICATIONS

Precipitated calcium carbonate is widely used as a fillter in the manufacture of tooth paste and powder and in rubber, plastics and paper industries. To some extent it is also used as an extendes pigment in paint industry.

ACTIVATED CALCIUM CARBONATE:-

Activated calcium carbonate is used in
Rubber Industry
Plastic Industry
It acts as a reinforcing filler.

PROPERTIES

PROPERTIES OF PURE CALCIUM CARBONATE:-

It is a white powder or colourless crystal. It is odorless or tasteless. It has specific gravity between 2.7 - 2.95. It decomposes at 825oC. It is non combustible, non-toxic, slightly soluble in water and soluble in acids with evolution of carbon dioxide.

Calcium Carbonate is one of the most stable, common and widely dispersed material. It occurs in nature as aragonite oyster shells, calcite, chalk, limestone, marble, marl and travertine.

Precipitated Calcium Carbonate is available under the following type of grades.

1. Light.
2. Medium.
3. Heavy.
4. Chemically pure - Finds use in laboratory.
5. Technical - Finds use in industry.
6. I.P. - Used in pharmaceutical industry.

PROCESS OF MANUFACTURE

The process of manufacture of Hydrated Lime, Chemical Lime, precipitated Calcium carbonate and Activated Calcium Carbonate from limestone, consists of a number of steps as described below:-

1. Grading of Limestone.
2. Calcination of limestone to produce quick lime and chemical lime.
3. Cooling of quicklime and chemical lime.
4. Hydration of quicklime.
5. Preparation of milk of lime.
6. Carbonation of lime slurry with carbon dioxide gas.
7. Filteration of calcium carbonate slurry.
8. Drying.
9. Dressing to prepare precipitated calcium carbonate.
10. Making grace calcium carbonate known as activated calcium carbonate.
11. Drying.
12. Packing.

MANUFACTURE OF ACTIVATED CALCIUM CARBONATE

For the manufacture of activated calcium carbonate, first of all precipitated calcium carbonate is produced as described in the above steps.

For activation the suspension from the carbonation towers is tested and admixed suitably according to the coating required.

The coated grades of calcium carbonate are used in special applications where high dispersing and low liquid adsorption properties are needed. The coating usually consists of fatty acids, or the wetting agents. They are applied either before or after the drying step.

Generally activated calcium carbonate is made by 3% coating of stearic acid on precipitated calcium carbonate.

PROCESS FLOW SHEET OF PRECIPITATED $CaCO_3$

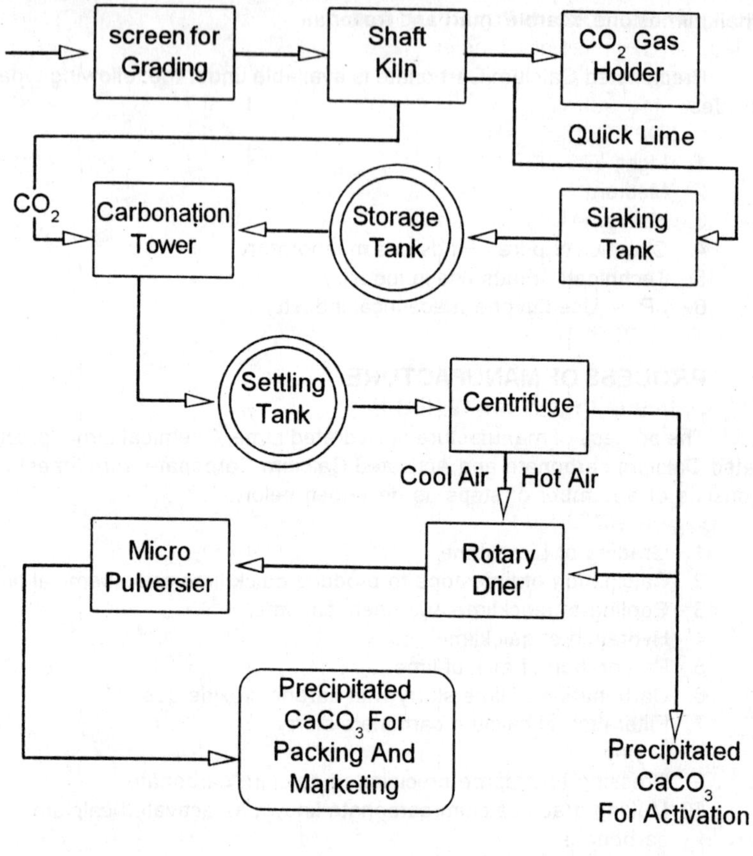

SUPPLIERS OF PLANT & MACHINERIES

KILN :

M/s. Andrew Yule & Company Limited,
Yule House, 8, Clive Raw,
P.B. No. 1164, Calcutta - 700 001.

DRYERS :

M/s. Andrew yuel & Company Limited,
Yule House, 8, Clive Row,
Post Box No. 1164, Calcutta - 1.

CALCIUM CARBONATE PLANTS :

M/s. G. Mirch Associates Private Limited,
Delstar, Huges Road,
Mumbai - 400 036.

TANKS :

M/s. Flowlink Industries Private Limited,
D-15, Commercial Complex,
Prashant Vihar,
Delhi-110 085.
Ph.: 7267006/7267007
Fax: 91-11-7267007

M/s. Annu Rashyan Udyog,
184, D.S.I.D.C Sheds,
Okhla Industrial Area-1,
New Delhi - 110 020.
Ph.: 6813624

SUPPLIERS OF RAW MATERIALS

LIMESTONE :-

M/s. Neej Chemicals,
A/6, Gautam Dhan Apartment,
Bajaj Road, Vile Parle (W),
Mumbai - 400 056.
(Factories At Kutach & Rajastan)

CARBON DIOXIDE GAS :-

M/s. Indian Oxygen Limited,
Oxygen House,
P - 34, Taratala Road,
Calcutta-700 088.
(Branches at all over India)

CAUSTIC SODA :

M/s. Gujarat Alkalies and Chemicals Limited,
P.O. Petrochemicals,
Dist. Baroda,
Gujarat-391 346.
Phone : 72681-82.

STEARIC ACID :

M/s. Nu-Chem plast,
A - 11, Rehman Market,
Pan Mandi, Sadar Bazar,
Delhi -110 006.
Ph : 777702.

PLANT ECONOMICS

Rated Plant capacity = 10.00 M.T/day
CALCIUM CARBONATE

LAND & BUILDING COST
(Land 4000 Sq.mts) Rs. 1,17,75,000.00

PLANT & MACHINERY

1. M.S.Tank FRP lined
2. Circulating pumps
3. Centrifuge
4. Rotary drier (Kiln)
5. Pulveriser
6. Packing unit
7. Lube type blower
8. Carbonation tower
9. Circulating Pumps
10. Dehydrator.
11. Compressor.
12. Gas Holder.
13. Water cooler.
15. Tools & jigs hose pipes and other maintennace workshop equipment
16. Slurry receining tank M.S. FRP
17. Vibrating screen & sieves
18. Piping & instrumentation
19. Water storage tank M.S.or FRP
20. Effluent treament unit
21. Shaft kiln
22. Drum Filter with vacum pump
23. Mixing tank M.S. FRP lined)
24. Carbon dioxide water scrubber
25. Carbon dioxide gas absorber.
26. Gas Reactivator .
27. Permanganate scrubber.
14. Settling Tank M.S. Rubber lined
28. Pump, blower, reboiler, CO_2 gas cooler and other .

FIXED CAPITAL

1. LAND & BUILDING	Rs.	1,17,75,000.00
2. PLANT & MACHINERY	Rs.	1,07,40,000.00
3. OTHER FIXED ASSETS	Rs.	32,16,500.00
TOTAL	Rs.	2,57,31,500.00

RAW MATERIALS

1. Lime Stone
2. Ethanolamine, Potassium Permanganate.
3. Other Chemicals Like Caustic Soda Stearic Acid.
4. Miscellaneous Consumables.
5. Packaging Polythene Lined Gunney Bags.

TOTAL WORKING CAPITAL/MONTH

1. RAW MATERIAL	Rs.	4,75,000.00
2. SALARY & WAGES	Rs.	2,59,375.00
3. UTILITIES & OVERHEADS	Rs.	2,50,000.00
TOTAL	Rs.	9,84,375.00

TOTAL CAPITAL INVESTMENT

TOTAL FIXED CAPITAL	Rs.	2,57,31,500.00
TOTAL WORKING CAPITAL FOR 1 MONTHS	Rs.	9,84,375.00
TOTAL	Rs.	2,67,15,875.00

TURN OVER/ANNUM

1. By sale of 2550 MT of Precipitated Calcium Carbonate.
2. By sale of 600 MT Activated Calcium Carbonate.

TOTAL Rs. 2,63,25,000.00

PROFIT = RECEIPTS - COST OF PRODUCTION
= 2,63,25,000.00 - 2,11,88,367.50
= 51,36,632.50

PROFIT SALES RATIO = Profit / Sales x 100 = *19.51 %*

RATE OF RETURN = Operating profit / T.C.I x 100 = *19.23 %*

BREAK EVEN POINT (B.E.P) = 69.71 %

Chapter- 7

CHEMICALS FROM PRAWN FISH HEAD

INTRODUCTION

Prawn fish or shrimp are processed for edible purposes after removal of head and other non-edible parts. These by products are used for several purposes such as preparation of fish meals, fish oils and other chemicals which are helpful for preparations of different medicines, pharmaceutical products.

Now a days, with the change of time these by products has been utilized and great success has been achieved with the progress of time.

There are several methods has been achieved to extract out the chemicals, hormones enzymes, from unutilised part of the fish. These chemicals are generally extracted from the pituitary glands obtained in the brain of the prawn fishes, shrimps and other varieties of fish.

The pituitary gland or hypophysis is small in size and is situated on the ventral side of the brain in a concavity called sella turcica in carps and is covered by duramater. It is connected to the brain by in fundibulum. In many fishes the gland gets detached when the brain proper is lifted.

The pituitary gland in fish is basically similar to those of other vertebrates in structure.

USES AND APPLICATIONS

1. The pituitary gland extract is used for induced breeding in the same fishes.

2. These extracts are useful for preparation of certain medicines and biological products.

3. The pituitary gland extract is injected into the body of the fish by following methods:

a) Intraperitoneal injection
b) Intramuscular injection

For induced breeding of the said fish.

PREPARATION OF PITUITARY GLAND EXTRACTS

1. Collection of Glands
2. Preservation of glands and storage
3. Preparation of Pituitary gland extract
4. Packaging & Preservation of Pituitary gland extract.
5. Storage.
6. Marketing.

PROCESS FLOW SHEET

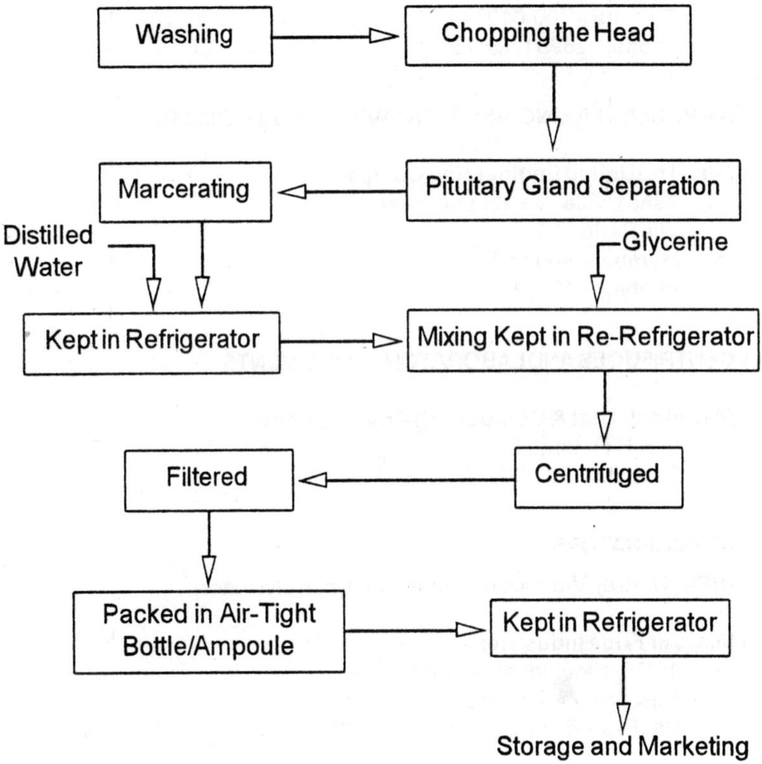

SUPPLIERS OF RAW MATERIAL

PRAWN FISH HEAD

Raw Materials Can be collected from local suppliers or prawn fish processing industries.

ABSOLUTE ALCOHOL, GLYCERINE, SALTS ETC.

M/s. BISCO Sales Corporation,
109, Sarup Building,
Malka Ganj Road,
New Delhi - 110 007.

GLASS AMPOULES SUPPLIERS

M/s. Gier Trading Company (Agency),
"Gier House",
4, Chatawala Lane,
Calcutta - 700 012.
Phone : 269810/267303.

AMPOULES FILLING & SEALING MACHINE (AUTOMATIC)

M/s. The United Engineering Company,
Ashok Villa, Valabhbhai Road,
Vile Parle (W),
Mumbai - 400 056.
Phone : 6127074

CENTRIFUGES AND LABORATORY EQUIPMENTS

M/s. Adair Dutt & Company (I) Private Limited,
5, B.B.D. Bagh East,
Calcutta - 700 001.

REFRIGERATORS

(BPL, Godrej, Videocon, Voltas, Allwyn, Kelvinator)

M/s. Air Frige Industries,
10/65, Kirti Industrial Area,
New Delhi - 110 015.
Ph./Fax : 531909, 731972, 01105436781

BASIS pituitary	:	2 mg/fish head
No. of fish	:	1,00,000 Nos./day
Production of pituitary	:	2,00,000 Mg/day (0.2 kg/day)
The volume of pituitary gland extract at the concentration (40 mg/ml of extract).		

Therefore, Total Quantity of Extract	:	5000 ml.
(5 kg extract/day.		

PLANT ECONOMICS

Rated Plant capacity = 5.00 Kgs/day
CHEMICALS FROM PRAWN FISH HEAD

LAND & BUILDING COST *(Total land 2 Acres)*	Rs.	64,50,000.00

PLANT & MACHINERY

1. Cutter, Chopper, Foreceps and other laboratory equipments
2. Bottles (Borosil)
3. Refregerator
4. Hand Centrifuge
5. Flasks (Round button)
6. Ampoules filling sealing (weighing) and labelling machine
7. Carton packaging machine

OTHER FIXED ASSETS

FIXED CAPITAL

1.	LAND & BUILDING	Rs.	64,50,000.00
2.	PLANT & MACHINERY	Rs.	26,63,900.00
3.	OTHER FIXED ASSETS	Rs.	19,50,000.00
	TOTAL	Rs.	1,10,63,900.00

WORKING CAPITAL REQUIREMENT/MONTH

RAW MATERIALS

1. Fish Head
2. Acetone Dehydrated Alcohol, Glycerine and chemicals
3. Glass Ampoules
4. Paper packaging material, carton labels, and other expenses

TOTAL WORKING CAPITAL/MONTH

1.	RAW MATERIAL	Rs.	4,61,000.00
2.	SALARY & WAGES	Rs.	2,92,500.00
3.	UTILITIES & OVERHEADS	Rs.	1,56,000.00
	TOTAL	Rs.	9,09,500.00

TOTAL CAPITAL INVESTMENT

TOTAL FIXED CAPITAL	Rs.	1,10,63,900.00
TOTAL WORKING CAPITAL FOR 3 MONTHS	Rs.	27,28,500.00
TOTAL	Rs.	1,37,92,400.00

TURN OVER/ANNUM

1. By sale of 15,00,000 Ampoules of 1 ml volume)
2. By sale of waste product 745 MT

TOTAL	Rs.	2,39,90,000.00

PROFIT = RECEIPTS - COST OF PRODUCTION

= 2,39,90,000.00 - 1,45,15,819.00

= 94,74,181.00

PROFIT SALES RATIO = Profit / Sales x 100 = 39.49 %

RATE OF RETURN = Operating profit / T.C.I x 100 = 68.69 %

BREAK EVEN POINT (B.E.P) = 37.79 %

Chapter- 8
DETERGENT CAKE & POWDER

INTRODUCTION

Detergents are defined as complete washing or cleaning products which contain among their ingredients an organic surface-active compound (Surfactant) that passes soil-removal properties. Frequently the term detergent is used synonymously with surfactant but common industry practice treats the surfactant as one component of a done here. Additionally this descussion treats primarily, only the so called synthetic detergents, excluding those products in which soap is the sole or predominant surfactant.

The synthetic detergent industry is one of the largest chemical process industries. The most recent estimates indicate an annual U.S production of synthetic detergents of about 3 million tonnes with an approximate annual value of 2 billion. The industry differs from many other chemical process industries, however, in that the bulk of its production is sold directly to individuals for house hold consumption primarily as branded products, rather than to industrial or institutional users.

PROPERTIES OF DETERGENTS AND USES

Detergents are very complex mixtures of many substances, all chosen to impart a particular action in cleaning. The modern concept of surface active agents, or surfactants includes soaps, detergents, emulsifiers wetting agent, and penetrents. They all owe their activity to amodification of the properties of the surface active agents have water attracting or hydrophilic, groups on one end of the molecule, water repelling or hydropholic, groups on the other. Detergent excel in possessing these special properties to effect soil.

DETERGENT CAKE AND POWDER USES

Detergent constitute about 95 percent of total surfactants. some of the important uses of detergent cake and powder are in:-

a). Hand Soaps and Shampoo.
b). Special protective creams : cream including cold creams, vanishing creams, absorption base creams and creams for special purposed such as depilatories, deodorantetc.
c). Cosmetics.
d). Cleaning and degresing of metals.
e). Cleaning of glass and containers.
f). Washing and treatment of food.
g). Cleaning of painted surfaces.
h). Cleaning of painted surfaces.

i). Household washing.
j). Removal of gelatine films.
k). For making antiseptic soaps.

DETERGENT CAKE FORMULA AND ITS MANUFACTURE

FORMULATION

INGREDIENTS

Alkyl Benzene Sulphate (65-85%) Active	20
Sodium Leuryl Sulphate	15
Tallow Coco Soap (80% : 20% Ratio)	35
Calcium Stearate	6-0
Titanium Dioxide	1-5
Tri-Sodium Ppolyphosphate	16.2
Perfume	0.3
Water	6.0
TOTAL	100.00

The manufacturing process of detergent bar can be divided into the following main head :

1. Igredient Dosing.
2. Slurry Preparation.
3. Cooling and refining.
4. Extrusion.
5. Conditioning.
6. Stamping.
7. Packing and forwarding.

PROCESS OF MANUFACTURE

DETERGENT POWDER PROCESS

Detergent powder is made from acid slurry by incorporating into it various additives and builders and spray drying the product so formed. On a cottage scale, the ingredients are mixed in open air. The following ingredients are used in detergents :-

1. Acid slurry
2. Optical Whitening agent
3. Foam Booster
4. Sodium carbonate
5. Trisodium polyphosphate
6. Trisodium phosphate
7. Sodium Perborate
8. Perfume
9. Sodium silicate
10. Sodium sulphate
11. Carboxy Methyl Cellulose (C.M.C)

In general the detergent contains 15 to 40% active material i.e. acid slurry, the rest being builders, fillers, dyes and other materials. Builders gives detergency. sodium tripolyphosphate and tetra sodium pyrophosphate are most outstanding alkaline builders. The amount of these vary from 30 to 50%. Small percentage, 1 to 3% of sodium carboxy methyl cellulose markedly improve the soil suspending power of detergents and prevent the redeposition of dirt. Brightening agents are al^o added in amount of 0.01 to 0.05%, sodium silicate lessons corrosion of aluminium washing machine.

The composition of a good quality detergent can be written as under:-

Acid Slurry	13%
C.M.C	1.0%
Trisodium phosphate	25.0%
Optical whitening agent	0.2%
Sodium perborate	1.0%
Trisodium polyphosphate	10.0%
Foam booster	1.0%
Sodium silicate	10.0%
Sodium carbonate	6.0%
Sodium sulphate	26%
Perfume	0.05%
Colour	0.05%
Moisture	7.7%

There are three processes which can be used for manufacture of detergent powder.

a) Pulverisation by blending all components in a pulveriser.
b) Cold spray process by crystallisation of a cold spray mix in current of cold air.
c) Hot spray process by rapid drying of cold spray mix in a current of hot air.

SUPPLIERS OF PLANT & MACHINERY

REACTION VESSELS AND STORAGE AND STORAGE TANKS

M/s. Flowlink Industries Private Limited,
D-15, Commercial Complex,
Prashant Vihar,
Delhi-110 085.
Ph.: 7267006/7267007
Fax: 91-11-7267007

M/s. Annu Rashyan Udyog,
184, D.S.I.D.C Sheds,
Okhla Industrial Area-1,
New Delhi - 110 020.
Ph.: 6813624

AGITATORS

M/s. Anup Engg. Company, Limited,
Anil Starch Premises,
Anil Road, Ahmedabad - 2.

M/s. A.P.V.Engineering Company Limited,
2, Jessore Road,
Calcutta - 700 028.

EVAPORATORS

M/s. Calcutta Chemicals Company Limited,
35, Panditia Road,
Calcutta - 700 029.

SUPPLIERS OF PLANT AND MACHINERY DRYERS

FORDETERGENT POWDER(NIRMA TYPE)

M/s. Alok Ashdown & Company Limited,
16, Bank Street Fort,
Mumbai-400 001.

SUPPLIERS OF PLANT & MACHINERY

M/s. D.S. Engineering & Mechanical Works,
D-2, Gali No. 4, Anand Parbat,
Industrial Area, New Rohtak Road,
New Delhi-110 005.

M/s. Mechanico Manufacturing Engineers,
15, Indl. Estate,
Okhla,
New Delhi -110 020.

SUPPLIES OF RAW MATERIALS

ALKYLBENZENE

M/s. Union Carbide,

M/s. U.S.A.Carboxy Methyl Cellulose

M/s. Cellulose Products of India Limited,
P.O. Kathwada Maize Products,
Distt. Ahmedabad.

OPTICAL WHITENING AGENT

M/s. Suhrid Geigy Limited,
Express Building, 14-E,
Church Gate, P.B. 11050,
Mumbai-400 020.

SODIUM SILICATE

M/s. Meera Chemicals,
Gali No.3, Bawana Road,
Samaipur, Delhi - 110 042.
Ph. : 7292914/7293914

PLANT ECONOMICS

Rated Plant capacity = 500.00 KG/day
DETERGENT CAKE & POWDER

LAND & BUILDING COST Rs. 1,21,000.00
(Area 350 Sq. Mt.)

PLANT & MACHINERY

1. Analgamator
2. Cake cutting Machine
3. Stamping Machine
4. Empty Drums for Mixing
5. Neutralizer
6. Mixer or Blender
7. Weighing Machine
8. Bhatti (Chulla)
9. Laboratory equipments
10. Trays/pan made of stainless steel
11. Pulverising machine (Grinding -machine)
12. Weighing Balance for packing
13. Miscellaneous items, like Blowers Trolleys and Bag Sewing Machine etc.

FIXED CAPITAL

1.	LAND & BUILDING	Rs.	1,21,000.00
2.	PLANT & MACHINERY	Rs.	1,81,000.02
3.	OTHER FIXED ASSETS	Rs.	5,000.00
	TOTAL	Rs.	3,07,000.02

RAW MATERIALS

1. Acid Slurry (LABS)
2. Sodium Tripolyphosphate
3. Carboxy Methyl Cellulose
4. Optical Whitening Agent
5. Foam Booster
6. Sodium Silicate
7. Sodium Sulphate
8. Acid Slurry
9. Soda Ash
10. Sodium Silicate
11. Marble chips powder
12. Packaging Material
13. Detergent Cake packaging

TOTAL WORKING CAPITAL/MONTH

1.	RAW MATERIAL	Rs.	1,00,150.00
2.	SALARY & WAGES	Rs.	10,000.00
3.	UTILITIES & OVERHEADS	Rs.	5,500.00
	TOTAL	Rs.	1,15,650.00

TOTAL CAPITAL INVESTMENT

TOTAL FIXED CAPITAL	Rs.	3,07,000.02
TOTAL WORKING CAPITAL FOR 3 MONTHS	Rs.	3,46,950.00
TOTAL	Rs.	6,53,950.02

TURN OVER/ANNUM

1. By sales of 30000 Kgs (30 MT)
2. By sales of 120000 Kgs. (120 MT)

TOTAL	Rs.	21,00,000.00

PROFIT = RECEIPTS - COST OF PRODUCTION

= 21,00,000.00 - 15,81,209.01

= 5,18,790.99

PROFIT SALES RATIO = Profit / Sales x 100 = *24.70 %*

RATE OF RETURN = Operating profit / T.C.I x 100 = *79.33 %*

BREAK EVEN POINT (B.E.P) = 34.05 %

Chapter- 9

DRY DISTEMPER

INTRODUCTION

Distempers as a class belong to water paints. Dry distemper is a powder mixture of pigment and binder which when dispersed in water gives the required water paint.

Distempers are manufactured in a wide range of bright cclours and find extensive use as well coatings on cemented surfaces just like white wash. Recently, distempers have replaced white wash and calcimine. This is mainly due to the superior retention powder, durability, and light fastness on exposure to exterior conditions throughout the year. Calcimine is a distemper in whiting as the principal pigment. It is sold in the form of dry powder to be mixed with water by the painter and is intended primarily for the decoration of plastered interior walls. Calcimine represent the latest expensive decorative coating available above the crude level of white wash or lime wash. It makes falt coatings with clear. Soft colour that do not fade and do not turn yellow in subsuced light.

TYPES OF DISTEMPER

There are two groups of materials that come within the general title of distemper. The first group includes the older types of distemper and the second are recently developed products often called emulsion paints, though the old oil-bound distemper is in fact also an emulsion paint.

PROPERTIES OF DISTEMPER

The following properties distemper have a good bearing on their choice for use in particular circumstances, especially when the conditions are not wholly favourable. Some comments are also made on the newer type emulsion paints, but as some of these are in a development stage it is advisable to consult the manufacturer for further details as to their use.

1. Permeability to Water
2. Contraction on Drying
3. Adhesion.

CHARACTERISTICS OF DRY DISTEMPER

Dry distemper is covered under oil free distemprs which is a soft distemper or ceiling white is a dispersion of whiting in glue solution in the following proportion by weight :

Whiting	83 parts
Water	35 parts
Skin Glue	2 parts

USES & APPLICATION OF DISTEMPERS

The importance of proper penetration of the surface will be evident from what has been said previously. The nature of these precautions and treatment will depend largely on whether or not the surface has been decorated already. The two sets of conditions are discussed below.

SURFACES NOT PREVIOUSLY DECORATED :

On the whole, little preparation is generally needed on new surfaces. It is advisable, however, to let constructional water dry out until the wall is at least surface dry; in view of the porous nature of the distempers, decoration often need not be deferred beyond on this point.

SURFACES PREVIOUSLY DECORATED :

Old non-washable distemper should always be completely removed before redecorating. Washable distempers that are dusty, but otherwise sound, can be redecorated with a similar distemper after dusting down. If the old surface of a washable distemper is dirty it should be well washed down and, if it is then found that much of the old decoration is removed in the process, it should be completely stripped before redecorating.

RAW MATERIAL FOR DISTEMPER (CASEIN BASED)

Various raw materials used in the manufacture of casein distemper are described below :

I. Opaque White Pigments
II. Pigments Of Low Opacity
III. Coloured Pigements
IV. Casein
V. Chemical Reagents
VI. Other Ingredients of the Non-Volatile Vehicle
VII. Anti Foaming Agents, Preservatives And Volatile Thinners

MANUFACTURING PROCESS

· DISTEMPER :

Dry distemper manufacture consists of through mixing of dry components of the formulation. Casein should be very finely ground. Generally the paint manufacture usually grinds and regrind the casein and shift it, returning the tails of the pulverizer. The reagent, plasticizer material and preservatives arethen added in a correct proportion and in corporated throughly in a dry mixer. The mixer has a set of revolving curved blades and is similar in construction to the dry mixer sometime used for blending pigments in the manufacturer of oil plant after mixing all the ingredients, the batch is passed through a stone mill or high speed pulverizer. It is then shifted again and sent back to the pulverizer until the whole mass has been reduced to a satisfactory degree of fineness. After this it is again mixed in a mixer and then packed.

Usually the dry distemper is packed in cartons, lined with moisture proof paper large quantity are packed in boxes, drums containing 25 or 100 pound materials.

For a white distemper the following is the general formulation :

	(% age)
Paris White	55
Lactic casein	10
Barytes	25
Slacked lime	6
Borax	4
Pigment q.s.	
Total	100

Formulation for Dry Distemper

Dry Distemper (White) :- Paint
U.S. patent 1,987,498

	(% age)
Titanium dioxide	15.00
Mineral filter	19.00
Special velvet filter	39.80
Casein	12.00
Mica	5.00
Borax glass	1.10
Sodium fluoride	1.00
Gelling agent	0.10
(Pectin or agaragor)	
Lime	7.00
Total	100.00

RAW MATERIAL SUPPLIER'S ADDRESSES

M/s. Borax India Limited,
Room No.-19, Bhagubhai Chembers,
363, Narsi Natha Street,
Mumbai - 400 009.
Ph: 3441711
3415204.

PARIS WHITE (CALCIUM CARBONATE) :

M/s. Balco Chemicals,
Gendigate Cross Road,
Opp. Ghantiyada,
Vadodara-390017.
Gujarat - 541 575
Ph: 444957.

SLAKED LIME :

M/s. Calcee Chemicals,
13-6, Janapathi Road,
Piduguralla Guntur Dist.,
Andhra Pradesh - 522413.
Ph: 2267
2767

BARYTES :

M/s. Alka Mineral & Chemicals,
25, Jilmil Industrial Area,
Shahdara,
Delhi -110 095.
Ph: 2285830
Fax: 5753125.

MANUFACTURERS OF RAW MATERIALS

ORGANIC PIGMENTS

M/s. Colour Chemical Limited,
22, Dadabhay Naroji Road,
Mumbai - 400 001.

IINORGANIC PIGMENTS

M/s. Olpherts Private Limted,
1/2, Moti Sil Street,
Calcutta - 700 013.

M/s. Chemo India,
Opp. Cotton Exchange Building,
160, Kalbadevi Road,
Mumbai.

EXTENDERS

M/s. Dinesh Chandra Industries,
Opp. Kamla Nehru Bagh,
P.O.B. No. 96, Porbander,
Gujarat.

METALALIC PIGMENTS

M/s. Metal Powder Company Limited,
Marvankulam,Thirumangalam,
P.O.Madurai, Distt.South India.

ZINC DUST

M/s. Associated Pigments Limited,
14, Netaji Subhash Road,
Calcutta.

LEAD OXIDE (RED LEAD, LITHORAGE)

M/s. Muraka Paints & Varnish Works Limited,
5-E, Delhousie Square,
Calcutta.

WHITE LEAD (BASIC LEAD CARBONATE)

M/s. Waldies Limited,
A-I, Gillander House,
Netaji Subhash Road,
Calcutta.

ZINC OXIDE

M/s. Pigments & Chemical Industries Private Limited,
32, Armenian Street,
Calcutta.

PLAYMERS & COPOLYMERS

M/s. Madhusuden Insopolymers,
(Prop) National General Agencies Private Limited,
Chandinali, Saki-Vihar Road,
Mumbai.

SUPPLIERS OF PLANT AND MACHINERIES

M/s. Kusum Engineering Company Limited,
25, Swallo Lane,
Calcutta.

MIXERS

M/s. APC Plant (Faridabad) Private Limited,
7, Convent Road,
Calcutta - 700 019.

COMPLETE PLANT SUPPLIERS FOR DRY DISTEMPER AND PAINT

M/s. T.R. Sharma Engineering Works,
A-156, Hari Nagar, Clock Tower,
New Delhi - 110 064.
Ph.: 5403729/5405328

PULVERIZER

M/s. Kaps Engineers,
Samraat Silk Mills Compound,
Lal Bahadur Shastri Marg,
Vikhroli (W),
Mumbai-400079
Ph: 022-5781933, Fax: 022-5785836.

PLANT ECONOMICS

Rated Plant capacity = 1.00 TON/day
DRY DISTEMPER

LAND & BUILDING COST Rs. 17,75,000.00
(Land 700 Sq.Mts)

PLANT & MACHINERY

1. Mild steel ball mill
2. Edge runner
3. Mixer (M.S.)
4. Vibrating screen
5. Weighing balance
6. Laboratory equipments
7. Pulverizer

FIXED CAPITAL

1.	LAND & BUILDING	Rs.	17,75,000.00
2.	PLANT & MACHINERY	Rs.	7,40,000.00
3.	OTHER FIXED ASSETS	Rs.	2,20,000.00
	TOTAL	Rs.	27,35,000.00

RAW MATERIALS

1. Paris white
2. Lactic casein
3. Barytes
4. Slacked lime

TOTAL WORKING CAPITAL/MONTH

1.	RAW MATERIAL	Rs.	3,15,250.00
2.	SALARY & WAGES	Rs.	50,125.00
3.	UTILITIES & OVERHEADS	Rs.	62,250.00
	TOTAL	Rs.	4,27,625.00

TOTAL CAPITAL INVESTMENT

TOTAL FIXED CAPITAL	Rs.	27,35,000.00
TOTAL WORKING CAPITAL FOR 3 MONTHS	Rs.	12,82,875.00
TOTAL	Rs.	40,17,875.00

TURN OVER/ANNUM

1. By sales of 300 Ton of dry distempers per annum
   TOTAL Rs. 75,00,000.00

PROFIT = RECEIPTS - COST OF PRODUCTION

= 75,00,000.00 - 61,40,342.50

= 13,59,657.50

PROFIT SALES RATIO = Profit / Sales x 100 = *18.13 %*

RATE OF RETURN = Operating profit / T.C.I x 100 = *33.84 %*

BREAK EVEN POINT (B.E.P) = 53.24 %

Chapter- 10
DEAD BURNT DOLOMITE

INTRODUCTION

The term 'Dolomite' is refereed to commercially is rock containing mineral Dolomite Colsite and magnesite. On heating dolomite loses carbon dioxide with an increase in volume, it is therefore, calcined at 15000C to convert it into a more stable form, i.e, dead burnt dolomite for the use in the manufacture of refractories. Large deposit of dolomite occur in the country and almost entire production of the mineral is used for refractory manufacture.

The places of availability of dolomite are Singbhum and Palamu districts of Bihar; Jabalpur, Bilaspur, Durg and Dhar districts of Madhya Pradesh; Shimuga district of Mysore; Sundergarh, Sambalpur and Korapur districts of Orissa; Alwar and Jaipur districts of Rajasthan and Darjeeling and Jalpaiguri district of West Bengal.

The major supply for the refractory industries, however comes from Orissa.

PRODUCTINTRODUCTION

Dolomite [$CaMg(Ca_3)2$] is a carbonate of Calcium and magnesium. The colour is grey, pink, white of various other colours as well.

Dolomite is used as refractory for furnaces, is the manufacture of magnesium compounds and magnesium metal, as building material, in fertilizers, stock feeds, heater making, ceramics, mineral ware, removal of sulphur dioxide from stock gases.

However, calcined dolomite is extensively employed in the manufacture and repair of banks and bottoms of open hearth furnace.

PROPERTIES

Dolomite has colour grey, pink, white and various other colours. It has vitreous lusture Sp.gr. 2.85.

Hardness : 3.5 - 4

It has good clearage in three dimensions, it is similar to colcite, but less soluble in acids, (reacts with acid. When powdered or with hot acid).

It is non combustible and non toxic.

USES AND APPLICATIONS

Dense fine-grained variety of crushed dolomite either in the raw state or more commonly after dead burning is used as a fefractory material is the manufacture of steel.

Dolomite used for refractory purpose is usually purer than used as flux.

Calcined dolomite crushed to peanut size is employed in the manufacture and repair banks and bottoms of basic open-hearth furnace.

For this purpose, Dolomite is calcined in a cupola with coke and the calcined material (double burnt dolomite) crushed, sized, and mixed with tar or other bonding materials.

Dolomite is used in the preparation of Dolomite Bricks .

MANUFACTURING PROCESS

Manufacturing process involves burning of Dolomite ore in a vertical shaft kiln. The kiln is usually oil fired.

The process can be divided into two main steps.

1. Crushing and grinding of Dolomite ore
2. Calcination in the kiln.

I. CRUSHING OF MINERAL :-

The Dolomite is brought into the factory by trailers. The Dolomite ore is broken into 1" size. For the purpose of crushing Jaw crusher is used.

II. CALCINATION :-

Calcining of Dolomite ore occurs in the kiln where the crushed Dolomite is fed from the top of the vertical shaft kiln. The shaft furnace is a vertical refractory lined cylinder in which a stationary (fixed bed) or descending column of solids is maintained through which an ascending stream of hot gas is forced. To minimise contamination furnace oil is used as fuel. The kiln shaft consists of three zones, preheating zones calcining zone and cooling zone.

The difference in the process of calcined Dolomite and dead burnt magnesia manufacture lies in the calcining temperature for the two. For the Dead Burnt Dolomite is in the range of 15000C and above so that carbon dioxide retained in Calcined Dolomite is about 2 to 10% whereas in dead burnt dolomite it is expelled completely.

SUPPLIERS OF PLANT & MACHINERIES

JAW CRUSHERS

M/s. International Engineering Company,
Lal Khan, Badarpur,
New Delhi -110 044.

M/s. Premier Machines Private Limited,
59, Nazafgarh Road,
New Delhi -110 015.
Ph./Fax : 530023, 5451286, 011-5195006

TANKS

M/s. New Ujagar Trailors,
F-134, 137, Mayapuri Industrial Area,
Phase-II,
New Delhi -110 064.

KILNS

M/s. McNally Bharat Engineering Company Limited,
44, Park Street,
Calcutta -700 016.

ELEVATOR

M/s. Sutdhar Machinery Manufacturers,
S. Plot No. 1, Rajendra Nagar,
Industrial Area,
P.O. Mohan Nagar,
Ghaziabad (U.P.).

VERTICAL KILN:

M/s. Calthenm Engineers & Consultants,
18/1A, Gorachand Lane,
Calcutta -700 014.
Tel: 033-2446309, 296119.
Tlx: 021-4898 ROMA - IN.
Fax: 91-33-2446309.

SUPPLIERS OF RAW MATERIALS

M/s. Bharat Mineral Chemical Industries,
1, Old Industrial Area,
Opp. Railway Goods Shed,
Alwar-301 001 (Rajasthan).

PLANT ECONOMICS

Rated Plant capacity = 20.00 MT/day
DEAD BURNT DOLOMITE

LAND & BUILDING COST *(Land Area 5000 sq.mt)*	Rs.	42,86,000.00

PLANT & MACHINERY

1. Jaw Crushers.
3. Oil Burner for the kiln
4. Fuel oil storage tank.
5. Bucket Elevator & Conveyors
6. Air cooling chamber
7. Lab equipments
8. Process control & instromentation
9. Misc. Viz. Motors, fittings, tools, jigs, fixtures etc.

FIXED CAPITAL

1. LAND & BUILDING	Rs.	42,86,000.00
2. PLANT & MACHINERY	Rs.	28,80,000.00
3. OTHER FIXED ASSETS	Rs.	11,00,000.00
TOTAL	Rs.	82,66,000.00

RAW MATERIALS

1. Dolomite Ore (MgO app: 20%)

TOTAL WORKING CAPITAL/MONTH

1. RAW MATERIAL	Rs.	2,07,000.00
2. SALARY & WAGES	Rs.	1,00,125.00
3. UTILITIES & OVERHEADS	Rs.	8,11,500.00
TOTAL	Rs.	11,18,625.00

TOTAL CAPITAL INVESTMENT

TOTAL FIXED CAPITAL	Rs.	82,66,000.00
TOTAL WORKING CAPITAL FOR 3 MONTHS	Rs.	33,55,875.00
TOTAL	Rs.	1,16,21,875.00

TURN OVER/ANNUM

1. 6000 M.T.
   Dead Burnt Dolomite. Rs. 2,40,00,000.00

PROFIT = RECEIPTS - COST OF PRODUCTION

= 2,40,00,000.00 - 1,69,33,902.50

= 70,66,097.50

PROFIT SALES RATIO = Profit / Sales x 100 = *29.44 %*

RATE OF RETURN = Operating profit / T.C.I x 100 = *60.80 %*

BREAK EVEN POINT (B.E.P) = 52.74 %

Chapter-11

GAS FILLING OF L.P.G. CYLINDER

INTRODUCTION

Through out the commercial life time of a hydrocarbon fuel, from production at the weelhead to combustion in chamber, considerations of fuel storage movement, loss, safety and contamination apply. These are determined largely by the properties of the fuel itself and are therefore controlled by suitable property specifications. They are also influenced significantly by the design of the handling equipment, the procedures adopted and in some cases by the use of appropriate fuel additives.

STORAGE OF HYDROCARBON FUELS

Bulk petroleum and hydrocarbons generally are most commonly stored in cylindrical tanks of welded steel construction up to about 100.000 Ton capacity mounted vertically on simple formulations of rubble and sand bituminmix.

For quantities up to about 250 nos. the cylindrical tanks may be carried horizontally to variations in temperatures. Low volatility fuels are stored at atmospheric pressure under a fixed roof, but the evaporation losses of volatile fuels are minimised either by storage under slight pressure by means of a control valve in the vent, or by the use of a floating roof, or floating innerblanket, to eliminate the vapour space. For fire safety, liquid-fuel tanks are separated from each other and surrounded by 'hung' walls to contains any leaks.

L.P.G. Required storage under pressure, ranging from 2 to 7 atm. for butane and propane, respectively, storage of liquefied gases is, therefore, effected in rugged metal tanks, either spherical or cylindrical with rounded ends. Surroundings hungs are not used in order to permit any leakafter to disperse freely in the atmosphere. Alternatively L.P.G. may be stored underground in natural or manmade cover or leached salt caverns. The fuel is trapped by the hydrostatic head of brine above it-which must be in excess of the fuel vapour pressure and is transferred to and from storage by displacement with brine. This method is relatively simple, inexpensive and from hurbles or epillages.

PROPERTIES

LIQUID HYDROCARBON GASES

Since the vander wall's forces between the lighter molecular of the paraffin hydrocarbons are relatively weak, these members exist as either gases or Vapours at ambient temperatures as shown from their boiling points (H.P) in figure and tables at 150°C.

In fact, methane is well above its critical temperature of 82.5°C and therefore cannot be liquefied under pressure. Ethane, propane and butane exist as Vapours, and pentane as a highly Volatile liquid. The olefins show similar properties.

Natural Gas (N.G) consist mainly of methane, plus decreasing preparations of ethane to heptanes together with traces of N_2 CO_2 and H_2S. Although pentane and heavier hydrocarbons hoil above ambient temperature, they vaporise in small proportions below abmient temperature just as water vapour exists in hurried air well below 100°C. Natural gas can be liquefied and stored as L.P.G. by cooling to about -118°C at a pressure of 13.5 atm. cooling to the boiling point of -162°C, of course, brings the pressure down to atmospheric liquefied petroleum gases (L.P.G.) comprising of mainly propane and butane but may include prepare, butanes, butadiene is obtain with traces of ethane, ethylene and the paraffins pentane to dodecane. Commercial propane and butane each contain approximately 95 percent of corresponding paraffins and olefins. At 15°C they can be stored at 7 and 2 atm respectively. On vaporisation the vapour liquid volume ratio ranges from about 600/1 for L.N.G. and over 250/- for L.P.G.

USES

L.P.G. is used mainly for cooking purposes in India. It is usually filled in small cylinders to the used in house hold cooking. It is also used for drying or in Industry with oxygen for cutting welding, brazing, heating etc. It is used in power production also or chemical feed stock, hot air hallooning. In fact, due to its smokeless burning it finds various uses.

It is used as industrial fuels, Boiler fuels, furnace fuels, also as internal combustion Engine fuel.

It is used as gas light (Petromax) fuel.

LPG BOTTLING PROCESS

The following steps to consider during whole operation of LPG filling in cylinders.

1. LPG Gas procurement from the refineries or suppliers sources.
2. Storage of LPG in the tanks or hortons sphere.
3. Empty cylinder testing for leakage of body or valves.
4. Cylinder filling with the specified quantity as mentioned for the cylinder size, volume etc.
5. Filled LPG cylinder testing.
6. Storage in the cool & dry place.
7. Marketing & distribution.

PROCESS FLOW SHEET

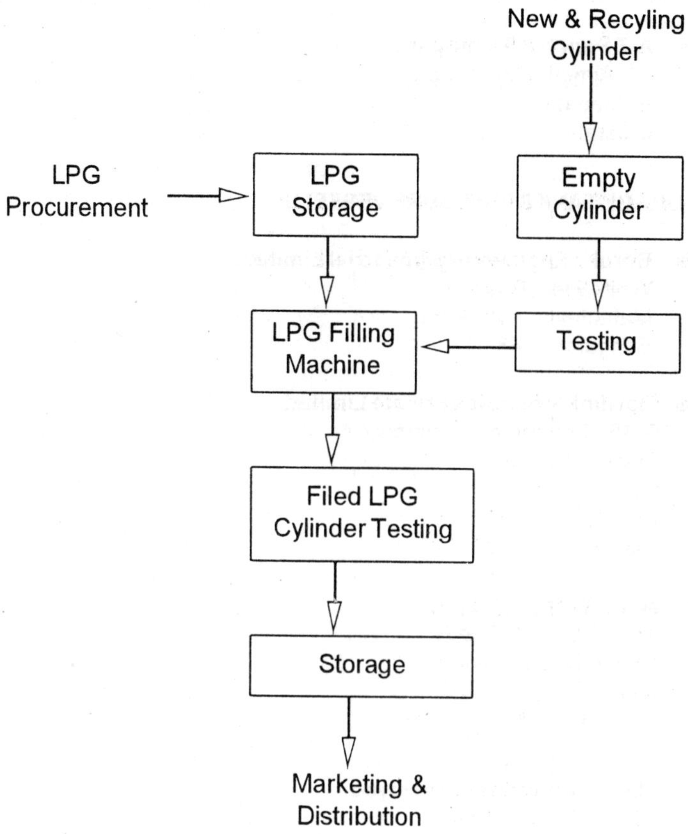

RAW MATERIAL SUPPLIERS

GOVERNMENT REFINERIES,

M/s. Uran

M/s. Mathura Refineries,

M/s. Koyali Refinery

MACHINERY SUPPLIERS

PUMPS & PUMPING SETS:

M/s. A-Z Panchal & Company,
13, Ajmeri, Udyognagar.
Ahmedabad,
Gujarat.

STORAGE TANK & PRESSURE VESSELS:

M/s. Boruka Engineering Industrial Limited,
White Field Road,
Mahadevapuram Post,
Bangalore - 48.

M/s. Flowlink Industries Private Limited,
D-15, Commercial Complex,
Prashant Vihar,
Delhi-110 085.
Ph.: 7267006/7267007
Fax: 91-11-7267007

M/s. Annu Rashyan Udyog,
184, D.S.I.D.C Sheds,
Okhla Industrial Area-1,
New Delhi - 110 020.
Ph.: 6813624

M/s. Annu Rashyan Udyog,
184, D.S.I.D.C Sheds,
Okhla Industrial Area-1,
New Delhi - 110 020.
Ph.: 6813624

PLANT ECONOMICS

Rated Plant capacity = 10000.00 /day
GAS FILLING OF L.P.G. CYLINDER

LAND & BUILDING COST	Rs.	40,80,000.00

(Land area required 10,000 sq.mts.)

PLANT & MACHINERY

1. Storage tanks(Horton's sphere)
2. Cylinder filling systems
4. Fire fighting arrangements and equipments
5. Testing equipments
6. Gen. Set

FIXED CAPITAL

1. LAND & BUILDING	Rs.	40,80,000.00
2. PLANT & MACHINERY	Rs.	57,60,000.01
3. OTHER FIXED ASSETS	Rs.	3,03,50,000.00
TOTAL	Rs.	4,01,90,000.01

WORKING CAPITAL REQUIREMENT/MONTH

RAW MATERIALS

L.P.G. Gas

TOTAL WORKING CAPITAL/MONTH

1. RAW MATERIAL	Rs.	99,40,000.00
2. SALARY & WAGES	Rs.	62,250.00
3. UTILITIES & OVERHEADS	Rs.	1,08,000.00
TOTAL	Rs.	1,01,10,250.00

TOTAL CAPITAL INVESTMENT

TOTAL FIXED CAPITAL	Rs.	4,01,90,000.01
TOTAL WORKING CAPITAL FOR 3 MONTHS	Rs.	3,03,30,750.00
TOTAL	Rs.	7,05,20,750.01

TURN OVER/ANNUM

By sale of 30,00,000 cylinders
of 14.2 kgs. Rs. 18,00,00,000.00

PROFIT = RECEIPTS - COST OF PRODUCTION

= 18,00,00,000.00 - 13,56,76,935.00

= 4,43,23,065.00

PROFIT SALES RATIO = Profit / Sales x 100 = 24.62 %

RATE OF RETURN = Operating profit / T.C.I x 100 = 62.85 %

BREAK EVEN POINT (B.E.P) = 25.50 %

Chapter-12
HYDROCHLORIC ACID (HCL)

INTRODUCTION

Hydrochloric acid is a solution of hydrogen chloride gas in water. It is also known as muriatic acid. Hydrochloric acid is an important acid, and is naturally present in the digestive system. The gastric mucosa produces about 1.5 litre per day of gastric juices, containing 0.05 to 0.1N. Hydrochloric acid content. Hydrochloric acid deficiency in gastric tract impairs the digestive process, particularly of carbohydrates and proteins while excessive acid causeses gastric ulcers. The atmosphere of each contains H_2O,CO_2 and HCl in the ratio of 20:3:1, giving an early ocean consisting of about 1-N HCl. Hydrogen chloride has also been detected in atmosphere of venus.

Anhydrous hydrogen chloride is a colorless gas that condenses to a colorless liquid and freezes to a white crystalline solid. The largely enthalpy of formation reflects the high thermal stability of hydrogen chloride.

Hydrogen chloride is highly soluble in water, which forms constant boiling mixtures & are frequently used analytical standards.

PROPERTIES & CHARACTERISTICS

Hydrochloric acid is colorless to slightly yellow, fuming liquid, have pungent smell. It is a strong, highly corrosive acid. The commercial acid contains maximum 38% of hydrogen chloride and has a specific gravity of 1.19. It is soluble in water, alcohol & benzene. Hydrochloric acid is non combustible.

It is highly toxic by ingestion and inhalation. It irritates eyes skin.

It is available in market in various grades such as 10% (diluted); technical (28,31,35,37%)

Hydrogen chloride gas is colorless, pungent gas which forms strongly in moist air and seriously effects both the skin and mucow menbrass. Contact into the gas or solution should be avoided (specially so far as the eyes are concerned). Most states in the U.S.A. accept 10 PPM as the maximum level of HCL gas can be tolered an eight hour period.

HCL condones to a liquid under 1 atom at a temperature of 85^{0}C and freezes at -114^{0}C.

USES & APPLICATION

It is used in pickling & metal cleaning, Industrial acidizing, general cleaning e.g. of membranes in deqalination plants, alcohol denaturant.

It is also used in acidizing of petroleum wells, chemicals intermediate, ore reduction, food processing industries like corn syrup, sodium glutamate etc.

It is also used in the derivation of various chemicals.

In steel pickling it provides an alternative to H_2SO_4 acid, inhabitants are added to allow the reaction in the any oxide film on the metal than attack on the metal itself, in galvanizing and in solder fluxes, in gelatial manufacturer in super refining in glucone and corn supar production from starch (as a hydrolying agent), and in rubber processing.

Important quantities of Hcl acid are used in the Dowell process for reactivating oil wells. Hcl acid reserves obstracting in rocks (such as lime stone) or improves the positively to make the rocks penetrable by oil.

Smaller quantities of Hcl acid are widely used in Industry, e.g. in dyestuff manufacture for combining with basic intermediates, in reduction process based on the use of nascent hydrogen (obtained from neutrals of HCL acid), in the production of gilicr. lel, In the removal of hair from skin and in the expeditin of impurities from clays & sand.

MANUFACTURING PROCESS

Hydrochloric acid is prepared by reacting H_2SO_4 acid with common salt. The reactions are represented by the following equations.

a. $$NaCl + H_2SO_4 \xrightarrow{150\text{-}300^0} NaHSO_4 + HCl$$

b. $$NaCl + NaHSO_4 \xrightarrow{600^0C} Na_2SO_4 + HCl$$

c. $$2NaCl + H_2SO_4 \xrightarrow{600^0C} Na_2SO_4 + 2HCl$$

PLANT & MACHINERY SUPPLIERS

M/s Chemech Engineering Works,
30 DSIDC,
Scheme-III, Phase-II,
Okhla,
New Delhi - 110 020
Ph. 633399.

M/s Chemfil Engineers,
B-4, DSIDC Industrial Complex,
Rohtak Road,
Nangloi,
Delhi - 110 041.
Ph. - 6448479

M/s Davindra Engineering & Manufacturing Company,
C-194/2, Mayapuri Industrial Area,
Phase-II,
New Delhi - 110 064,
Ph. - 591232.

RAW MATERIAL SUPPLIERS

COMMON SALT

M/s Sanjay Chemicals,
54, IVth West Cross Road,
Gandhi Nagar,
Vallore - 6.

M/s Chinai Chemicals,
311/3, Rakhial Road,
Octroi Naka,
Ahmedabad - 23,
Gujarat.

PLANT ECONOMICS

Rated Plant capacity = 1.50 MT/day
HYDROCHLORIC ACID

LAND & BUILDING COST	Rs.	4,00,000.00

(Land require area 500 sq mt.)

PLANT & MACHINERY

1. Manuheim Furnace
2. Karbate Cooler
3. Coke Packed Tower
4. Scrubber.
5. Storage Tanks.
6. Pumps & Motors (Polypropylene)
7. Other Jigs, Fixtures, etc.
8. Testing Equipment etc.
9. Miscellaneous

FIXED CAPITAL

1. LAND & BUILDING	Rs.	4,00,000.00
2. PLANT & MACHINERY	Rs.	2,83,000.00
3. OTHER FIXED ASSETS	Rs.	1,35,000.00
TOTAL	Rs.	8,18,000.00

TOTAL WORKING CAPITAL/ANNUM

1. RAW MATERIAL	Rs.	72,475.00
2. SALARY & WAGES	Rs.	27,250.00
3. UTILITIES & OVERHEADS	Rs.	20,500.00
TOTAL	Rs.	1,20,225.00

TOTAL CAPITAL INVESTMENT

TOTAL FIXED CAPITAL	Rs.	8,18,000.00
TOTAL WORKING CAPITAL FOR 3 MONTHS	Rs.	3,60,675.00
TOTAL	Rs.	11,78,675.00

TURN OVER/ANNUM

1. By Sale of 450 MT of HCl
2. 257.73 MT of salt cake

TOTAL Rs. 25,11,840.00

PROFIT = RECEIPTS - COST OF PRODUCTION

= 25,11,840.00 -18,02,258.50

= 7,09,581.50

PROFIT SALES RATIO = Profit / Sales x 100 = *28.25 %*

RATE OF RETURN = Operating profit / T.C.I x 100 = *60.20 %*

BREAK EVEN POINT (B.E.P) = 45.35 %

Chapter-13
HYDROGENATION OF NON-EDIBLE OILS

INTRODUCTION

Primarily, hydrogenation is a means of converting liquid oils to semisolid.

For hydrogenation to take place, gaseous hydrogen liquid oil, and the solid catalyst must be brought together at a suitable temperature. In ordinary practice it may be assumed that the hydrogen is first caused to dissolve in the oil, with the hydrogen-laden oil then brought into contact with the catalyst by mechanical means. In the usual type of equipments, reaction is brought about by agitating the suspension of the catalyst and oil in closed vessel in an atmosphere of hydrogen. Agitation of the catalyst oil mixture serves the double purpose of promoting solution of hydrogen in the oil and continuously renewing the oil at the catalyst surface. The solubility of hydrogen and other gases in oil increases linearly with temperature and, of course, pressure.

USES AND APPLICATIONS

It is used in the impregnation and coating of papers, fiber boards, leather cork, textile, and rubber coated fabrics for electrical insulation and to make them resistant to greases, oil and water. In the manufacture of polishes and finishes, it is used in wax blends where increase in grease and solvent resistance, hardness and melting point is desired. Hydrogenated castor oil is also used in lubricating greases, sealants and polting compounds as a plasticizer for plastic, as blending agent and viscosity readucer in hot melts and in the manufacture of metal caster oils. The major application of hydrogenated castor oil is in the manufacture of lubricating greases and protective coatings.

PROCESS OF MANUFACTURE

Fatty acids and enadible fats high in free fatty acids, when hydrogenated, are usually saturated as nearly as possible, although there is some partial hydrogenation of soft greases and marine oils for soap making. The hydrogenation of fatty acids is quite similar to the hydrogenation of vegetable oils to produce hard oils, except that temperature above 300°F and some times above 300°F are avoided high pressure are depended on to accelerate the reaction. The converters which must be built of type 316 stainless steel or other alloy resistance to corrosion, are usually designed for a working pressure of 200-300 lbs. Hydrogenation is relatively difficult. 0.2 -0.5% of nickel is required, and the catalyst is largely in activated with one usage.

PROCESS OF MANUFACTURE
HYDROGENATION OF CASTOR OIL

The main reaction in the hydrogenation of castor oil is the conversion of triricinolein into hydroxy stearin. Although other unsaturated glycerides are also hydrogenated their percentage in castor oil is very small and it may be assumed that castor oil is very small and it may be assumed that astor oil consists of only triricinolein and most calculations are done with this assumption.

Hydrogenation is carried out in the presence of a catalyst. Nickel is the most widely used catalyst, other catalysts such as palladium and platinum may also be used but they are costly. Hydrogenation of castor oil differs from the manufacture of vanaspati in which the aim is selective hydrogenation of unsaturated compounds into less unsaturated compounds and obtain a product with melting point of 37°C. In vanaspati manufacture thus very little fully saturated glycerides are produced, but in the manufacture of hydrogenataed castor oil the aim is to fully saturate the oil so that the melting point is raised to about 85°C. The hddrogenation of castor oil is non-selective and more drastic than vanaspati manufacture and requires higher temperature higher pressure and higher concentrations of catalyst. However, since the hydrogenation is non-selective, the catalyst can be reused more number of times in this case in the case of vanaspati manufacture where often only active catalyst is used.

Hydrogenation results in the addition of hydrogen at the double bonds in the fatty acid chain. The degree of unsaturation is measured by iodine value (weight in gm o iodine required for complete reaction with 1 kg oil). To reduce the iodine value by one unit 1 tonne of oil will theoretially require 0.08 kg hydrogen equivalent to about 900 litres at normal temperature and pressure. However, in actual practice a little more than the theoretical amount is required to compensate for the loss of hydrogen by leakage and unabsorbed losses to atmosphere. In the hydrogenation process, the iodine value of castor oil is reduced from 84-88 to about 2 for full saturation. Assuming that the change in iodine value is about 84 full saturation of 1 ton oil will required about 75600 lts of hydrogen theoritically. In actual practice the requirements may be 80,000 litres per tonne of oil hydrogenated if the oil is to be fully hydrogenated.

SUPPLIERS OF RAW MATERIALS

NICKEL CATALYST

M/s. Menna Chemicals,
22, Appollo Street,
End Floor,
Mumbai - 400 001.

BLEACHING BARTH

M/s. Vimal Organics Limited,
D-35, Bulandshahar Road,
Industrial Area, Ghaziabad-09 (U.P).
Ph./Fax: 0575-750765/754913

SUPPLIERS OF PLANT AND MACHINERY

BOILER

M/s. Indcon Boilers,
D - 170.
Okhala Industrial Area,
Phase-1,
New Delhi - 110 020.

STORAGE TANK & PRESSURE VESSELS

M/s. Annu Rashyan Udyog,
184, D.S.I.D.C Sheds,
Okhla Industrial Area-1,
New Delhi - 110 020.
Ph.: 6813624

PLANT AND MACHINERY

1. Raw oil Storage Tanks
2. Oil Pumps
3. Weigh Bridge
4. Oil Receiving Tanks
5. Caustic Scribber
6. Caustic Pump
7. Gas Circulator
8. Oil Water Gravity Separators
9. Gas Cooler
10. Chemical Pumps
11. Transportation and others
12. Filter press with pumps:
13. Vacuum Pumps:
14. Hardening Machine
15. Catalyst press
16. Catalyst storage tank.
17. First through oil tank
18. Finished hard oil tank.
19. Catchalls:
20. Boiler
21. Electrical and water installation

PLANT ECONOMICS

Rated Plant capacity = 10.00 MT./day
HYDROGENATION OF CASTOR OIL

LAND & BUILDING COST	Rs.	24,90,500.00
(Land required area 3000 sq. mts.)		

FIXED CAPITAL

1. LAND & BUILDING	Rs.	24,90,500.00
2. PLANT & MACHINERY	Rs.	62,15,000.00
3. OTHER FIXED ASSETS	Rs.	5,00,000.00
TOTAL	Rs.	92,05,500.00

RAW MATERIALS

1. Castor oil
2. Hydrogen gas
3. Raney nickel alloy
4. Caustic soda flakes
5. Hyflosupercel
6. Miscellaneous (filter cloth and other chemicals, gunny bags etc.)

TOTAL WORKING CAPITAL/MONTH

COST OF RAW MATERIALS	Rs.	69,28,302.50
SALARY & WAGES / MONTH	Rs.	1,36,375.00
UTILITIES AND OVERHEADS	Rs.	2,33,600.00
TOTAL	Rs.	73,98,277.50

TOTAL CAPITAL INVESTMENT

TOTAL FIXED CAPITAL	Rs.	92,05,500.00
TOTAL WORKING CAPITAL FOR 3 MONTHS	Rs.	2,18,94,832.50
TOTAL	Rs.	3,11,00,332.50

TURN OVER/ANNUM

1. Receipt by sale of 3000 Tons of Hydrogenated Castor Oil. Rs. 11,40,00,000.00

PROFIT = RECEIPTS - COST OF PRODUCTION

= 11,40,00,000.00 - 9,61,08,285.65

= 1,78,91,714.35

PROFIT SALES RATIO = Profit / Sales x 100 = *15.69 %*

RATE OF RETURN = Operating profit / T.C.I x 100 = 57.53 %

BREAK EVEN POINT (B.E.P) = 36.55 %

Chapter-14
H-ACID

INTRODUCTION

The study deals mainly with the H-Acid, and important dyes intermediate, which is mainly used for the manufacture of Reactive, Direct and Acid Dyes.

The study analyses the present and future structure of the H-Acid industry in India, with a view to estimating the future demand for H-Acid.

This study also considers the feasibility aspect for the establishment of an H-Acid, and also analyses the technical and financial viability of the project.

USES AND APPLICATION

H-Acid is used in many direct and reactive dyes e.g. Direct black E, Direct green. Direct blue 2B, Reactive Magentas, Reactive Voilet 3B. If H-Acid is fused with caustic, chromotropic acid (1:3 Dihydroxy Naphthalene 3:6 Disulfonic acid) is formed. The intermediate is used for some important chromotropeazodyestuff. H-Acid is also used for hydroxyketone clase of dyes. The N-acy1 (N-acetyle, N-Benzoly, N-P-Teluenesulfony1) red and voilet azo dyes. With aniline and amonoacetanildie. Acetyl-H-acid gives Amodo-napthol-red G and amodo-Naphthol red 6B, respectively. (The latter is more stable than G barand) By the alkaline coupling of diazatized Nadoecylabiline on N-acetyl-H-acid, a member of classical carbonian range, carbolan crimsor B (C.I.acid red 138) is obtained.

A wool dye, C.I. Acid blue 6,17185, is formed by acid coupling of 4-amono-3-nitro acetanilide with H-acid. On hydrolyzing with dilute acids or alkalines H-acid gives 4-5 Dihydraxy-1, Naphthalene disulfonic acid.

PROPERTIES

H-Acid is cold in the market as in the form of centrifuged cake having 50-60%, purity, it's grey in colour and very alightly soluble in water. Solubility of H-acid, at 18°C water- 0.993%; and 100°C in water 8%.

It's rapid soluble in soda ash solution, H-acid with ferric chloride gives brownish red colour. This acid salt fluoresces bluish red which turns red voilet on dilution with alkali H-acid couples twice first acid and than alkaline.

PRESENT STATUS OF THE INDUSTRY

At present there are approximately 15-20 units manufacturing H-Acid. Of these, only four units are in the organised sector, namely, actual products and Amr Dye-Chem, Zenith Steel Tubes and Pipes Ltd., and Piramed Rasayan, while all the remaining II units are in the small sector.

MANUFACTURING PROCESS

Napththalene is first broken up in a Naphthalene crusher as it comes in the form of hot pressed lumps. The sulfonator is charged with sulfuric acid mono hydrate and the mass is cooled to 20 to 25°C by circulating cold water in the jacket. Throughout this cooling process the mass is continuously agitated. At this temperature the grounded of flaked Naphthalene is slowly changed in the sulfonator, so that the temperature does not rise beyond 32-35°C. The temperature is raised to 85°C and solution is stored for 1 to 1 1/4 hours. The temperature is raised to 143°C, by passing steam and the solution is again stirred for 1 hours. The mass is cooled by circulating cold water and after that 98% sulfuric Acid is charged within 1 to 2 hours. The batch temperature is maintained at the room temperature and Cleum of 62% strength is added. The mass is again stirred for 30 minutes at 30-35°C. The temperature is then raised to 146 - 150°C, over a period of 4-5 hours. The temperature is brought down to 55-60°C. And further quantities of 62% Oleum is added.

The temperature is again raised to 155-156°C and at this temperature the solution is stirred for 3-4 hours. The heating process is stopped and the temperature is brought down to 100°C by adding water. This is the stage where Naphthalene is converted into Nitro T-Acid. (1 Nitro 3:6:8 T Sulfuric Acid).

This nitrated Naphthalene Sulfonic Acid slurry is then added to Calcium Carnonate slurry already kept at 80-85°C for a long period, The over mass is filtered in a notch called Gypsum notch, the mass is washed and Nitro T-Acid solution is collected and reduce to Amono T-Acid (KOCH Acid). The boiling mass is then filtered washed and cooled in a tank, where KOCH Acid is isolated with 30% Hydrochloric Acid is filtered and washed, the wet pitated KOCH Acis is dissolved in the solution of water and caustic lye to a positive alkaline pH. The dissolved KOCH acid is then fused with Caustic Flakes at 165°C for 1 to 2 hours. The solution is kept under pressure at high temperature for 2 to 3 hours. The fused mass is then drowned in water and taken for isolation where N-Acid is isolated by 98% sulfuric acid at high temperature. The temperature. The material can be dried at 90°C in tray dryer. The H-Acid can be sold either in wet cake form or dried form.

SUPPLIERS OF RAW-MATERIALS OF H-ACID

SODAASH (SODIUMCARBONATE) :-

M/s. BharatChemical Company,
331, Samuel Street, Vadgadi,
Mumbai - 400 003.

CAUSTICSODA : (SODIUM HYDROXIDE):-

M/s. Alchemicals Private Limited,
Opp. Patallia Talao, Saraspur,
Ahmedabad - 380 018 (Gujarat).

OLEUM:-

M/s. Atul Prdocuts Limited,
Arvind Asoka Aruna Mills,
Hospital Premises,
Near Ashoka Mills Limited,
Naroda Road, Ahmedabad -2,

SUPPLIERS OF RAW MATERIAL

NAPTHALENE:-

M/s. Bhavaree Coke Company Limited,
Kusunda, Dhandbad Dist.
Bihar.

NITRICACID:-

M/s. Ashoka Chemical Industries,
6, Karballa Mohamed Street,
Calcutta - 700 001.

CALCIUMCARBONATE:-

M/s. Dorr Oliver Limited,
16, Queens Road,
Mumbai -400 020.

HYDROCHLORICACID:-

M/s. Andhra Sugars Limited,
Venkaterayapuram, P.B. No.1.
Tanuka, Hyderabad (A.P).

PLANT ECONOMICS

Rated Plant capacity = 0.40 TON/day
H-ACID

LAND & BUILDING COST	Rs.	8,90,000.00

(Land area requirement 1000 sq.mt.)

PLANT & MACHINERY

1. Sulphonator
2. Nitrator with Jacket
3. Neutralization tank
4. Reduction Tank
5. Filter press
6. Centrifuge rubber lined
7. Storage tanks
8. Boiler
9. Chilling plant
10. Air Compressor
11. Boiler
12. Air Compressor
13. Dryer
14. Isolation of Koch acid wooden tank.
15. Koch acid slurry preparation tank
16. Autoclave (M.S.)
17. Isolation of Acid lead lined/Brick lined
18. Carboys for sulphuric acid oleum and caustic
19. Pumps valves pipe lines and other ancilliaries
20. Lab. equipments
21. Dryer
22. Chilling plant
23. Effluent treatment system

FIXED CAPITAL

1. LAND & BUILDING	Rs.	8,90,000.00
2. PLANT & MACHINERY	Rs.	13,17,000.00
3. OTHER FIXED ASSETS	Rs.	2,55,000.00
TOTAL	Rs.	24,62,000.00

RAW MATERIALS

1. Naphthalene
2. Sulphuric acid
3. Calcium carbonate
4. Hydrochloric acid
5. Other Misc. Chemicals
6. Oleum
7. Nitric acid
8. Iron fillings
9. Caustic soda (Solid & Lye)

TOTAL WORKING CAPITAL/ANNUM

1. RAW MATERIAL	Rs.	90,18,000.00
2. SALARY & WAGES	Rs.	7,75,500.00
3. UTILITIES & OVERHEADS	Rs.	20,40,000.00
TOTAL	Rs.	1,18,33,500.00

TOTAL CAPITAL INVESTMENT

TOTAL FIXED CAPITAL	Rs.	24,62,000.00
TOTAL WORKING CAPITAL FOR 3 MONTHS	Rs.	29,58,375.00
TOTAL	Rs.	54,20,375.00

TURN OVER/ANNUM

1. By Sale of 120 M.T. of H-Acid	Rs.	1,68,00,000.00

PROFIT = RECEIPTS - COST OF PRODUCTION

= 1,68,00,000.00 - 1,34,10,082.50

= 33,89,917.50

PROFIT SALES RATIO = Profit / Sales x 100 = 20.18 %

RATE OF RETURN = Operating profit / T.C.I x 100 = 62.54 %

BREAK EVEN POINT (B.E.P) = 44.36 %

Chapter-15
HYDROGEN GAS PLANT

INTRODUCTION

Hydrogen the lightest and most abundant element has an atomic number of one and an atomic weight of 1.00782519 on the 12°C scale. The single atom compromising the hydrogen nuecleus has a single orbiting electron filling on half of the IS electron sell. Hydrogen atoms designated H can exist in a pure state under certain circumstances. Normally however, pure hydrogen exists as H_2 the hydrogen molecule and the lightest of all gases.

Hydrogen H_2 is a product of many reactions but it is present at only extremely low levels in the earths atmosphere (0.1 PPM level). The H_2 molecule exists in two forms designated ortho-hydrogen and para-hy-drogen depending upon the nuclear spins of the atoms. Many physical and thermo dynamic atoms properties of H_2 depend upon the nuclear spin orientation, but the chemical properties of the two forms are the same.

Hydrogen gas is a very stable molecule because of its high bond strength (436 KJ/Mal or 104 KCal/mal). It is not particularly reactive under ordinary conditions, but at elevated temperature and with the acid of catalysts, it undergoes many reactions. Hydrogen forms compounds with almost every other element, often by direct reaction of the elements. The explanation of its ability to form compounds with such chemically dissimilar elements as alkali metals, halogens, transition metals and carbon lies in the intermediate electronegatively of the hydrogen atom.

USES AND APPLICATION

Hydrogen is an important industrial chemical in petorleum refining and in the synthesis of ammonia and methanol. These three areas account for more than 96% of the current industrial hydrogen consumption. The balance is consumed in the manufacture of various chemicals (eg. cyclohexane, benzene by toluene dealkylation, oxo-alcohols, and aniline)., metallurgical processing, reducing gas blanketing, vegetable oil hydrogenation, and in the electronics industry.

Even larger amounts of hydrogen will be produced and used in the future. More acidic and heavier crudes will be treated in the refineries. Desulfurization and adjustment of the H_2 concentrations can substantially increase requirements. In all coal gasification processes leading to the prepartion of a synthesis gas, hydrogen is generated by the shift reaction and, after isolation is used for a great number of hydrogasification reactions.

PROPERTIES

HYDROGEN:

Hydrogen gas diffuses rapidly through many materials inculding metals. This property is used in separation hydrogen from other gases and in purifying hydrogen on an industrial scale. Hydrogen diffusion through metals is also used as an analytical technique for hydrogen determination in gas chromatography. Hydrogen is only slightly soluble in water but is soewhat moer soluble in organic compounds.

For instance at 0°C and 0.1 MP a (1 atm) pressure, the solubility of H_2 inwater (STP) is 0.0214 cm3/g; in benzene the solubility is 0.0585 cm3/g.

Solid hydrogen usually exist, in the hexagonal close packed from Lo = 378 pm and Co = 616 pm production of hydrogen through electrolysis is used industrially. Electrolytic production of hydrogen may have a central role in any future hydrogen based energy system.

B.I.S. SPECIFICATIONS

OXYGEN:

IS: 309 - 1974 in for compressed oxygen gas.

It prescribes requirements and methods of sampling and test for compressed oxygen gas for industrial use.

IS: 6207 - 1971 is for trolleys for oxygen cylinders. It specifies sizes, material construction and other requirements.

IS: 1090 - 1965.

COMPRESSED HYDROGEN:

It covers two grades of the material. Grade - I provides a material having reduced oxygen and moisture content suitable for special industrial uses. Such as prefocus lamps, mercury vapour lamps, semi-conductor industries etc. Grade - II generally used and is suitable for cooling generators gas welding, cutting of special steels, and filling matereological of ballons. Prescribes requirements and methods of sampling and test.

IS: 8198 - (Part II) 1976 - is for code of practice for steel cylinders for compressed hydrogen gases.

It covers filling, inspection, testing maintenance and use of portable steel cylinders for the storage and transportations of hydrogen gas in cylinders exceeding 500 ml. water capacity:

These B.I.S. specification may be consulted for quality adjustment as well as storage of the products.

MARKET SURVEY

Oxygen and hydrogen gases are manufactured large as well as in small scale sector. These gases are used for steel manufacturing Ammonia and methanol manufacturing, rocket propulsion, metal cutting, medical use, and welding and in high altitude flying.

Owing to the bulk use in various industries, the demand of hydrogen is vary good.

Hydrogen gas being widely used in hydrogenation of oil of making vanaspati Ghee and various petrochemical industries, Ammonia synthesis industries has bulk demand at present and is likely to increase in near future. With the rapid industrialization of the country. So its demand will increase many fold.

PROCESS OF MANUCACTURE

The manufacture of Hydrogen and Oxygen by water electrolysis of water is accomplished in electrolysis cell. The cell is usually unit incorproatin bipalar electrodes and asbestos diaphragms to separate the hydrogen and oxygen streams. Since the electrtolysis is carried out in a alkaline electrolyte, the use of an inexpensive anode such as Ni is facilitated. Owing the universally favoured electrolyte.

$$2\,H_2O \longrightarrow 2H_2 + O_2$$

Based on

$$E_r = E_o \quad \frac{RT}{4F} \quad 2.303 \log (PO_2\, PH_2)$$

The reversible potential for the over all process is 1.23 V at normal temperature and pressure. Inpractive, however no gas evolution is observed below 1.65 V and the actural operating voltage is 1.8, 2.6 V. The energy efficiency of the process is therefor of the order of V15 - 65% equation 2 also shows that the magniture of the reversible sible potential of the process increases by about 90 MV for a tenfold increases in operating pressure. High pressure gas therefore, may be generated at the cost of only a minimal increase of electrolysis voltage. Several of the filter press electrolysis talk advantage of this fact and are constructed for operations at 3.04 MP a (30 atms). The theoretical energy requirement for 100 M^3 of Hydrogen and 50 M^3 of Oxygen is 32 Kwh of which 279 Kwh has to be supplied as electrical energy the balance could be heated. The Hydrogen gas so obtained is 99.7% pure and can be utilized directly for the hydrogeneation of the edible oils.

SUPPLIERS OF PLANT & MACHINERY

ELECTROLYTIC CELLS:

M/s. Bharat Heavy Plate & Vessels Limited,
Nattayya Palem B.H.P.V.,
Visakhapatnam - 12 (A.P).

GAS HOLDERS:

M/s. Anup Engineering Limited,
Anil Starch Premises,
Anil Road,
Post Box No. - 1164,
Ahmedabad - 380 002,
Gujarat.

COMPRESSORS:

M/s. K.C.P. Limited,
Ramakrishna Building,
38, Mount Road,
Chennai - 600 006.

PRESSURE VESSEL:

M/s. Bird & Company (Private) Limited,
Chartered Bank Buildings,
Calcutta - 700 001.

WATER TREATMENT EQUIPMENTS:

M/s. Doshi Ion Exchange Chemical Industries,
Plot No. /24-25-26,
Phase -II, G.I.D.C.,
Vatra, Ahmedabad - 382 445,
Gujarat.

SUPPLIERS OF RAW MATERIALS

POTASSIUM HYDROXIDE (ELECTROYTE):

M/s. Andhra Sugars Limited,
Venkatarayapuram,
Tanuku - 534 215,
Andhra Pradesh.

ADDRESSES OF GAS CYLINDER SUPPLIERS

M/s. Acetylene Industrial Gas Cylinders Limited,
4, Saradamal Street,
Gokulam Colony,
Chennai - 17.

PLANT ECONOMICS

Rated Plant capacity = 5000.00 M.CUB./day
HYDROGEN GAS PLANT

LAND & BUILDING COST	Rs.	14,00,000.00
(Area required 1000 Sq.mts.)		

PLANT & MACHINERY

1. Water treatment unit complete with all accessories
2. Electrolyzer with all accessories.
3. Rectification unit
4. Gas Holders
5. Compression unit equipped with all the accessories.
6. Gas storage tanks(Pressure Vessels) Capacity 300 M.Cub.each.
7. Miscellaneous equipments & tools Viz., Pipe fitting, Valves etc.

FIXED CAPITAL

1. LAND & BUILDING	Rs.	14,00,000.00
2. PLANT & MACHINERY	Rs.	30,00,000.00
3. OTHER FIXED ASSETS	Rs.	8,60,000.00
TOTAL	Rs.	52,60,000.00

WORKING CAPITAL REQUIREMENT/MONTH

RAW MATERIALS

1. Water Treatment Chemicals
   (Potassium Hydroxide)
2. Electrolyte (KOH) 250 kgs.
3. Miscellaneous.

TOTAL WORKING CAPITAL/MONTH

1. RAW MATERIAL	Rs.	26,250.00
2. SALARY & WAGES	Rs.	63,125.00
3. UTILITIES & OVERHEADS	Rs.	15,26,000.00
TOTAL	Rs.	16,15,375.00

TOTAL CAPITAL INVESTMENT

TOTAL FIXED CAPITAL	Rs.	52,60,000.00
TOTAL WORKING CAPITAL FOR 3 MONTHS	Rs.	48,46,125.00
TOTAL	Rs.	1,01,06,125.00

TURN OVER/ANNUM

1.	By sale of 750000 M.Cube Oxygen	Rs.	75,00,000.00
2.	By sale of 15,00,000M.Cube Hydrogen	Rs.	2,25,00,000.00
	TOTAL	Rs.	3,00,00,000.00

PROFIT = RECEIPTS - COST OF PRODUCTION

= 3,00,00,000.00 - 2,20,41,602.50

= 79,58,397.50

PROFIT SALES RATIO = Profit / Sales x 100 = 26.53 %

RATE OF RETURN = Operating profit / T.C.I x 100 = 78.75 %

BREAK EVEN POINT (B.E.P) = 56.38 %

Chapter-16

INDIAN MADE FOREIGN LIQUOR (IMFL)

INTRODUCTION

Gin, vodka, and related spirits like aquarit are distinguishable from whisky, rum and brandy which themselves have a number of common characteristics. The most evident difference is in colour, with gin an vodka normally being colourless white whisky, rum and brandy vary in shade from straw-coloured to the deepest brown. This immediate difference is linked with distinguishing features of composition and flavour which are reflected in the methods of production of the two troup of sprits. The aurd whisky comes from the Gaelic word wisge-beatha, as the Irish called it, incoming the water of life.

The colour in whisky, rum and brandy oves it origin to the practice of ageing or maturing these spirits in wooden casks, which as containers have previously used for transporting some compatible liquid such as slerry, wine or molasses. Residues of previous contents, together with substance extracted from the wood itself, serve to give the maturing spirit a brown colour which in interest of standardization, is supplmented by the addition of caremel. The requirement for maturation in wood is now codified in lay standing whisky is the potable spirit obtained by distillation of an aquons extract of an infusion of matted barly and after cereals that has been ferriented with strains of sacctromyus ceramisial. Various types of whisky are produced in a number of different countries in the world. They differ principally in the nature and proportion of the cerels used as a raw materials along with matted barly and also in the type of still used for distillation. The principal types of whisky are also characterised of particular geographical regions of the world.

USES AND APPLICATIONS

Whisky is a kind of wine generally used by human beings. It is very useful for children if given a little doze say about one tea spoon in milk or water every day. It kills to cold and cough and the effect larger quantity will work as wine.

Apart from the above it is also used for the extraction of several drugs and for manufacture of several medicinal preparations. Whisky also kinds used in preparation of assences and flavours. It is used as a process material in the preparation of numerous organic compounds including synthetic drugs and dyestuffs especially for crystallization and purification.

There are two types of whisky, one is white and the other is brown. The white brandy is made from the juice of fruit and the brown from the pulp. White brandy is used for the use by human beings and the brwon for other purposes.

PRODUCTION OF BRANDY

Brandy : Brandy is a distillate or a mixture of distillates obtained solely from the fermented juice, mash, or wine of fruit, or from the residue there of, distilled at less than 190o proof (95%) in such a manner as to produce the taste, aroma, & characteristics generally attributed to it. The most imported category of brandy is fruit brandy, distilled solely from the juice or mash of whole, sound, ripe fruit or from standard grape, intrus, or other fruit wine. Brandy derived exclusively from one variety of fruit is so designated.

Ethyl Alcohol : Ethanol C2 H5 OH is completely miscible with water and forms a constant boiling point mixture with it at 96% alcohol by weight. It is clear, colourless, inflammable liquide with a density of 0.7939 at 100 percent alcohol or at 200o proof. It is a good solvent for essential oils, esters, tannins, various organic acids and certain other organic compounds. It is, therefore, a very important industrial solvent.

PRODUCTION OF RUM

Rum is produced from cane-sugar or sugar by products, the most common raw material being cane juice, syrup or molasses. The raw material used largely determines the type of rum produced. Cane juice is best suited for the production of rum with a light aroma. Finely ground sugar-cane is pressed in to a dry mass. Finely ground sugar-cane is pressed in to a dry mass, and the cane juice so obtained is used as such or after concentration. Syrup, a thick, viscous liquid, is obtained by evaporating water from cane-juice by vaccum distillation. Most rum is produced from molasses, which is especially is a by-product in the production of sugar. It remains as the mother liquor when sugar is separated from can juice by repeated crystallization. Depending on the sugar-cane variety, production methods and other factors such as climate, it contains some 50 - 60% sugar.

Rum is an alcoholic distillate from the fermented juice of sugar cane, its syrup, molasses, or other by products, distilled at less than 190o proof (95%) in such a manner that the distillate possesses the taste, aroma, and characteristics generally atributed to rum, and bottled at not less than 80o proof (40%) & also includes mixtures solely of such distillates.

MANUFACTURING PROCESS OF WHISKY

1. PRESSING:

The grapes are picked usually at the time when they contain the most sugar and carted to the winery for pressing. If the grapes are to be used for the production of white wine/brandy they are crushed and pressed so that only the juice shall be fermented it for red wine, the wntire pulp after crushing is placed in the fermenting vats in order to extract the colour during fermentation. The crushing and pressing are don by rollers and screw or hydraulic press.

2. FERMENTATION

There are two types of fermentation: -

1. Alcoholic
2. Acidic Fermentation.

ALCOHOLIC FERMENTATION

The alcoholic fermentation is due to the presence of various yeasts of which the most important is the so-called 'true wine yeast' saccharonyes elliposidues. The exymose, or enzyme present in the yeast cells acts on the dissolved sugar, changing to the alcohol and carbon dioxides, these yeasts are present on the skins of the grapes, so that under ordinarily faverable conditions the yeast will begin to ferment almost immediately as shown by the increase in temperature formation of gas bubbles and change from a sweet taste to an acid and alcoholic one. On account, however, of the presence of other less desirable yeasts the wine make often adds to the must pure cultures of special yeasts, thereby securing better control of the fermentation and a cleaner product.

3. BOTTLING

When the brandy has ceased froming a deposit is bright and clear and has reached its optimum quantity. It is bottled the object being to prevent further deleterious change by protecting it from oxidation of the action of micro-organisms. After bottling, the brandy improves the several months and then remains with little change except for a very gradual development of the highest qualities of flavour for many years, if kept under suitable conditions.

MANUFACTURERS OF ALCOHOLIC BEVERAGES

M/s. Mohan Meaking Breveriwa Limited,
P.O. Solan Brewery,
Himachal Pradesh.

M/s. The Rampur Distillary and Chemical Company Limited,
Rampur - 244 901,
Uttar Pradesh.

M/s. Carew & Company Limited,
Rosa, Shahjehanpur Dist.,
Uttar Pradesh.

M/s. Daurala Sugar Works,
Daurals,
Meerut Distt.,
Uttar Pradesh.

SUPPLIERS OF PLANT & MACHINERY

M/s. A.P.V. Engineering Company Private Limited,
41, Choranghee Road,
Calcutta.

M/s. Chemical Plant & Equipment Limited,
7, Lower Chitpore Road,
Calcutta.

M/s. Garlick & Company Private Limited,
Haines Road,
Mumbai - 400 011.

STORAGE TANK

M/s. Flowlink Industries Private Limited,
D-15, Commercial Complex,
Prashant Vihar,
Delhi-110 085.
Ph.: 7267006/7267007
Fax: 91-11-7267007

M/s. Annu Rashyan Udyog,
184, D.S.I.D.C Sheds,
Okhla Industrial Area-1,
New Delhi - 110 020.
Ph.: 6813624

BOILER

M/s. Delhi Engineering Compnay,
S-17, Industrial Estate,
Badli, Delhi - 110 042.
Ph. : 7292500

PLANT ECONOMICS

Rated Plant capacity = 1200.00 GLN/day
I.M.F.L. (ALCOHOL)

LAND & BUILDING COST	Rs.	97,50,000.00
(Total land required 4000 sq.mts.)		

PLANT & MACHINERY

1. Fruit Crushing Mill
2. Cleaning Tank
3. Scrubber
4. Fermentor
5. Rectifying Column
6. Product Storage tank
7. Cooling Tower
8. Bottles Washing Machine
9. Bottles Filling and Sealing Machine
10. Mixing Tank
11. Seed Tank
12. Filter Press
13. Analyser
14. Baby Boiler
15. Storage Tank
16. Pumps & Piping
17. Miscellaneous
18. Condensers with Accumulater

FIXED CAPITAL

1. LAND & BUILDING	Rs.	97,50,000.00
2. PLANT & MACHINERY	Rs.	34,01,000.00
3. OTHER FIXED ASSETS	Rs.	5,44,600.00
TOTAL	Rs.	1,36,95,600.00

RAW MATERIALS

1. Grape & Other fruits
2. Yeast, variable amount required
3. Other Chemicals i.e. Sodium sulphite, minerals acids enzymes etc.

TOTAL WORKING CAPITAL/MONTH

1. RAW MATERIAL	Rs.	53,00,000.00
2. SALARY & WAGES	Rs.	2,13,625.00
3. UTILITIES & OVERHEADS	Rs.	6,99,000.00
TOTAL	Rs.	62,12,625.00

TOTAL CAPITAL INVESTMENT

TOTAL FIXED CAPITAL	Rs. 1,36,95,600.00
TOTAL WORKING CAPITAL FOR 3 MONTHS	Rs. 1,86,37,875.00
TOTAL	Rs. 3,23,33,475.00

TURN OVER/ANNUM

1. By sale of 3,60,000 gallons of Alcohol in different packings — Rs. 9,36,00,000.00

PROFIT = RECEIPTS - COST OF PRODUCTION

= 9,36,00,000.00 - 8,30,62,864.50

= 1,05,37,135.50

RATE OF RETURN = Operating profit / T.C.I x 100 = *32.59 %*

BREAK EVEN POINT (B.E.P) = 55.03 %

Chapter-17

INTEGRATED COMPLEX OF ESTERS AND ALLIED PRODUCTS

INTRODUCTION

India is one of the big country, having a Vast Scope of chemicals for industrial uses, dosmestic uses and other various uses in various fields. The chemical products are categorised into different fields having different applications. Though there are a number of manufacturers exist, still the market diversifying day by day. These are large number of consumers whose demand for the products are increasing with tremendous growth rate. The competetion is also very high. There is also increase in number of producer/manufacturers of Esters of different ranges.

The di-octyl phthalate being an important plasticizer is used extensively in the PVC processing industries. For plastic materials to exhibit flexibility, resiliency and melt flow, it must be "plasticizers" either within itself or by the addition of an added substances, which is known as plasticizers without this it would not be possible to make plastic sheeting film and other flexible forms of plastics.

PLASTICIZERS :

The Plasticizers is a material incorporated in plastic to increase its workability, flixibility and to impart specific properties. Thermosetting resins like phenolics are sometimes made with small amounts of plasticizers for ease information during an intermediate stage. But these uses are small as compared to those in the related field of surface coatings. Because of its especially suited for beneficial modification by plasticizers. Thus PVC industry absorbs the Lion's share of plasticizers today. The production of new and high quality of plasticizers help in diversifying use of PVC in good packaging refrigerators, gasketings etc.

There are different types of diethyl phthalates. The four diethyl phthalates viz. Dimethyl phthate, diethyl phthalate, dibutyl phthalate and dioctyl phthalate have been reserved for small scale Industries. All these diethyl phthalates can be manufactured by esterifying with appropriate alcohols in presence of a catalyst. The process is essentially the same for different types of phthalates and modifications are necessary only in the alcohol recovery and product purification system.

Plasticizers can be divided into two broad categories namely :

a) Primary plasticizers and

b) Secondary plasticizers

Wire Enamels: Wire Enamels are used for coating of winding wires.

PROPERTIES

Chemical Formula :

D.O.P.	$C_{24}H_{38}O$
Mol. wt.	390
Sp. gr. at 25°C.	0.982
Refractive index	1.4850
Viscosity at 20°C	82 CPS

Dioctyl phthalate D.O.P. or di (2 ethhexyl) phthalate formula C_6H_4 (COOCH$_2$CH (C_2H_2) C_4H_2)2

It is light coloured odourless liquid insoluble in water miscible with mineral oil. It is combustible. It is is largest of all groups and consists of esters of phthalic acid. They have good alround properties including reasonable low temperature characteristics and they are easy to be incorporated into resins. But the compounds made with them do not have good flame-resistance. They are mono-menic primary plasticizers of the greatest popularity.

PROPERTIES OF D.B.P. :

Plasticizer acts as a lubricants between the long molecules of the polymer which must move past or over each other when the polymer is dinstincted or flexed. the plasticizer, acting some what as oil on a bearing, lubricates by reducing intermolecular friction.

S. No.	PLASTICIZER	SP.GR.	BOILING POINT	REFRACTIVE	M.W.
1.	DMP	1.190	282	1.515	194
2.	DEP	1.120	298	1.503	222
3.	DBP	1.045	340	1.490	278
4.	DOP	0.978	230 AT 5MM HG.	1.485	390
5.	DIPHENYL PHTHALATE	1.280	MB - 69	1.5572	318.3
6.	DIMETHYL GLYCOL PHTHALATE	1.170	340	1.502	282
7.	DYBUTYL GLYCOL PHTHALATEE	1.060	370	1.482	366

PROPERTIES OF N-BUTYLACETATE:

It is a Colourless Liquid with a Fruity Odor.

Molecular Wt.	=	116.16
Sp. Gr.	=	0.8836 200C/4
Melting Point	=	76.8°C
Boiling Point	=	126.5°C

It is soluble in alcohol and ether in all properties at room temperature. It is soluble in most hydrocarbons. It is slightly soluble in water. (0.7 gm per 100 gms at room temperature).

8

Flash Point (closed cup)	= 720F
Ignition Temperature	= 7900F
Vapour Density	= 4
Explosive limit (% by volume in air)	= lower 1.7 Upper 15
Maximum allowable Concentration (PPM By Volume)	= 200 to 500

PROPERTIES OF WIRE ENAMEL :-

1. Appearence	Brown/Reddish liquid
2. Clarity	Clear
3. Viscosity on Ford CupNo4	80 Secs - 100 Secs at 30°C
4. Flash Point	42°C

USES AND APPLICATIONS

D.O.P.:

D.O.P. is used for compounding with P.V.C. as a plasticizer.

D.O.P. is an important plasticizer for the vinyl resins. This acts as a softening agent and at the same time increase toughness of the resin. It adds more flexibility to the resins in which it is applied. It is added 25 per cent of 40 per cent of the weight of the resins used. Since, the other thermoplastics like polyethylene etc., are costly. P.V.C. will replace these resins because of cheapness and other quality.

D.B.P.:

Plasticizers are Indispensable for thermoplastic, as it impart specific advantage to finished product. They are also used in adhesives, suuface coatings etc.

In general, DBP find uses with processing of folowing plastics :-

1. Cellulose Nitrate.
2. Ethyl Cellulose.
3. Vinyl.

ETHYLACETATE :

1. Uses by Medical practitioners in medicine.
2. It is used as a solvent.
3. Ethyl acetate is also used in variesorganic synthesis.
4. It is used as a flavouring agent.
5. In refumery.
6. In the preparation of smokeless powders.
7. As artificial fruit essence.
8. In the preparation of Nitro Cellulose varnishes lacquers and dopes, Nitro celluloseplastics and some pharmaceuticals and Rayon.

BUTYLACETATE :

The bulk of butyl Acetate Production is used in the protective Coatings industry as a solveent and thinner. At one time it was the most important lacquere solvent in thee medium boiling range, but in theeee last few years it has met several competition for Methyl Isobutyl Ketone.

WIREENAMELS :

It is used for coating thee surface of wire to protect from moisture, coorrosion etc.

JELLYCOMPOUND :

Jelly cable filling compound is used in teelephone cable for long time protection of cables from moisturee, water, and coorrosion.

RAW MATERIAL

1. Phtalic Anhydride
2. ActylAlcohol.

CATALYST:

Sulphuric Acid.

Refining Agent:

Chemical Reaction:

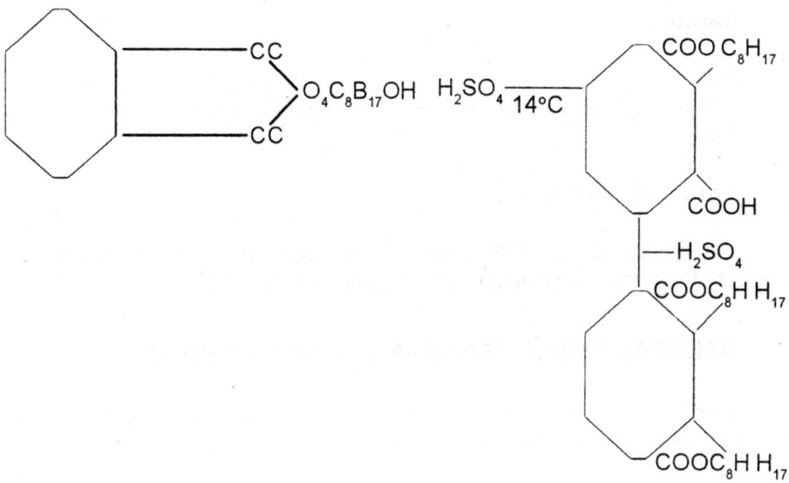

PROCESS

DOP is manufactured in the estrification reaction kettle by the reaction of phthatic anhydride and octyl alcohol. Sulphuric acid is used as acatalyst. Temperature is maintained anywhere between 120-180°C.

The whole process consists of the following steps:-

1. Reaction between Ph. Anhydride and octyl alcohol.
2. Distillation.
3. Packing & Forwarding.

The following materials are required or 50 kgs batch of D.O.P.

Phtalic anhydride	20.25 kg.
Octyl alcohol	32.05 kg.
Sulphuric acid	0.5 kg.
Activated charcoal	0.2 kg.

The calculated quantities of the alcohol and phthalic anhydride alongwith sulphuric acid are heated in the vessel. The reaction mixture is stirred and heated at 150°C to 200°C. The reaction needs six hours to complete. The completion of the reaction may be studied by taking the sample out of the reaction vessel and allow to stand. If we get the clear layer of water then the reaction is complete. Density of the liquid can also be helpful in testing the completion of the reaction.

PROCEESS OF DIBUTYL PHTHALATE

DBP is manufactured by the reaction of Butyl alcohol on phthalic anhydride. In the presence sulphuric acid which serves as catalysts on heating about 125°C - 140°C.

Reaction :

$$C_6H_4(CO)_2O + 2C_4H_9OH \xrightarrow[\text{Catalyst}]{H_2SO_4} C_{16}H_{22}O_4 + H_2O$$

Temp 125 - 140°C

If proper condition of temperature & pressure are maintined during the reaction, then this will correspond to a yield of about 90%.

MANUFACTURING PROCESS OF ETHYL ACETATE

Incase of Batch process to manufacture ethyl acetate the following ratio of reactants are recommended.

10 parts by wt of 8% acetic acid
10 parts by wt of 95% ethyl alcohol
0.33 parts by wt of 50 to 66°Be H_2SO_4

Incase of continuous process acid of any concentration can be used but it is particularly applicable to the utilization of dilute acetic acid, such as that obtained from ethyl alcohol by fermentation.

The process starts with acetic acid, excess 95% ethyl alcohol, and about 1% 66°Be sulphuric acid are mixed and continously passed through a preheater to an esterifying column. The column and other equipments are generally constructed of copper.

TYPICAL FORMULATIONS

For 1 Ton Ethyl Acetate

1. Ethyl Alcohol (95%)	-	1,240	lbs
2. Acetic Acid (100%)	-	1,375	lbs
(8%)	-	17,250	lbs
3. Sulphuric Acid (66°Be')	-	15 to 150	lbs

PROCESS OF BUTYL ACETATE

Acetic acid and n-butyl alcooohol (10 per cent excess) are charged into a batch still. About 0.1 per cent sulfuric acid (66o Be) is added as catalyst. The acetic acid should be free from other acids, but its water content is not critical; 80 per cent to glacial acetic acid is most commonly used. The amount of water present determines the length of distillation and limits the capacity of thee equipment. The butyl alcohol should contain a minimum of other alcooohols or isomers.

Basis : 1 Ton Butyl Acetate

n - Butyl Alcohol	-	645 Kgs.
Glacial Acetic Acid	-	500 Kgs.
Sulphuric Acid (66oBe')	-	3 Kgs.

Chemical Reaction :

$$C_4H_9OH + CH_3COOH \xrightarrow{H_2SO_4} CH_3COOC_4H_9 + H_2O$$

95% yield

PROCESS OF WIRE ENAMEL

All the basic raw materials i.e Dimethyl terephthalate and ethylene glycol 1:2 proportion weight by weight taken in a resin kettle fitted for vaccum distillation. Several metal may be used.

The construction popular being mild steel, although stainless steel, copper, iron, and nickel have been used.

In this cases of manufacturing, before starting reaction, inert gas should flash over the reactor to sweept out the oxygen in the condenser. After that start the process for production, i.e. heat the kettle to 190oC and continued the reaction until acid value of the resin come down to 30-34.

The reaction is enhances in presences of 0.2 - 0.5% glycerol. The catalyst used about 0.5% in the reaction.

PROCESS OF JELLY COMPOUND

Formulation :

	Parts by wt.
HDPE	25
Petroleum Jelly	15
Calcium Carbonate	30
Carbon Black	10
Mercapto Benzothiazol	0.5
Stearic Acid	2
Polymerized Trimethyldihydroguinoline	6
Diazocarbonamide	1
Petroleum oil	1
Dioctyl Phthalate	2

SUPLIERS OF PLANT & MACHINERY

VACCUM PUMPS

M/s. K.G. Khosala & Company Private Limited,
1, Deshbandhu Gupta Road,
Karol Bagh,
New Delhi-110 005.

M/s. S.L.M. Manek Lal Industries Limited,
Bank of India Building,
Ahmedabad, Gujarat.

STORAGE TANKS

M/s. Flowlink Industries Private Limited,
D-15, Commercial Complex,
Prashant Vihar,
Delhi-110 085.
Ph.: 7267006/7267007
Fax: 91-11-7267007

READER & DISTILLATION PLANT:

M/s. A.P.V. Engineering Company Limited,
41, Chowringhee Road,
Calcutta.

M/s. D.C.M. Chemical Works (Engineering Division),
Bara Hindu Rao,
Delhi-110 006.

OTHER SUPPLIERS OF PLANT & MACHINERY

M/s. A.P.V. Engineering Company Limited,
2, Jassore Road,
Dum Dum,
Calcutta - 700 028.

M/s. Sweter Gas,
D-1, Industrial Estate,
Barielly (U.P.).

SUPPLIERS OF RAW MATERIALS

M/s. Herdillia Chemicals Limited,
Air India Building,
Nariman Point,
Mumbai-400 021.

M/s. National Organic Chemical Industries,
Mafatlal Centre,
Nariman Point,
Mumbai - 400 021.

ETHYLALCOHOL:

M/s. Alembic Chemical Works Limited,
Alembic Road,
Baroda-3 (U.P).

PHTHALIC ANHYDRIDE:

M/s. Asiatic Chemical Company,
47, Abdul Rehman Street,
Mumbai-400 003.

OCTYLALCOHOL:

M/s. Indian Explosive Limited,
34, Chowinghee Road,
Calcutta - 700 016.

ACTIVATED CHACOAL:

M/s. Birlex Chemicals,
Outside Bhatanwada Gate,
P.O. Box No. 106,
Amritsar (Punjab).

PLANT ECONOMICS

Rated Plant capacity = 36.00 M.T./day
INTEGRATED COMPLEX OF EASTERS

LAND & BUILDING COST Rs. 1,73,00,000.00
(Land Area required 5 Acres)

PLANT & MACHINERY

1. Storage Tank for DBP/DOP
2. S.S. Lined Storage Tank
3. Shell & Tube Heat Exchanager
4. Boiler
5. S.S. Washing Vessel
6. Miscellaneous, Pumps, Valves, Vessels, Pipelines, Barrels etc
7. Laboratory Testing Equipments
8. Automatic Weighing and Filling Machine
9. Water, Storage Tank (PVC)
10. S.S. Lined Mild Steel Reactor
11. Plate & Frame type Filter Press
12. Alcohol Seperator
13. Miscellaneous Equipments
14. Instrumentation and Process Control Equipments
15. Pollutions Control Equipments
16. S.S. Lined Vacuum Distillation Column

FIXED CAPITAL

1.	LAND & BUILDING	Rs. 1,73,00,000.00
2.	PLANT & MACHINERY	Rs. 2,54,50,000.00
3.	OTHER FIXED ASSETS	Rs. 78,50,000.00
	TOTAL	Rs. 5,06,00,000.00

WORKING CAPITAL REQUIREMENT/ANNUM

RAW MATERIALS

1. Phthalic Anhydride
2. Sulphuric Acid
3. Phthalic Anhydrides
4. Sulhpuric Acid (66 Deg. Be)
5. Xylene
6. Glycerol
7. HDPE· Resins
8. Calcium Carbonate
9. Mercapto Benzothiazole
10. Diazocarbonamide
11. Dioctyl Phthalate
12. Activated Charcoal
13. Acetic Acid (100%)
14. n-Butyl Alcohol
15. Polymerized Trimethyl Dihydro Quinoline
16. Octyl Alcohol (2-Ethyl Hexanol)
17. Activated Charcoal
18. Butyl Alcohol (Normal)
19. Mono Ethylene Glycol
20. Phenol
21. Butyl Titanate
22. Petroleum Jelly
23. Carbon Black
24. Stearic Acid
25. Petroleum Oil
26. Dimethyl Phthalate
27. Ethyl Alcohol (95%)
28. Sulphuric Acid (66 Deg. Be)
29. Acetic Acid (Glacial)
30. Sulphuric Acid (66 Deg. Be)

TOTAL WORKING CAPITAL/ANNUM

1.	RAW MATERIAL	Rs. 40,52,37,450.00
2.	SALARY & WAGES	Rs. 49,80,000.00
3.	UTILITIES & OVERHEADS	Rs. 1,86,38,000.00
	TOTAL	Rs. 42,88,55,450.00

TOTAL CAPITAL INVESTMENT

TOTAL FIXED CAPITAL	Rs. 5,06,00,000.00
TOTAL WORKING CAPITAL FOR 3 MONTHS	Rs. 10,72,13,862.50
TOTAL	Rs. 15,78,13,862.50

TURN OVER/ANNUM

1. D.O.P. 1200 MT
2. D.B.P. 1200 MT.
3. Ethyl Acetate 1200 MT.
4. Butyl Acetate 1200 MT.
6. Cable Filling Jelly Compound 3000 MT
5. Dihydro Quinoline

TOTAL Rs.54,60,00,000.00

PROFIT = RECEIPTS - COST OF PRODUCTION

= 54,60,00,000.00 - 47,10,63,999.75

= 7,49,36,000.25

PROFIT SALES RATIO = Profit / Sales x 100 = *13.72 %*

RATE OF RETURN = Operating profit / T.C.I x 100 = *47.48 %*

BREAK EVEN POINT (B.E.P) = 40.80 %

Chapter-18
Mini Sugar Plant

INTRODUCTION

Sugar is a universal sweetening agent and sugar - cane is the primary age - old source of it. Sugar cane is a very important industrial crop, accounting for about 60% of sugar production in the world.

From the times immemorial the word "sugar" is being used variously to express delight as well as distrust sarcastically. Sugar has been used in human diet through the functions of pancreas, depending on the quantity6 of sugar consumed. It is must for human diet when taken directly or indirectly through various carbohydrate containing food stuffs.

Sugar as sucrose is important for energy and metabolic activities.

PROPERTIES

Sugar is a white crystalline solid or powder chemically known as a carbohydrate. It is also known as sucrose having the chemically formula 612 H22 O11 5-1/2H2O. It chars on heating leaving carbon like mass. Following varieties of sugar are commercially recognised and made for various uses.

RAW SUGAR

For its manufacture, the cane juice is clarified simply by means of lime and heat, i.e. by defection and is not subjected to sulphitation or carbonation. Milk of lime is added in sufficient quantity of neutralize the juice, and the mixture heated to boiling point. The flocculent precipitates, i.e. muds and scums, are removed, and the clear yellow or brown juice is evaporated in multiple - effect evaporators and the raw sugar crystallized in vaccum pans.

CUBE SUGAR

It is made in India for refined crystalline sugar of fine grains by shaping it mechanically into cubes. The cubes should have sufficient hardness so as not to break during packing and transport and also disintegrate quickly in solution.

IICING SUGAR

It is made by pulverizing superior vacuum pan sugar or refined sugar in ball mill or other disintegrators with or without the addition of any edible starch. The starch, when added, is uniformly extended in the sugar and does not exceed 5 per cent by weight. The icing is packed in hermetically sealed tin containers.

This sugar is mostly used for dusting confectionery, and for dressing cakes, pastries and other bakery products.

ALCOHOL AND ITS USES

The importance of molasses is as a major raw material for producing alcohol. Many sugar mills also have distilleries and as their adjunct, it helps them to improve their profitability. There are also independently established distilleries, which secure the required molasses under allocation by the State Governments.

Since its price is determined by the cost of the end-product, the entire quantity of molasses has been subject to price control. The industry has been representing to the government that a higher price should be paid per tonne of molasses, or there should be a free sale quota for being disposed off more profitably.

An output of 225-250 litres of alcohol can be secured out of every tonne of molasses, allowing for wastage and use of molasses for various other purposes.

BAGASSE AS RAW MATERIAL FOR PAPER AND BOARDS

The other major by-product is bagasse. As in the case of molasses, the output of bagasse will increase directly in proportion to the increase in the quantity of cane crushed. About 28 percent of the cane handled is wet bagasse. This is directly fed into the boilers of sugar mills as fuel, for reducing the cost of rising steam and avoiding the use of coal or other dearer fuels. It is now recognised that the use of bagasse as fuel in the boilers should be minimised with pre-treatment so that there can be greater efficiency in the boilers.

USES

1. As such sugar used as sweetner in food product, like Jam, Jellis, Bread, Biscuits, Cake etc. Industry.
2. It has largest used as domestic purposes also.
3. It is also used as raw material for the fermentation Industry.

PRODUCT USES & APPLICATIONS

The various end used uses of sugar are mainly in the following products:-

1. Beverages.
2. Bakery, cereal and allied products.
3. Confectionery and related products.
4. Canned, bottled, and frozen foods, jellies etc.
5. Ice Cream and dairy products.
6. Sweets
7. Used inhouseholds, restaurants and hotels in a number of food and specially products.
8. Pharmaceuticals.

RAW MATERIALS

The various raw materials required in sugar production are:-

1. Sugar Cane.
2. Chemicals and auxilliary materials.

(a) Limestone (b) Coke (c) Sulphur
(d) Superphosphate (e) Soda (f) Hydrochloric acid
(g) Sodium hydrosulphite (h) Flocculents

PROCESS OF MANUFACTURE

In India, the factories make mainly the white direct consumption sugar which is 99.8% pure. Some limited quantity of raw or brown sugar (97 - 98% pure) is also made for the purpose of export. Sugar is produced in vacuum pan evaporators. The method of manufacture consists of the following steps:-

1. Extraction of Juice.
2. Clarification.
3. Evaporation.
4. Crystallization
5. Centrifugation.
6. Drying
7. Bagging
8. Store
9. Market.

BY PRODUCTS OF SUGAR INDUSTRY

The by-products of sugar industry are:

(i) Bagasses
(ii) Molasses
(iii) Filter cake or press mud.

SUPPLIERS OF PLANT & MACHINERY

COMPLETE SUGAR PLANT

M/s. Kambro Engineers,
B-30, Er,
Entrepreneur Industrial Estate,
Bala Nagar,
Hyderabad-37 (A.P).

SUPPLIERS OF RAW MATERIALS

QUICKLIME

M/s. Kotak Chemicals Private Limited,
240, Dr. DN. Road,
Mumbai - 400 001.

SODA ASH

M/s. Associated Lab. Requisties,
144, Holly Bhavan,
1,10, New Marine Lines,
Mumbai-400 020.

CAUSTIC SODA

M/s. The Andhra Sugars Limited,
Venkataraya puram
Mandapa ka Limits,
Tannuku -534215 (A.P.)

SODIUM HYDRO SULPHITE

M/s. Keaar Sugar Works Limited,
100, Swami Vivekanand Road,
Goregoan (West),
Mumbai-400 062.

SUPER PHOSPHATE

M/s. Kathari Sugars & Chemicals,
Kothari Buildings,
115, Nungam Bakram High Road,
Chennai - 600 034.

SULPHUR

M/s. Chawla Chemical Industries Limited,
6, Homji Street,
2nd Floor,
Haji Adam Mension,
2nd Floor,
Mumbai-400 001.

PLANT ECONOMICS

Rated Plant capacity = 4,50,000 MT./ANNUM
SUGAR PLANT

LAND & BUILDING COST Rs. 7,20,00,000.00
(Land required area 100 acres)

PLANT & MACHINERY

1. Pully coveyor belt system Cap:105 tons/hr.
2. Cane cutter(consist of cylinderical shaft revolving at 400-500 R.P.M. fitted with knives
3. Roll crushing unit (rolls are groo-ved) capacity to crush 105 tons per hour driver by 1 nos.
4. Strainer made by stainless steel
5. Plate type Heat Exchanger
6. Clarification tank made by S.S. 304 bottom conical shape, Cap. 10,000 litres.
7. Filtration unit
8. Sulphitation tank made by S.S. conical shape
9. Sulfur furnace
10. Tripple effect Evaporator capacity to evaporate
11. Crystalizer (Cylinderical tank - consisting cooling cold with agitator)
12. Centrifugal Machine
13. Drier
14. Pumps, fittings, lines
15. Vertical type oil fired boiler
16. Miscellaneous equipments [weighing Bridges (Cap.30 MT), material handling Eqpts.packaging eqpts. etc.
17. D. G. Sets.

FIXED CAPITAL

1.	LAND & BUILDING	Rs. 7,20,00,000.00
2.	PLANT & MACHINERY	Rs. 45,00,00,000.00
3.	OTHER FIXED ASSETS	Rs. 5,65,00,000.00
	TOTAL	Rs. 57,85,00,000.00

TOTAL WORKING CAPITAL/ANNUM

1.	RAW MATERIAL	Rs. 35,44,40,000.00
2.	SALARY & WAGES	Rs. 1,02,45,600.00
3.	UTILITIES & OVERHEADS	Rs. 2,66,80,000.00
	TOTAL	Rs. 39,13,65,600.00

TOTAL CAPITAL INVESTMENT

TOTAL FIXED CAPITAL	Rs. 57,85,00,000.00
TOTAL WORKING CAPITAL FOR 3 MONTHS	Rs. 9,78,41,400.00
TOTAL	Rs. 67,63,41,400.00

TURN OVER/ANNUM

1. By selling sugar 4,50,000 Qts.	Rs. 60,75,00,000.00
2. Molasses 90,000/- MT.	Rs. 13,50,00,000.00
3. Bagasse 1,35,000 MT.	Rs. 4,05,00,000.00
4. Pressed Mud 22500 MT.	Rs. 33,75,000.00
TOTAL	Rs. 78,63.75,000.00

PROFIT = RECEIPTS - COST OF PRODUCTION

= 78,63,75,000.00 - 62,93,87,052.00

= 15,69,87,948.00

PROFIT SALES RATIO = Profit / Sales x 100 = *19.96 %*

RATE OF RETURN = Operating profit / T.C.I x 100 = *23.21 %*

BREAK EVEN POINT (B.E.P) = 61.69 %

Chapter-19

MENTHOL CRYSTALS FROM MENTHOL OIL

INTRODUCTION

Menthol is a white crystalline chemical product. It is manufactured either from natural source or is produced synthetically. Laevo ro Racemic forms are only therapeutically active. Melting point of natural or synthetic laevomenthol lies between 41 and 44°C.

Menthol is utilized by a wide spectrum of users for its following properties, namely (a) flavouring agent (b) anti-pruritic (c) cooland and (d) cariminative

Two varieties of menthol are produced in India the crystals and the flakes. The crystals are preferred by most users probably because of history and past usage and there fetch a better price than flakes.

PROPERTY AND STRUCTURE

Menthol is natural leavo-menthol obtained from the volatile oils of various species of menthol synthetic leavo menthol or racemic menthol

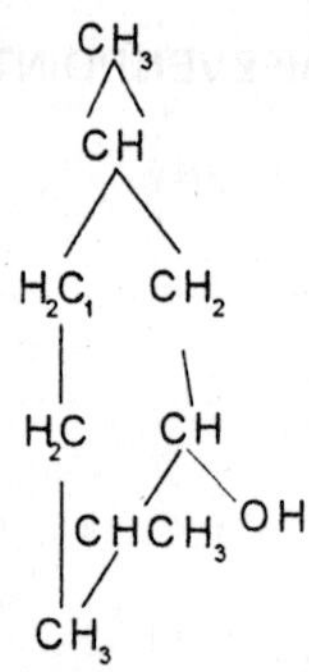

Menthol-4-isopropyl Cyclohexane-3-01

Menthol contains three asymmetric carbon atoms. It may therefore exist in four externably compensated optically active forms. Two of the common stereo isomeric menthols are leavo rotary 1-mention occurring naturally or produced synthetically and racemic oil menthol produced synthetically.

Monocyclic, saturated, secondary terpene alcohol, occurs in nature in the form of 1-menthol-d-neo-menthol. The type mostly required industry is 1-menthol white crystal with cooling odour and task.

Mol. wt.	156.26
Sp. Cr.	0.89
N.P.	42-43°C
B.P.	212°C

Soluble in alcohol, light petroleum solvents, glacial acetic acid and fixed or volatile oils. Slightly soluble in water. Charaiterised by low toxicity and combustible nature.

USES AND APPLICATIONS

Menthol posses a distinct peppermint flavour. It also possesses cooling and stimulating action in high degree on the stain and mucous membrane. Its flavour coolness and stimulating properties are widely exploited in various industries eg pharmacential and in the manufacture of a number of consumer items such as mouth washes, tooth paste, chewing gum, jellies, Cigarettes, alcoholic liquors and in the chest rub. Boils carbundes, coryza qastrodynia, headache, leery ngitis nausia, nausalquia pharyngills stindeseases accornpried by itchiy of it.

In pharmacy and Medicine, Menthol finds application in the treatment of certain skin conditions such as uptocoria because of its local anaersthetic properties it also helps in allewiating nause and gastrodynin. Since menthol also posses counter irritant properties it has been employed in the treatment of headache and other form of neuralgia.

The other common use of menthol is as a flavaouring agent principal use in peppermint and line havours. It has found application also in the flavouring of cigarettes, snuff, confectionery aid chewing gum. It is also very useful for imparity acceptable flavours to tooth paste and other cosmetic preparations.

PRESENT MANUFACTURERS

M/s. Crystal and Chemical Laboratories,
67, Halwasiya Meerut,
Lucknow (U.P).

M/s. Camphor and Allied Products Limited,
M.G. Road,
Mumbai-400 004.

M/s. Crystal Chemicals Private,
I-15, Swinhoe lane,
Calcutta - 700 001.

M/s. Mentha and Allied Products Private Limited,
1/10 Asaf ali Road,
New Delhi-110 002.

M/s. Richardson Hindustan Limited,
Tiecicon House, E. Moses Road,
Mumbai-400 011.

PREPARATION OF MENTHOL CRYSTAL

Preparation of Menthol Crystal from Mentha Arvensis (which is in our country name Pudina herb).

THEORY

Menthol oil is first prepared by steam distillation of Mentha Arvensis. Now mentha oil arround 1.5 - 1.8% of which 70-80% will be menthol crystal. Yield of mentha oil depend upon the origin of herbs and methods of cultivation.

RAW MATERIAL

1. Pudina Herbs (Mentha Arvensis)
2. Boric Acid

Put 20 kgs of pudina herbs on dry basis distillation plants. Added to it around 40 litres of water in the distillation plawn, heat the distillaiton plawnt at 100°C initial 2 hours. Then cool down and heat the contents to 80-95°C about six hours.

At this time piperment oil will be distilled away through the jacket, on cooling of the piperment vapour to produce piperment oil and collect in the receiver.

Now produce piperment oil around 13.6 - 14 kgs

This piperment oil contents around 70-80% of menthol. Now piperment oil is cool down to 15°C to seperate out Menthol crystal. Now centrifuge the precipited crystal to seperate out menthol crystal and menthol oil. By first stage it will separate out around 60-65% of menthol crystal.

Now residual oil is taken and added 0.01% of Boric Acid to it and cool down the oil to 5°C to residual menthol crystal seperate out. It will be arround 10-12%

It has been found that the 9.8-10.5% kgs of menthol crystal will be obtained. Pack it in a close container. Store it in a cool place for long preservation.

SUPPLIERS OF PLANT AND MACHINERY

CHILLING PLANT OR REFRIGERATION UNIT (FREEZER)

M/s. Frick India Limited,
Jeevan Vihar-3,
Parliament Street,
New Delhi - 110 001.

M/s. Air Fridge Industries,
10/65, Kirti Nagar,
New Delhi-110 015.

COMPLETE PLANT SUPPLIER FOR MENTHOL CRYSTAL PLANT

M/s. Rank and Company,
A-95/3, Wazirpur Industrial Area,
Delhi - 110 052.
Ph.: 7125402

RAW MATERIAL SUPPLIERS

M/s. Anant Ram Hari Ram Agarwal,
2068/70, Katra Tobacco,
Khari Baoli, Delhi -110 006.

M/s. Berlia Chemicals & Traders Private Limited,
Rang Mahal, II Floor,
212/216, Smuel Street,
Vadgadi, Mumbai.

PLANT ECONOMICS

Rated Plant capacity = 1.00 TON/day
MENTHOL CRYSTALS FROM MENTHOL OIL

LAND & BUILDING COST *(Land required area 1000 sq.mt)*	Rs.	15,00,000.00

PLANT & MACHINERY

1. Fractional Chilling unit
2. Jacketted Vessel
3. Centrifuge Machinery
4. Storage Tanks (SS lined)
5. Pipe-fitting and Misc.instruments
6. Laboratory equipments

FIXED CAPITAL

1. LAND & BUILDING	Rs.	15,00,000.00
2. PLANT & MACHINERY	Rs.	30,00,000.00
3. OTHER FIXED ASSETS	Rs.	5,00,000.00
TOTAL	Rs.	50,00,000.00

TOTAL WORKING CAPITAL/MONTH

1. RAW MATERIAL	Rs.	78,00,000.00
2. SALARY & WAGES	Rs.	88,800.00
3. UTILITIES & OVERHEADS	Rs.	1,21,000.00
TOTAL	Rs.	80,09,800.00

TOTAL CAPITAL INVESTMENT

TOTAL FIXED CAPITAL	Rs.	50,00,000.00
TOTAL WORKING CAPITAL FOR 3 MONTHS	Rs.	2,40,29,400.00
TOTAL	Rs.	2,90,29,400.00

TURN OVER/ANNUM

1. By processing of 300 Tons of Menthol Crystal
2. By processing of 240 tons of Dementholized Oil

TOTAL	Rs.	10,86,00,000.00

PROFIT = RECEIPTS - COST OF PRODUCTION

= 10,86,00,000.00 - 10,33,39,068.00

= 52,60,932.00

***PROFIT SALES RATIO = Profit / Sales x 100** = 4.84 %*

***RATE OF RETURN = Operating profit / T.C.I x 100** = 18.12 %*

BREAK EVEN POINT (B.E.P) = 61.00 %

Chapter-20

ORGANIC MANURE

INTRODUCTION

Vegetation like all living things, requires certain foods for its survival and growth. For this purpose fertilizers or manure are the materials to be added to the soil and sometimes to foliage to supply nutrients to sustain plants and promote their abundant and fruitful growth. The elements that constitute these plants foods are divided into three classes.

1. Primary Nitrogen (N), phosphorus (usually expressed as P_2O_5), and potassium (expressed as K_2O)

2. Secondary - calcium (Ca), magnesium (Mg) and Sulphur (S)

3. and Minor or so called micro nutrients iron (Fe), manganese (Mn), copper(Cu) Zinc(Zn), boron(B) and molybdenum. In addition to their role as nutrients calcium and magnesium are important in adjusting the pH and filth of the soil.

Most of the manures of organic origin (animal or plant) contain several plant nutrients (particularly N & P as well as smaller quantities of K and trace elements) although in considerably lower concentration than in inorganic fertilizers organic manures however should be valued not only for their nutrient content but rather for thin beneficial effect on the soil. The organic matter promotes the microbial processes in the soil, improves the soil structure, aeration and water holding capacity. It has a regulating effect on the soil temperature, delays the fixation of mineral phosphoric acid,and supplies organic decomposition acid, and supplies organic decomposition products Which aid the growth. Moreover, it is a source of slow and uniformly active nitrogen and consequently has a beneficial influence on the protein content of plants.

TYPES OF ORGANIC MANURES

The organic materials available for utilization as plant nutrient sources can be put into the following categories according to their source of origin

- Animal Wastes
- Human Wastes
- Crop Residues
- Green Manures
- Municipal Organic Waste
- Slurry Obtained from bio-gas plants
- Micro trial inoculants
- Blue green algae
- Azolla

PROPERTIES

The magnitude of the projected demand for fertilizer or manure, and the parallel demands on capital, raw meterials, and energy, it is unfortunate that crops donot utilize applied fertilizer very efficiently. Nitrogen utilization by the first crop following application ranges from a low of about 30% for vegetables to a high of about 60% for grain crops, on average, no more than one half of applied fertilizer nitrogen is used by crops.

The fertilizer of manure Industry requirs a number of special terms peculiar to fertilizers, some of which are traditional.

Analysis: Denotes the concentration of plant nutrients. the term high analysis is used to denote fertilizers of relatively high nutrient concentration.

Grade:- Denotes the nutrient content expressed in %age. For example 10-10-10 usually denotes a fertilizer containing 10% N, 10% P2O5 and 10% K2O. Three values are generally given, even if one or more nutrients are missing eg:- 46-0-0 for urea and 18-46-0 for diammonium phosphate. Other nutrients are rarely indicated but occasionally a grade such as 4-10-10-4-2-1 is given, the last three number indicating secondary or micro-nutrients in this case Mg, Mn and Cu. respectively.

Unit:- refers to 1% of a ton of nutrient in the metric system, 1 unit in 10 Kg and a 10-10-10 fertilizer contains 10 units or 100 kg N, 10 units or 100 kg of P2O5 and 100 kg of K2O.

B P L:- (Bone Phosphate of Lime) is the phosphate content of phosphate are expressed as tricalcium phosphate.

A.P.A.:- (Available Phosphoric Acid) is the phosphate content available to plants as determined by an solubility fast.

USES & APPLICATIONS

Organic manures are known to improve crop production by improving the properties of the soil. Manures provide humus to the soil improving its properties and serving as a reservoir of major plant nutrients. The use of organic manure results in adequate availability of micro-nutrients. It provides for recycling and use of organic wastes and minimises the pollution of land and water resources.

The addition of oroganic manure improves the structure, texture and filth of the soil. Sandy soils become more compact and clay soil more open. The aggregation of soil particles is brought about by the production of poly-saccharides as a result of a microtrial metabolism. A belter structure provides better penetration and aeration at the root, Soils provided with organic manure have belter permeability and greater capacity to hold water. Besides, erosion of soil us controlled when the soil is rich in organic manure.

Organic manure increases thebuffering capacity of the soil and prevents rapid changes in pH as well as acidity and alkalinity. Since most organic manure is prepared from plants and animal residue, they contain most of the elements needed by the plants. Organic manure does affect the availability of plant nutrients in many ways.

PROCESS OF MANUFACACTURE

FROMFARMYARDMANURES

A sufficient quantity of dry litter should be spread under each animal in the evening for absorption of the urine. The material consisting of dung and urine socked in it should be collected every day and placed in trenches about 6 metres long, 2 metres wide and 1 metre dcep. The additions should be in section of 1 meter length. When each section is filled up to a height of about 0.5 metre above the ground level, the top of the heap should be rounded off to the shape of a dome andplastered over with a slurry of low-dung & earth.

Two such trenches are sufficint for filling up twion the waste materials by turns during a whole year for a farmer owing three or four heads of cattle. By this means it is possible to obtain 5-6 ton of good quality manure per year per head of cattle. Application of 25 kg superphosphate for each tonne of manure prevents loss of nitrogen and makes the manure a more balanced plant food. Superphosphate should be applied overeach layer of urine soaked litter and dung added to the pit. A quality of 12.5 kg would be sufficient for spreading on the 4-5 layers of the manure in each metre section of the pit. The manure trench should be kept protected from the son & rain.

COMPOSTING

Composting, the biochemical degradation of organic material, is a sanitary process for treating municipal, agricultural, and industrial wastes, compost cannot be considered a fertilizer. Its main value seems to be its high organic content as a soil conditioner, which may provide poor soils with better filth, water holding capacity and improved nutrient holding capacity. Composting converts organic materials to a humus like substance, a process constantly carried on in nature.

Present day composting plants generally provide for five basic steps in processing the refuse.

(1) Preparation
(2) Digestion
(3) Curing
(4) Finishing
(5) Storing

Preparation:- Processing of the refuse prior to composting involves several operations, which typically may include receiving, sorting, mag netic separation, grinding, and adding sewage sludge. The receiving equipment is designed to act as a refuse reservoir and to provide an even flow of refuse through the plant. It usually consists of a hopper and some device that beigins moving refuse through the plant at the rate at which subsequent operation can process it.

Digestion:- Digestion or decomposition is carried out either in open windrows or in enclosures. The principal objective is to create an environment in which micro-organisms will rapidly decompose the organic portion of the refuse. Most modern plants use aerobic rather than an aerobic decomposition. In aerobic decomposition, micro-organisms requiring free oxygen degrade the waste. To furnish the oxygen, air is introduced into windrows by turning and into enclosed systems by forced draft and agitation, Heat, which is generated profusely, reached 140oF to 160 F (60o to 70oC) or higher. the heat destroys pathogenic organisms, weed seeds, flyora, etc. Decomposition proceeds rapidly and does not produce excessively unpleasent odors.

Curing:- Curing time to permit additional stabilization depends on the use to be made of compost. compost can be applied with little curing to fields or gardens that are not to be planted for some manters. It planting is to take place immediately, stabilization must have advanced to be point at which further decompsition will not rob the soil of nitrogen.

Finishing:- Screening, grinding, or a combination of similar processes is done to remove plastics, glass; and other materials from the compost that might be objectionable in its use. It the compost is to be utilized as an erosion control measure in isolated places, it can be applied without being ground or screened. Additional upgrading, such as pelletizing or fertilying with commercial fertilizer, may also be accomplished to satisfy various markets.

Storage:- The demand for compost in quantity is greatest in the, spring and fall. A plant must, therefore provide storage space for upto at least six months of production. The compost can be stored out doors in piles.

SUPPLIERS OF PLANT & MACHINERY

STORAGE TANKS

M/s. Chemsphere Engineers & Construction Limited,
Jai Hind Building,
1, Bhuleshwar,
Mumbai - 400 002

M/s. G.R. Engg. Works Private Limited,
Poonam Chambers,
Dr. A.B. Road,
Worli, Mumbai - 400 018

TANKS (CONICAL BOTTOM)

M/s. Chem Resist Lining,
35, Arcot Road,
Kodambakam,
Chennai - 600 024

HIGH PRESSURE VESSALS

M/s. A C C Vickers Babcock,
Express Towers,
18th Floor,
Nariman Point,
Mumbai - 400 021

PLATE & FRAME FILTER PRESS

M/s. Arunoday Engineering Works,
Near Somnath Temple,
Bilmara,
Gujarat.

DRYER (TRAY)

M/s. Ace Industries,
Gala No. 14, Alpine Industrial Estate,
Marol Military Road,
Andheri (E),
Mumbai - 400 054

PULVERIZER

M/s. Anu Designers & Fabricators,
C-I/12, G.I.D.C. Estate,
Opp. Ambica Nagar Society,
Odhav,
Ahmedabad - 382 415
Gujarat

GRINDING MILLS

M/s. Mercantile Engineers,
4/5, Jhandewalan Extension,
New Delhi - 110 005.

PLANT ECONOMICS

Rated Plant capacity = 20.00 TON/day
ORGANIC MANURE

LAND & BUILDING COST	Rs.	21,30,000.00

(Land required 3000 sq. mts.)

PLANT & MACHINERY

1. Cement Storage Tank
2. Mixing Tank (Conical Bottom)
3. Separator & Cooling Tank
4. Plate & Frame Filter Press
5. Cabinet Dryer
6. Pulverizer
7. High Pressure vessel (Jacketted)
8. Grinding Mill
9. Boiler
10. Miscellaneous Accessories and Fitting
11. Packaging Machine

FIXED CAPITAL

1. LAND & BUILDING	Rs.	21,30,000.00
2. PLANT & MACHINERY	Rs.	13,95,000.00
3. OTHER FIXED ASSETS	Rs.	2,60,000.00
TOTAL	Rs.	37,85,000.00

WORKING CAPITAL REQUIREMENT/MONTH

RAW MATERIALS

1. Sewage Sludge, Night Soil, Animal & Human Waste
2. Sulphuric Acid & Other Chemists

TOTAL WORKING CAPITAL/MONTH

1. RAW MATERIAL	Rs.	1,95,000.00
2. SALARY & WAGES	Rs.	81,600.00
3. UTILITIES & OVERHEADS	Rs.	1,08,500.00
TOTAL	Rs.	3,85,100.00

TOTAL CAPITAL INVESTMENT

TOTAL FIXED CAPITAL	Rs.	37,85,000.00
TOTAL WORKING CAPITAL FOR 3 MONTHS	Rs.	11,55,300.00
TOTAL	Rs.	49,40,300.00

TURN OVER/ANNUM

1. By sale of 6000 Tonne/annum of organic manure Rs. 1,20,00,000.00

PROFIT = RECEIPTS - COST OF PRODUCTION
= 60,31,346.00

PROFIT SALES RATIO = Profit / Sales x 100 *= 50.26 %*

RATE OF RETURN = Operating profit / T.C.I x 100 *= 122.08 %*

BREAK EVEN POINT (B.E.P) = 27.26 %

Chapter-21
POTASSIUM IODATE

INTRODUCTION

Potassium iodateisthemajor chemical usedforlodizationof edible common salt. It is also used as feed additives and asmaturing agents. Besides this it is used as dough conditioner in bread industries for bread manufacturing. Now the Govt. of India has passed an act to lodize the common edible salt at any cost considering the health factors of approximate 900 million Indian people. Besides this the export of common salt without lodization is not possible in the overseas countries. The export of salt is opened in international market only when the salt is iodized as per BIS or ISO 9000 specification.

PROPERTIES

- Chemical Formula = KIO_3
- It is white crystalline powder.
- It is odorless in nature.
- It is soluble in water and dilute Sulphuric Acid.
- It is insoluble in Alcohol.
- It's Specific Gravity is 3.979
- Melting Point - 560° C (Partial decomposition)
- It has low toxicity in nature.
- It has solubility in water 9.16 at 25° C ; 32.2 at 100° C
  Grades C.P, F.C.C.

USES AND APPLICATIONS

- It is used for lodization of edible Salt.
- It is used in analysis or testing of Zinc and arsenic.
- It is used in lodometry in medicine manufacturing.
- It is used as a reagent.
- It is used as feed additives.
- It is used in foods as maturing agent and dough Conditioner.

Specification and Requirements of Potassium Iodate

Table-1: Requirements for Potassium Iodate

Sl. No. (1)	Characteristic (2)	Requirement AR Grade (3)	Requirement FD Grade (4)	Requirement Tech Grade (5)	Method of Test (Ref to Cl No. in Annex A) (6)
i)	Potassium iodate (as KIO_3), percent by mass, Min	99.9	99.0	99.0	A-3
ii)	Matter insoluble in water, percent by mass, Max	0.003	--	--	A-4
iii)	Free acid, percent by mass, Max	0.002	--	--	A-5
iv)	Free alkali, percent by mass, Max	0.002	--	--	A-5
v)	Bromate, bromide, chlorate and chloride (as Cl), percent by mass, Max	0.02	0.01	0.1	A-6
vi)	Iodide (as I), percent by mass, Max	0.001	0.002	0.005	A-7
vii)	Nitrogen compound (as N), percent by mass, Max	0.002	--	--	A-8
viii)	Sulphate (as SO_4), percent by mass, Max	0.01	--	0.1	A-9
ix)	Iron (as Fe), percent by mass, Max	0.001	--	--	A-10
x)	Heavy metals (as Pb), ppm, Max	10	10	--	A-11
xi)	Sodium (as Na), percent by mass, Max	0.01	--	0.05	A-12
xii)	Loss on drying, percent by mass, Max	0.05	0.5	--	A-13
xiii)	Arsenic (as As), ppm, Max	--	3	--	A-14
xiv)	pH (5 percent solution)	5.5-9.0	5.5-9.0	5.5-9.0	A-15

MANUFACTURING PROCESS

Method - 1

Potassium Iodate can be prepared from potassium Iodide by electrolytic oxidation or by passing Chlorine through The Alkaline solution.

POTASSIUM IODATE

There are three methods for manufacturing of potassium Iodate, which are specified as follow :-

Method -1 :-

Potassium Iodate can be prepared from potassium Iodide by Electrolytic oxidation Process.

Chemical Reaction :-

$$KI + \_6H_2O \xrightarrow[\text{4000 Amp.}]{\text{Electric Current}} KIO_3 + 3H_2 + 3H_2O$$

This process is applicable only when the large capacity of production is required to be utilised and power availability is sufficient. Potassium Iodide can be collected by evaporating the solution from electric cell and Hydrogen Gas can be collected in Gas Holder.

Method - 2 :-

Potassium Iodate can be prepared from potassium Iodide by dissolving in the Potassium Hydroxide solution and then by passing the Chlorine gas in it.

Chemical Reaction :

$$2KI+6KOH+3Cl2 \xrightarrow{\text{heat}} 2KIO3+6KCl+3H2$$

This process is hazardous in operation. As any leakage of Chlorine in atmosphere will prove fatality. Again the Chlorine Gas is highly corrosive in nature. It will damage and Corrode the tanks in short spanv.

Therefore the above two process is eleminated for production of Potassium Iodate in sufficient quantity.

Method - 3 :-

This is widely used to prepare the Potassium Iodate. But in this process the Potassium Iodate is poduced as minor product which can be isolated from the major product and can be dried and packed in air tight containers.

In this process the Iodine solid (crude or resublimed) is dissolved in the hot Alkali solution or hot potassium Hydroxide solution to produce potassium Iodide as major product and Potassium Iodate as minor product. The mixture of above two products will be obtained in the crystal forms by evaporating the finished solution to dryness. The crystal mixture is now dissolved with stirring in the Ethyl Alcohol.

The Potassium Iodate is insoluble in Ethyl Alcohol but Potassium Iodide is completely soluble in Ethyl alcohol. So Potassium Iodate can be recovered as residue by filteration, washing and drying operations. Similarly the dissolved Potassium Iodide present in Ethyl Alcohol can also be recovered afterwards by evaporating and the Ethyl alcohol by solvent recovery unit. The Potassium Iodide crystals can be dried and packed in air tight containers. The recovered Ethyl Alcohol can be recycled in the next batch.

Chemical Reaction :-

Step-1 : $$6KOH+3I_2 \xrightarrow{\text{Heat}} 5KI+KIO_3+3H_2O$$

Step-2 : $$5KI+HIO_3+3H_2O \xrightarrow[\text{and drying}]{\text{Evaporation}} 5KI+KIO_3$$

Step-3 : $$5KI+KIO_3+C_2H_5OH \xrightarrow{\text{Dissolving completely}} KIO_3 \text{ (UndissolvedResidue)} + (5KI+C_2H5OH \text{ in solution form})$$

Step-4 : $$KIO_3+(5KI+C_2H_5OH \text{ in solution form}) \xrightarrow{\text{Filtration}} KIO_3 \text{ (Removal as Reside)}$$

Step-5 : $$(5KI+C_2H_5OH)\text{solution} \xrightarrow[\text{Condensation for Ethyl Alcohol Recovery}]{\text{Evaporation and}} KI\text{(Removal as crystal)}$$

RAW MATERIAL MANUFACTURERS/SUPPLIERS

IDOINE

M/s. Auto Laboratories Private Limited,
408, Navratan,
69, P.D. Mello Road,
Mumbai - 400 009.
Ph : 3429027/3425058
Fax : 91-22-3425022

POTASSIUM HYDROXIDE FLAKES/POWDER

M/s. Atul Product Limited,
Ashoka chambers,
Rasala marg,
Mithakhali Cross Road,
Ellis Bridge,
Ahmedabad - 380 006.
Ph.: 0272-40411
Fax : 2023057

ABSOLUTE ETHYL ALCOHOL

M/s. Kolhapur Sugar Mills Limited,
Udyog Bhawan,
Walchand Hirachand Marg,
Ballard Estate,
Mumbai - 400 038,
Ph. : 2614381/2614382/2614383
Fax : 022-2616356

CONTAINER

M/s. Varahi Plastics Private Limited,
WZ-8/1 Industrial Area,
Kirti Nagar,
New Delhi -110 015.
Ph. : 5451504

PLASTIC FILMS

1. **M/s. A.R. Co-Extruded Film Private Limited,**
Najafgarh Road,
Ganesh Market,
Nangloi, Delhi - 110 041.

PLANT AND MACHINERY SUPPLIERS

M/s. Air Flow Private Limited,
13/1090,
Hardian Singh Road,
Karol Bagh,
New Delhi -110005.
Ph. : 5721236/5727286

TANKS (ALL TYPES)

M/s. Flowlink Industries Private Limited,
D-15, Commercial Complex,
Prashant Vihar,
Delhi - 110 085.
Ph.: 7267006/7267007
Fax: 91-11-7267007

M/s. Annu Rashyan Udyog,
184, D.S.I.D.C Sheds,
Okhla Industrial Area-1,
New Delhi - 110 020.
Ph.: 6813624

BOILER

M/s. Delhi Engineering Compnay,
S-17, Industrial Estate,
Badli, Delhi - 110 042.
Ph. : 7292500

PLANT ECONOMICS

Rated Plant capacity = 252.00 KGS./day POTASSIUM IODATE

LAND & BUILDING COST
(Land 5000 sq.fts)

PLANT & MACHINERY

1. M.S. Body with FRP Linning, Jacketted Tank
2. PVC water storage tank (Sintex type)
3. Evaporator FRP lined
4. S.S. stirrer
5. S.S. Lined Condenser
8. Boiler, oil fired
6. S.S.Tank for Ethyl Alcohol Storage
7. Feeding Pump (Centrifugal type)
10. Filtration unit (S.S. body)
9. Fluidized Bed Dryer (S.S. lined)
11. Pumps, Valves, Motors, M.S. Tanks, Pipes Fitting and Miscellaneous, Machineries
10. Weighing Balance electronic type
12. Laboratory Equipments, Analytical Equipments

FIXED CAPITAL

2.	PLANT & MACHINERY	Rs.	20,20,000.02
3.	OTHER FIXED ASSETS	Rs.	4,30,500.00
	TOTAL	Rs.	24,50,500.03

WORKING CAPITAL REQUIREMENT/MONTH

RAW MATERIALS

1. Potassium Hydroxide powder/flakes
2. Iodine Crude (99% pure)
3. Absolute Ethyl Alcohol
4. Packaging containers with labels

TOTAL WORKING CAPITAL/MONTH

1.	RAW MATERIAL	Rs.	24,77,750.00
2.	SALARY & WAGES	Rs.	41,875.00
3.	UTILITIES & OVERHEADS	Rs.	1,01,100.00
	TOTAL	Rs.	26,20,725.00

TOTAL CAPITAL INVESTMENT

TOTAL FIXED CAPITAL	Rs.	24,50,500.03
TOTAL WORKING CAPITAL FOR 3 MONTHS	Rs.	78,62,175.00
TOTAL	Rs.	1,03,12,675.03

TURNOVER

1. By sale of 15600 kgs. of Potassium Iodate,
2. By sale of 60000 kgs. Potassium Iodide,

TOTAL Rs. 4,56,00,000.00

PROFIT = RECEIPTS - COST OF PRODUCTION

= 4,56,00,000.00 - 3,38,14,981.51

= 1,17,85,018.49

PROFIT SALES RATIO = Profit / Sales x 100 = 25.84 %

RATE OF RETURN = Operating profit / T.C.I x 100 = 114.28 %

BREAK EVEN POINT (B.E.P) = 20.57 %

Chapter-22

PVC STABILIZERS

INTRODUCTION

PVC is required to be stabilized during high temperature processing on three counts: firstly, discolouration of compound, secondly, evolution of HCL and thirdly, development of unsaturation followed by severe cross-linking which can catastrophically raise the torque/melt viscosity leading to mechnical damage to processing equipments.

Though, the need for stabilization was long felt and though it was soon discovered how stabilizers worked, it took many decades of careful work to realize the cause of such unstability of PVC.

The PVC stabilisers can be grouped in four types:

(i) Lead Based Stabilizers
(ii) Mixed Metal Based Stabilizers
(iii) Non Metal Based Stabilizers
(iv) Tin Based Stabilizers.

PROPERTIES

Excellent stabilizers do act in a variety of ways, with both preventive and curative measures to stabilize PVC.

1. HCL Absorption
2. Elimination of Labile Chlorine
3. Prevention Of Auto Oxidation
4. Additioin to Ppolyene Sequence
5. Carbenium Ion Elimination
6. Tin Based Stabilizers

USES AND APPLICATIONS

Tin stabilizers can be used universally for most of PVC application.

However, they can be used with PVC or its copolymers, graft or even blends, irrespective of whether PVC is produced by suspension, emulsion or mass process.

It can not be used in most transparent applications such as bottles, films, sheets.

VARIOUS TYPES OF TIN BASED STABILISERS

There are two types of tin stabilizers available, known as organo-tin stabilizers, which is used for processing of PVC products for better results in processing and afterward results.

(i) Non-sulphur containing tin stabilizers.
(ii) Sulfur containing tin stabilizers

FORMULATIONS

These various formulated compound mixture known as single-pack stabilizer system.

(I) Tin Stabilizer Formulation

FORMULATION-1

Dibutyl tin maleate	Parts per weight
Epoxydised soyabean oil	10
Stearic acid	1.6
Light solvent Naphtha (mineral spirit)	2

Process :-

Dissolve dibutyl tin maleate in light solvent naphtha with heating. Then add stearic acid till homogenous mixing. Then add the epoxydised-soyabean oil in it and homogenised the mixture till uniformly mixed. Then 2-3 parts of above mix can be used in 100 parts of PVC resin ready for product making.

FORMULATION-2

		Parts by wt.
Di - n - Octyl tin Maleate	-	1
Light Solvent Naphtha	-	2 - 3
Epoxydised Soyabean Oil	-	10
Stearic Acid	-	2

Process :- The process is same as in the formulation - I.

SUPPLIERS OF CHEMICALS

M/s. Shanker Dyes & Chemicals,
119, Tilak Bazar,
Delhi-110006.
Ph : 2520589
239574

M/s. IA Chemical & Associates,
10184, Arya Samaj Road,
Karol Bagh,
New Delhi -110 005
Ph : 5727778.

PLANT & MACHINERY SUPPLIERS

M/s. Quality Steel Fab India,
5 A/31 A, N.I.T.,
Faridabad - 121 001
Haryana.

M/s. Raja Industries,
C - 210, Mayapuri Industrial Area,
Phase - II,
New Delhi -110 064.
Ph. : 5403554
5400521
5402507.

STORAGE TANKS

M/s. Flowlink Industries Private Limited,
D-15, Commercial Complex,
Prashant Vihar,
Delhi - 110 085.
Ph.: 7267006/7267007
Fax: 91-11-7267007

M/s. Annu Rashyan Udyog,
184, D.S.I.D.C Sheds,
Okhla Industrial Area-1,
New Delhi - 110 020.
Ph.: 6813624

PLANT ECONOMICS

Rated Plant capacity = 100.00 KGS/day PVC STABILIZERS

LAND & BUILDING COST
(Land 100 Sq.Mts)

PLANT & MACHINERY

1. S.S kettle with M.S. Jacket
2. Weighing Balance
3. S.S. Storage Tank
4. 1 HP Motor with Pump Centrifugal Type
5. Pipes, Fittings, Tanks
6. Testing Equipments for Laboratory

FIXED CAPITAL

1. LAND & BUILDING	Rs.	Rental
2. PLANT & MACHINERY	Rs.	1,09,000.01
3. OTHER FIXED ASSETS	Rs.	50,000.00

WORKING CAPITAL REQUIREMENT/MONTH

RAW MATERIALS

1. Barium Stearate
2. Epoxydised Soyabean Oil
3. Cadmium Stearate
4. Triphenyl Phosphite

TOTAL WORKING CAPITAL/MONTH

1. RAW MATERIAL	Rs.	3,21,250.00
2. SALARY & WAGES	Rs.	9,500.00
3. UTILITIES & OVERHEADS	Rs.	8,400.00
TOTAL	Rs.	3,39,150.00

TOTAL CAPITAL INVESTMENT

TOTAL FIXED CAPITAL	Rs.	1,59,000.02
TOTAL WORKING CAPITAL FOR 3 MONTHS	Rs.	10,17,450.00
TOTAL	Rs.	11,76,450.02

TURN OVER/ANNUM

1. By sale of PVC stabiliser
   30,000 Kgs.

   TOTAL Rs. 48,00,000.00

PROFIT = RECEIPTS - COST OF PRODUCTION

= 48,00,000.00 - 43,09,811.01

= 4,90,188.99

PROFIT SALES RATIO = Profit / Sales x 100 = 10.21 %

RATE OF RETURN = Operating profit / T.C.I x 100 = 41.67 %

BREAK EVEN POINT (B.E.P) = 39.94 %

Chapter-23

PHENYL (BLACK AND WHITE)

INTRODUCTION

A disinfectant is basically an agent which destroys pathogenic organism. A good disinfectant should also be a deodorant possessing good keeping qualities. And it would be effective against microorganism of widely varying types.

Phenyl type disinfectants fall in the category of black oil disinfectants and are extensively used for sanitation purposes, for drains, floor, stables etc. and are prepared from coal tar distillates containing high boiling tar acids. These are, however, less, affected in contact with organic matter.

Phenyl is being used since very beginning for killing insects grown in nallahas, lavatory and kooradan. Most of the diseases causes due to insects.

USES & PROPERTIES

A phenyl type disinfectant which destroys pathogenic organism, must also have the following properties.

1. It should not be poisonous to higher organism.
2. It should not have corrosive or caustic action on animal tissues.
3. It should not leave any unpleasant odour or stain in the area distinfected.
4. It should also be a deodorant.

It is basically an agent which destroys pathogenic organism and hence it is uses are numerous. It is extensively used in for sanitation purposes for drains, floors, stables, etc. As these are slightly soluble in water, have to be emulsified for use as disinfections.

MANUFACTURING PROCESS

HIGH BOILING TAR ACID BLACK FLUIDS (PHENYL):

Formulation		(%)
H.B.T.A (Boiling range 90% between 220°C - 310°C)	-	40
Creosote Oil (5- 7% Tar acids)	-	25
W.W. Rosin	-	12
Castor Oil (Commerial grade)	-	7
Linseed oil	-	3
Soyabean Oil	-	2
Caustic Soda	-	3.4
Soft Water	-	7.6

PROCESS :-

The castor oil and linsecd oil are mixed together in a saponification vessels and heated slowly to 90oC. A pre-prepared 33% Caustic soda solution in water is then slowely added with stirring. After the complete addition the mixture is boiled for a few minutes for the complete saponification of the fats. The castor oil accelerates and assists the saponification of otherwise slowly reacting linseed oil and soyabean oil. After the complete saponification of the fats rosin's is added and again the mixture kept in boiling stage for the saponifation of rosin.

During the saponification process whatever water is lost by it evaporation is compensated by adding water.

When the saponification is over heated, is stopped and sufficient quantities of water added to get a soap solution. To this soap solution, is added with stirring the high boiling tar acid and Creosote oil followed by the remaining quantities of water. The disinfectant thus formed is stirred for a period of 15 minutes to get a stable emulsion in water which can be packed and put into the market.

RAW MATERIAL SUPPLIERS

ROSIN

M/s Delhi Rosin & Turpentine Mfg. Company,
Bharwain Road,
Hoshiarpur (Punjab).

CAUSTIC SODA

M/s Alkali and Chemical Corporation of India Limited,
34, Chowringe,
Calcutta - 700 016.

CREOSOTE OIL (LIGHT)

M/s. Indian Rosin & Turpentine Company Limited,
Cutterbuck Ganj,
Bareilly (U.P.)

SUPPLIER OF PLANT AND MACHINERY

TANKS

M/s Acmec India Corporation,
16, Manu Mansion, Old Custom House Road,
Mumbai - 400 001.

M/s. Flowlink Industries Private Limited,
D-15, Commercial Complex,
Prashant Vihar,
Delhi - 110 085.
Ph.: 7267006/7267007
Fax: 91-11-7267007

M/s. Annu Rashyan Udyog,
184, D.S.I.D.C Sheds,
Okhla Industrial Area-1,
New Delhi - 110 020.
Ph.: 6813624

STEAM JACKETTED VESSELS

M/s. Harayana Engineers & Fabricators,
12/6, Mathura Road,
Faridabad - 121003
(Haryana).

BOTTLE FILLING & SEALING MACHINE

M/s. Aal Mach Machinery,
1/4103/2, Phase IV,
Vatva,
Ahmedabad - 382445.

BOILER

M/s. Delhi Engineering Compnay,
S-17, Industrial Estate,
Badli, Delhi - 110 042.
Ph. : 7292500

PLANT ECONOMICS

Rated Plant capacity = 1000.00 KGS/day
BLACK & WHITE PHENYL

LAND & BUILDING COST Rs. 8,10,000.00
(Land Area required 600 sq. mts.)

PLANT & MACHINERY

1. M.S. tank
2. Emulsifier, storage tanks,
3. Liquid disinfectant (Phenyl) storage tank
4. Lab testing Equipments
5. Bottle filling & sealing M/c & other ancillaries
6. Steam Jacketted kettle
7. Caustic soda Preparation tank
8. Pumps, valves, motors, starters
9. Raw Material storage tank
10. Boiler

FIXED CAPITAL

1. LAND & BUILDING	Rs.	8,10,000.00
2. PLANT & MACHINERY	Rs.	6,86,000.00
3. OTHER FIXED ASSETS	Rs.	2,00,000.00
TOTAL	Rs.	16,96,000.00

RAW MATERIALS

1. For Black Phenyl:- High boiling tar acid (H.B.T.A.)
2. Casein (fine powder)
3. Borax
4. Sodium Dodecyl Benzene Sullphonate
5. Packaging material glass bottles
6. Rosin
7. Linseed Oil
8. For White Phenyl:- High Boiling Tar Acid
9. Creosote oil
10. Cresylic Creosote
11. Caustic Soda
12. Soyabean Oil
13. Castor Oil

TOTAL CAPITAL INVESTMENT

TOTAL FIXED CAPITAL	Rs.	16,96,000.00
TOTAL WORKING CAPITAL FOR 3 MONTHS	Rs.	20,62,821.00
TOTAL	Rs.	37,58,821.00

TURN OVER/ANNUM

1. BY sale of 1,50,000 Kgs of Black Phenyl.
2. By sale of 1,50,000 Kgs. of white Phenyl.

TOTAL Rs. 1,00,50,000.00

PROFIT = RECEIPTS - COST OF PRODUCTION

= 1,00,50,000.00 - 90,82,481.78

= 9,67,518.22

***PROFIT SALES RATIO = Profit / Sales x 100** = 9.63 %*

***RATE OF RETURN = Operating profit / T.C.I x 100** = 25.74 %*

BREAK EVEN POINT (B.E.P) = 63.09 %

Chapter-24

SODIUM META SILICATE

INTRODUCTION

The most common crystalline soluble silicates are of the meatasilicate family Na_2. NH_2O. The anhydrous sodium metasilicate $Na_2 SiO_3$ contains SiO_2 Chains, where X as the hydrates ($Na_2H_2Si_4$ X H_2O, where X = n-1) contains silicate monomer. The structure variations in the series with x-4, Sodium metasilicate pentahydrate, 5 sodium metasilicate hexa hydrate, sodium metasilicate octa hydrate and 8 sodium metasilicate mono hydrate, appear to result primarily from the order and co-ordination of the hydrated sodium ion.

The standard penta hydrate form contains 98% or more calculated Na_2SiO_3. $5H_2O$ and is covered by a tentative A.S.T.M. specification.

An anhydrous form is also available. Greatly incuased quantities of metasilicate have been used in recent years because of the ability of this non caustic form of alkali to built up-fairly high alkalinitics. The benefits of soluble silica as a detergent aid have been presented in elaborate explanations but in the presence of soap it would appear that the meager colloidal properties of silicate are for out weighed by those of the soap.

PROPERTIES, USES & APPLICATIONS

Sodium Metasilicate, Anhydrous
Na_2SiO_3. A crystalline silicate
Properties: Dustless white granules;
m.p. = 1080oC
total Na_2O content 51.5%;
total Na_2O in active form 48.6%
Density = 2.61 or 75 lb/in ft.

Soluble in water, precipitated by acids and by alkaline earth and heavy metalions. pH of 1% solution 12.6

Non-toxic, non-combustible.

Derivation:- Crystallized from a melt of Na_2O and SiO_2 below 1089°C.

Sodium - m - Silicate (Na_2SiO_3) is a colourless crystalline substances. It is available in powder form also, containing 51.7% of Na_2O and 46.2% SiO_2.

Sodium - Silicate pentahydrate is a white grannular material containing 29.0% of Na_2O. It is very soluble in cold and hot water.

USES

Laundry, dairy and metal cleaning; floor cleaning; base for detergent formulations bleaching aidis de-inking paper.

Also available as the pentahydrate, whose properties are m.p. 72.2°C; total Na_2O content 29.3%; totla Na_2O in active form 27.8%; Density 1.75, or 55 lb per Cn ft.

Beyond that uses of sodium - m - silicates are in

a) Manufacture of Silica Gel.
b) In Soaps and Detergents
c) Adhesives, Especially Box Board Type
d) Pigments
e) Water Treatment
f) Bleaching and Sizing of Textiles and Paper Pulp
g) Ore Treatment
h) Soil Solidification & Dilling Mud.

REQUIREMENTS FOR SODIUM METASILICATE

1.	Total alkalinity (as Na_2O percent by mass, Min	49.0	28.0	21.0 -	A-6
2.	Ratio of total alkalinity (as Na_2O) to total soluble silica (as Si_2O) (Na_2O:SiO_2)	<	1:1 ± 0.05	> -	A-8 or A-12
3.	Loss on evaporation, percent by mass, Max	2.0	43.5	59.0-	A-9
4.	Matter insoluble in water, percent by mass, Max	<	0.5	> -	A-3
5.	Free alkalinity (as Na_2O) percent by mass, Max	2.0	1.0	0.8	Appendix A -

* *Specification for sodium silicate.*

MANUFACTURING PROCESS

This is a process for producing sodium metasilicate, Na2SiO3, from silica and soda ash utilizing a molten reaction pool supported in a bed of solid silicate. Interposed between the upper periphery of the vessel and the refractory top of the furnace are a series of cooling chambers which will be more fully described hereafter.

The vessel is substantially filled with a body of comminuted sodium metasilicate which forms a bed that supports a action pool of the molten silicate. A mixture of sand and soda ash in the proper proportions is continuously fed to the pool by three screw conveyors mounted in the refractory side wall . The mixture fed by the conveyors floats out on the surface of pool and into the pool wherein it reacts to form the metasilicate. Heat to maintain the pool in molten condition and to cause the reaction to proceed is supplied by two pairs of burners , one pair being mounted in each of the end walls of the furnace.

The burned gases leave the furnace through the passages 29 formed in the end walls of the furnace. In order to effect desired thermal economy, the furnace shown in preferably of the regenerative type wherein the air for combustion an/or fuel gas is preheated by heat withdrawn from the flue gases. It will of course be understood that in accordance with the usual regeneratigve practice, only one pair of burners 28 is used at a time, and the burned gases are withdrawn from the furnace through the passage 29 at the end of the furnace opposite that in which the operating burnes are located.

The molten silicate is withdrawn from the furnace through a forehearth generally designated and provided with the burners for maintaining the metasilicate in molten condition as it passes there through. As in the case of the main part of the furnace, the stream of metasilicate flowing through the forehearth is supported on a bed of comminuted metasilicate. Sodium metasilicate is used in cleaning compositions.

RAW MATERIAL REQUIREMENTS

Basis : 1 tonne 40°be Sodium Metasilicate (Water Glass)

Sodium Carbonate (Dense, 57%)	-	156 kgs
Sand	-	293 kgs
Gas (250 kcal)	-	150 m^3
Water	-	160 gals
Steam	-	520 kgs
Electricity	-	21.6kwh

SUPPLIERS OF RAW MATERIALS

SODA ASH

M/s. Tata Chemical Limited,
Bombay House,
24, Bruce Street,
Fort, Mumbai-400 001.

CAUSTIC SODA

M/s. Shreeram Food & Fertilisers Limited,
P.B. No. 221, Najafgarh Road,
New Delhi - 110 015.

SILICA

M/s. Tanwar Rajput & Company,
10, Small Industrial Area,
Kota - 7 (Rajasthan).

SUPPLIERS OF PLANT & MACHINERY

CENTIFUGE

M/s. Bunching Schimt Limited,
66, Ring Road,
Lajpat Nagar - III,
New Delhi, - 110 024.

CRYSTALLISERS

M/s. Berry Borox Commercial House,
135, Cannin Street,
Calcutta.

TANKS

M/s. Flowlink Industries Private Limited,
D-15, Commercial Complex,
Prashant Vihar,
Delhi - 110 085.
Ph.: 7267006/7267007
Fax : 91-11-7267007

M/s. Annu Rashyan Udyog,
184, D.S.I.D.C Sheds,
Okhla Industrial Area-1,
New Delhi - 110 020.
Ph.: 6813624

SUPPLIERS OF COMPLETE PLANT & MACHINERY

M/s. Arun Enterprises (Delhi),
F-11, DSIDC Industrial Complex,
Rohtak Road,
Delhi - 110 041.
Phone: 5714 108
7224 199.

PLANT ECONOMICS

Rated Plant capacity = 5.00 TON/day
SODIUM META SILICATE

LAND & BUILDING COST	Rs.	9,45,000.00

(Total land required 5000 sq.ft.)

PLANT & MACHINERY

1. Vertical Boiler
2. Digesters with Agitator
3. Storing with Metasilicate
4. Dissolver
5. Setting tank
9. Coal fired Tank Furnace
6. Solidification System
7. Regenerative Furnace
8. Overhead PVC Tank
10. Testing Equipments

FIXED CAPITAL

1. LAND & BUILDING	Rs.	9,45,000.00
2. PLANT & MACHINERY	Rs.	25,50,000.00
3. OTHER FIXED ASSETS	Rs.	6,70,000.00
TOTAL	Rs.	41,65,000.00

WORKING CAPITAL REQUIREMENT/MONTH

RAW MATERIALS

1. Sodium Carbonate
2. Sand
3. Packaging material

TOTAL WORKING CAPITAL/MONTH

1. RAW MATERIAL	Rs.	1,93,200.00
2. SALARY & WAGES	Rs.	92,500.00
3. UTILITIES & OVERHEADS	Rs.	80,200.00
TOTAL	Rs.	3,65,900.00

TOTAL CAPITAL INVESTMENT

TOTAL FIXED CAPITAL	Rs.	41,65,000.00
TOTAL WORKING CAPITAL FOR 3 MONTHS	Rs.	10,97,700.00
TOTAL	Rs.	52,62,700.00

TURN OVER/ANNUM

1. By sale of 1500 MT of Sodium Metasilicate
   TOTAL Rs. 90,00,000.00

PROFIT = RECEIPTS - COST OF PRODUCTION

= 90,00,000.00 - 60,57,574.50

= 29,42,425.50

PROFIT SALES RATIO = Profit / Sales x 100 = 32.69 %

RATE OF RETURN = Operating profit / T.C.I x 100 = 55.91 %

BREAK EVEN POINT (B.E.P) = 45.89 %

Chapter-25

SILICONE EMULSION (MOULD RELEASING AGENT)

INTRODUCTION

Silicones are synthetic polymers having an inorganic skeleton of alternate silicone and oxygen atoms, the silicone valencies not taken up by oxygen being saturated with organic grpoupe and other groups. they occupy an intermediate position between inorganic and organic compounds. because of this dual nature they have many properties which have made them very useful in many applications. silicones are produced in several forms including fluids, rubbers and resins. silicones emulsions are formed from silicone fluids and water with the help of a suitable emulsifier, and find various applications.

The term silicone denotes a polymer with the structural formula (RnSiO(4-n)1/2)m where n is between 0 and 3 and m is 2 or more. It contains a repeaating silicone oxygen chain having organic groups R, attached to a significant portion of the silicone atom by silicone carbon bonds. In commercial silicones most of the R groups are methyl, longer alkyl, fluoroalky, phenyl, vinyl and a few others. Silicone fluids the Si-O chain is unbranched.

Silicone fluids are generally, dimethyl polysiloxane, methyl hydrogen polysiloxane or silicones consisting of copolymers of dimethyl siloxane with methyl phenyl, methyl-hydrogen, diphenyl, methyl-alkyl and other siloxanes. Linear poly-dimethyl siloxanes or dimethyl polysiloxanes are the most important of all the silicones. These fluids with hexamethyl disiloxane. For relating low viscosity fluids are manufacured by reacting dimethyl silicone fluids the process is run for several hours at 180°C in glasslined kettles with acid chloride catalysts or at lower temperature with sulphuric acid. Alkaline catalysts are used for the production of high viscosity fluids or gums. Silicone fluids have m.wt. of 2000 to 15000 and viscosities from 10 to 10,000 pcs.

USES AND APPLICATIONS

Silicone emulsion is used basically as a mould releasing agent for plastic and rubber mouldings of various shape, size of products.

SILICONE OIL EMULSION (MOULD RELEASING AGENT)

Formulation :-

		Parts bt wt.
DC - 200 Silicone oil	-	200
"Carbopol - 934"	-	2
Dodecylamine	-	1
Sodium Hydroxide (10% Solution)	-	6
Water	-	200

PROCESS OF MANUFACTURE

First of all weigh the ingredients separately in desire quantity. Then carefully disperse the "Carbopol - 934" in the water and mix to a thin, cloudy dispersions without lumps. add the sodium hydroxide lye solution in it and stir homogeneously with mild agitation. Then add Dodecylamine in it with stirring. The dispersion will gel immediately. Lastly, add the DC - 200 silicone oil in a slow, steady stream with good mixing. A white, stabble emulsion forms immediately. This emulsion is packed in air tight container.

PLANT & MACHINERY SUPPLIERS

M/s. SSP Private Limited,
19, DLF Industrial Area - II,
13/4, Mathura Road,
Faridabad - 121003.
Phone: - 0129 - 275968
Fax: - 0129 - 277441

STORAGE TANKS

M/s. Flowlink Industries Private Limited,
D-15, Commercial Complex,
Prashant Vihar,
Delhi-110 085.
Ph.: 7267006/7267007
Fax: 91-11-7267007

M/s. Annu Rashyan Udyog,
184, D.S.I.D.C Sheds,
Okhla Industrial Area-1,
New Delhi - 110 020.
Ph.: 6813624

RAW MATERIAL SUPPLIERS

SILICONE OIL

M/s. Dadia Chemical Industries,
Plot No. R - 381, T.T.C,
M.I.D.C. Belapura Road,
Thane - 400701,
Phone: - 7691669,
Fax: - 2873480.

DODECYLAMINE, CARBOPOL - 934

M/s. Fine Organics,
15/2, Neelkanth Market,
M.G. Road,
Ghatkopar (East),
Mumbai - 400 077,
Phone: - 5116900
5116902
5153041
Fax: - 91 - 022 - 5153215,
Telex: - 011 - 73311 FINE IN

SODIUM HYDROXIE (CAUSTIC SODA)

M/s. Noida Chemicals,
C - 10, Sector - 7,
Noida - 201301 (U.P),
Phone - 89 - 24718, 573 - 5151.

PLANT ECONOMICS

Rated Plant capacity = 500.00 Kgs/day
SILICONE EMULSION

LAND & BUILDING COST	Rs.	10,00,000.00
(Land 500 sq. mts.)		

PLANT & MACHINERY

1. Stainless Steel Storage Tank
2. Stainless Steel Tank
3. Stainless Steel Mixing Tank
4. PVC Water Tank (Sintex Type)
5. Testing Equipment
6. Pipes, Pumps, Valves, Fittings, Instrumentation

FIXED CAPITAL

1.	LAND & BUILDING	Rs.	10,00,000.00
2.	PLANT & MACHINERY	Rs.	2,41,000.00
3.	OTHER FIXED ASSETS	Rs.	4,00,000.00
	TOTAL	Rs.	16,41,000.00

WORKING CAPITAL REQUIREMENT/MONTH

RAW MATERIALS

1. Silicone oil (Dc - 200)
2. Carbopol - 934
3. DoDecylamine
4. Sodium Hydroxide (10% solution)

TOTAL WORKING CAPITAL/MONTH

1.	RAW MATERIAL	Rs.	21,64,365.00
2.	SALARY & WAGES	Rs.	55,125.00
3.	UTILITIES & OVERHEADS	Rs.	72,250.00
	TOTAL	Rs.	22,91,740.00

TOTAL CAPITAL INVESTMENT

TOTAL FIXED CAPITAL	Rs.	16,41,000.00
TOTAL WORKING CAPITAL FOR 3 MONTHS	Rs.	68,75,220.00
TOTAL	Rs.	85,16,220.00

TURN OVER/ANNUM

1. By sale of 150,000 kgs of Silicone Emulsion Mould Releasing Agent

TOTAL	Rs.	3,15,00,000.00

PROFIT = RECEIPTS - COST OF PRODUCTION

= 3,15,00,000.00 - 2,91,52,799.60

= 23,47,200.40

PROFIT SALES RATIO = Profit / Sales x 100 = 7.45 %

RATE OF RETURN = Operating profit / T.C.I x 100 = 27.56 %

BREAK EVEN POINT (B.E.P) = 49.09 %

Chapter-26
TEXTILE AUXILLIARIES

INTRODUCTION

The oldest textile auxiliary is soap, and it has been in use for about 2000 years. Turkey red oil was manufactured in 1834. The major development of textile auxiliaries was started during 1st world war in Germany. The crease resistance process was developed by Total Broadhwest Lee Co. Ltd. Manchester in 1928. This led to the production of a variety of cross linking agents and softeners.

CLASSIFICATIONS OF TEXTILE AUXILIARIES

These may be broadly classified, depending on the purpose for which they are used, into two groups - (1) those which are used in textile processing to serve some purpose or purposes and after these purposes are served, thhey have to be removed from the textile material being processed and (2) those whichh continue to form an integral part of the material being processed by way of either chemical reaction with the textile substrate or mechanical deposition of water soluble or water insoluble substances in the textile substrate and are expected to remain on the material more or less permanently, with standing the subsequent rigorous action of varying degrees, exerted on the end products during the use by the consumers. These two classes may be called temporary and permanent textile auxiliaries respectively. the temporary textile auxiliaries may be defined as those which are helpers or assistants and are additives to the usual processing solutions (scouring, bleaching, dyeing, aftertreating, finishing etc.) for improving the efficiency of the process and /or the effect obtained on the textile material being processed. Thus under the category of temporary textile auxiliaries is included a variety of products, having diverse properties.

Detergents used in kier-boil-ing of cotton fabrics and wetting agents used in tthe mercerrising liquors, especially in the mercerisation of grey cotton cloth help caustic soda to come into intimate contact with the cotton fibres and wetting agents used in the mercerising liquors, especially in the mercerisation of grey cotton cloth help caustic soda to come into intimate contact with the cotton fibres by efficient wetting and penetration of the liquors into the fabric to bring about either the saponification of the fatty matter present in the fibres or on the warp yarn (kier-boiling) or seelling and subsequent mercerisation of the fabrics (mercerising). After these processes are carried out, the detergent and the wetting agent are removed from tthe material along with the caustic soda used and thhe impurities removed from the fabric.

Levelling agents used in dyeing acid dyes on wool or nylon, or in class of (normal dyeing) vat dyes on cotton or carriers and dispersing agents used in the dyeing of disperse dyes on polyester fibres, and soluton aids used in dissolving sparingly soluble dyes in printing pastes, which normally contain a small amount of water, are some examples of temporary textile auxiliries. their presence in the processing media (dye solutions or printing pastes) is absolutely necessary from the point of view of obtaining level shades, good depth and optimum colour value in dyeoing and printing.

Textile auxiliaries belonging to the second group, the permanent one, are usually found in finishing processes. Softeners, water-profing and water repelling agents, crease resisting finishing formulations, flame retardants, rot proofing agents, antistatic agents, binders and fixers used in pigment printing and dye fixing agents are some examples of types of products falling in this group of textile auxiliaries. In this case also some are semi permanent while others are permanent. Deposition of water insoluble chemicals to impart a particular finishing effect is the basis of the use of semi permanent textile auxiliaries, while chemical reaction with the fibre substances forms the basis of producing permanent or durable effects on textiles. In these cases, emphasis is laid on the production of finishes, which loast 25 or 50 home launderings and repeated dry cleanings.

The important textile auxiliaries are, therefore, classified according to their fuctions as agents for

1. Sizing
2. Desizing
3. Scouring
4. Mercerizing
5. Bleaching
6. Dyeing
7. Printing & Finishing.

SUPPLIERS OF TEXTILE AUXILIARIES

M/s. **Ahura Chem. Products (Pvt.) Limited,**
Sion Road,
Sion East,
Mumbai.

M/s. **Arofen Limited,**
63, Apollo Street,
Mumbai.

M/s. **CIBA-Geigy of India Limited,**
Royal Insurance Building,
14-J, Tata Road,
Mumbai.

LIST OF CHEMICALS USED AS TEXTILES

AUXILIARIES FOR COTTON YARN

Sizing

1. Adhesives & Binders	Starch, Gums, Casein, Gelatine, Poly Vinyl Alcohol.
2. Lubricant	Tallow, The Fat of Beef or Mutton or Both. Sizing
3. Softner	Spalm Oil, Tarkey Red Oil, Stearine.
4. Hygroscopic Agent	Glycerine
5. Antiseptic Agent	Salaeyic Acid & Its Compound & Sodium Silicofluoride.
Desizing	
6. Enzymes	Bacterial Enzymes, Malt Enzymes & Pan Desizing Creatic Enzymes
7. Wetting Agents	Non Ionic Polyehylene Oxide Conden Sate/Ester Linked Alkaline Sulphonate
Scouring	
8. Sodium Hydroxide	Scouring Alkyl Derivatives of Napthalene Sulphonic Acid, Sulphated Alcohol, Gardionol, Lissapol, Lorol .
9. Mercerizing	
Mercerizing	
10. Phenolic Compounds	Cresylic Acid, Solvent Cyelohexame
11. Bleaching	Calcium or Sodium Hypochlorates
12. Optical Brightening Agent	Tinopol, Uvitex, Blanchopor, Unimol.
13. Stain Removing Agent	Trichloro Ethylene Per Chloro Ethylene, Carbon Tetra Chloride
14. Drying	Weting & Pentrating Agent Such as Polyethylene Glycol Alkyl Aryl Sulphonates
15. Lebelling Agents	Fatty Amide Sulphonates.
16. Dispersing Agent	Sulfated Fatty Esters & Amides
17. Sequestring Agent	E.D.T.A.
18. Dye Fixing Agent	Cationic Surfactants.
19. After Washing Agent	Cation Surfactants.
20. Printing	Clycerol, Wheat Starch, British Gum
21. Finishing	Glycol, Melamine Formaldehyde, Phenols, Copper & Quinolinate.

DETAILS OF TEXTILE AUXILIARIES CHEMICALS & THEIR MANUFACTURE FOR DIFFERENT PROCESS

STARCH

Milling of corn, zea may provide corn starch. Steeped corn is coarsely ground in an attrition mill to break loose the germ. The mill gap during this step must be adjusted to maximize the amount of germ feeds but minimize rupture of germ. Germ is removed from the aqueous slurry in a cyelone separator. The Germ fraction is processed for corn oil. The cyclone underflow is milled a second time for complete release of the starch grannules. Following the second milling, the kernal suspension contain starch, glutten & fibre. The collected fibre is combined with glutten for feed use.

The starch glutten suspension, is concentrated by centrifugation. The concentrated starch is passed through hydrocyclone to remove the last traces of protein. Strach suspension may be processed dry or marketed as unmodified starch.

GLUE/GELATINE

Manufacture of Animal glue is essentially a treatment of a collagen source with heat and water in order to hydrolyziet to a soluble product as rapidly and as efficiently as possible. The resulting solution is filtered, centrifuged to remove fat, concentrated to a suitable solids content, chilled to get the concentrate extruded or cut into particles, dried, grounded and packed.

CASEIN

It is a cheese product derived from milk first milk is processed i.e. cooling homogenization. Paste urization cleaming is done to store milk for long time than cheese is manufactured. Casein is precipitated by acidification which can be accomplished by natural souring of milk.

POLYVINYL ALCOHOL

Polyvinyl alcohol is manufactured by base-catalyzed methanolysis of polyvinyl acetate. Sodium Hydroxide is the usual base. The degree of hydrolysis during alcoholysis is controlled and is independent of molecular weight.

GELATINE

Gelatine is manufactured by hot water extraction followed by freezing & filtration of Agar. The freezing allows removal of the soluble salts. Manufacture involves the following steps:

1. Extraction
2. Filtration
3. Gelation
4. Thawing
5. Drying
6. Washing & drying
7. Cleaning or Washing of Agar Raw Materials
8. Freezing
9. Filtration
10. Bleaching
11. Bleaching or Chemical Treatment .

PALM OIL & TURKEY RED OIL

These oils are manufactured by extraction (solvent) process and further refining of the oil from the oil seed.

FORMULATION

Water	150 gal.
Soda Ash	50 oz.
1% Copper Sulfate Solution "Pearl"	50 cc.
Cornstarch	80 lb .
35% Hydrogen Peroxide	135.4 fl. oz.
Tallow	1 lb.

These are filled into the starch kettle in the order given and with constant stirring. The processing temperature of 208oF. is reached in 30 minutes and maintained for another 15 minutes. The paste is used for slasher sizing of 19/1 and 26/1 warp yarns.

Sizing for Backs of Axminster Rugs

U.S. Patent 2,542,344

Sulfite Waste Solids	28 - 50.3
Starch	20- 35.2
Clay	42.3 - 0.0
Ethylene Glycol Diabietate	9.7 - 14.5

This is dispersed in water with hheat to give a viscosity of 200 to 2000 cp.

U.S. Patent 2, 576,921

Arrowroot Starch	2 g
Gelatin	1 oz.
Alum	1/4 oz.
Alcohol	1 fl. oz.
37% Formaldehyde	1 fl. oz
Water To make	1 qt.

LIST OF RAW MATERIAL SUPPLIERS

ETHYLENE

M/s. National Organic Chemicals Industries Limited,
Mafatlal Centre,
Nariman Point,
Mumbai-400 021.

ALUM

M/s. K. P. Chemical Works,
99/15, Jawahar Nagar,
Goregaon (West),
Mumbai-400 062.

ALUMINIUM SALTS

M/s. Hemkunt Chemical Industries,
2 "O", Vijay Chamber,
2nd Floor, 1140,
Tribhuvan Road,
Mumbai-400 004.

OXYGEN

M/s. Indian Oxygen Limited,
Calcutta.

PLANT AND MACHINERIES SUPPLIERS

FILTER PRESS:

M/s. Amar Engineering Works,
WZ - 8, Raja Garden,
New Delhi-110 015.

GENERATOR SETS:

M/s. Jeevan Diesels (Delhi),
2867, Shahganj,
Shardhanand Marg,
Delhi-110 006.
Ph. 522 335

SUPPLIERS OF REACTORS (STAINLESS STEEL)

M/s. Gohel Chemical Engineering Industries,
21, Shri Jaiaram Industrial Estate,
Rakhial, Ahmedabad,
Gujarat.

DRYERS

M/s. Allied Group Industries,
B-18, Sector - VII,
Noida - 201 301,
U.P.

HEAT EXCHANGER

M/s Arun Enterprises,
F - 11, DSIDC Industrial Complex,
Rohtak Road,
Delhi-110 041.

PLANT ECONOMICS

Rated Plant capacity = 2000.00 KGS/day
TEXTILE AUXILLIRIES

LAND & BUILDING Rs. 23,00,000.00
(Land 3000 sq.mt.)

PLANT & MACHINERY

1. Corn Storage
2. Attrition Mill
3. Miller
4. Hydro Cyclone
5. Agar Storage House
6. Extrator
7. Freezer
8. Bleaching Tank
9. Washing Tank
10. Tripple Effect Evaporator
11. Absorption Lower
12. Heat Exchanger
13. Boiler
14. Automatic Packing Machine
15. Washing Tank Made of Brick, Cement & Clay
16. Steping Tank
17. Cyclone Separator
18. Centrifuge Separator
19. Dryer (Electrical)
20. Bleaching Tank
21. Filter Press (Rotary)
22. Rotary Dryer (Steam)
23. Dryer Steam
24. Chemical Reactor
25. Distillation Column
26. Boiling Pan
27. Tripple Effect Evaporator
28. Chemical Treating Tank
29. D.G.Set

FIXED CAPITAL

1. LAND & BUILDING	Rs.	23,00,000.00
2. PLANT & MACHINERY	Rs.	47,10,000.00
3. OTHER FIXED ASSETS	Rs.	8,00,000.00
TOTAL	Rs.	78,10,000.00

WORKING CAPITAL REQUIREMENT/MONTH

RAW MATERIALS

1. Corn
2. Ethylene
3. Refined Oil
4. Activated Carbon
5. Agar
6. Oxygen
7. Alum
8. Aluminium Salts

TOTAL WORKING CAPITAL/MONTH

1. RAW MATERIAL	Rs.	4,87,500.00
2. SALARY & WAGES	Rs.	2,36,000.00
3. UTILITIES & OVERHEADS	Rs.	91,600.00
TOTAL	Rs.	8,15,100.00

TOTAL CAPITAL INVESTMENT

TOTAL FIXED CAPITAL	Rs.	78,10,000.00
TOTAL WORKING CAPITAL FOR 3 MONTHS	Rs.	24,45,300.00
TOTAL	Rs.	1,02,55,300.00

TURN OVER/ANNUM

1. By SALE OF 150 MT Corn Starch
2. Glycerol 150 MT
3. Ethylene Glycol 150 MT
4. Gelatine 150 MT
5. Bye product fatty acid 120 MT

TOTAL Rs. 1,54,20,000.00

PROFIT = RECEIPTS - COST OF PRODUCTION

= 20,94,384.00

PROFIT SALES RATIO = Profit / Sales x 100 = *13.58 %*

RATE OF RETURN = Operating profit / T.C.I x 100 = *20.42 %*

BREAK EVEN POINT (B.E.P) = 70.96 %

Chapter-27

UNSATURATED POLYESTER RESIN

INTRODUCTION

Polyester resins are prepared by reacting a dihydric alcohol with a mixture of unsaturated and saturated dibasic acids. The basic resin, so obtained is not usable because of its high viscosity and poor reactivity. It is diluted with a reactive unsaturated compound called monomer and supplied to the user. The remaining polymer chemistry is carried out at the casteomers end where with the help of a catalyst and an accelerator, the resin is further polymerized (cross-linked) to produce a three dimentional influsible structure.

RAW MATERIAL

The four types of components used in the manufacture of Polyester resins is mentioned in the list of commonly used. Raw materials given in table.

Components of Polyester Resins

Saturated Acid	Unsaturated Acid	Glycols	Monomer
Pthatic Anhydride	Maleic Anhydride	Ethylene Glycol	Styrene
Isothalic Acid	Fumeric Acid	Diethylene Glycol	Dialel
Ferepthalene Acid	Chloromaleic Acid	Propylene Glycol	Phthalate
Adipic Acid	Mesaconic Acid	Neopennily Glycol	Vinyltolekene
Selaic Acid	Itaconic Acid	Dipropylene Glycol	Triallel
Aelaic Acid	Chlorosumar is Acid	Trimethyolpropane	Cyanuvate
Het Acid	Cinnarmic Acid	Dianol -3-3	Chlorostyrne
Tetrachlorophthalic		Dianol -3-3	Methylstyrene
Nadic Methyl		Dibutylene	Divinyl
Anhydride		Glycol	Benjevs
Acrylic Acid		Hexanediol	Methylmetha
Methacrylic Acid		Glycerol	Crylate
Glyco Puntane			
Dianhydride		Dieyctopenta	Acrylete etc.
Dianhydride		Diene etc.	
Trimethiltic			
Anhydride etc.			

PROPERTIES AND USES

The over small properties of a polyester resin are decided by its formulation and reaction conditions. The properties that are decided by formulation are called 'Formulation dependent' properties and the properties decided by reaction conditions are called ('Reaction dependent by properties.). A list of these properties is shown below:

PROPERTIES

A. FORMULATIONDEPENDENT PROPERTIES

1. Reactivity
2. Flammability
3. Optical properties
4. Corrosion resistance
5. Mechanical properties
6. Heat distortion temperature

B. REACTIONDEPENDENT PROPERTIES

1. Acid value
2. Viscosity.
3. Curing characteristics geltimse, peak exotherm etc.

B is phenol Fumarates have the highest heat destortion temperature followed by isophthale and orthophthalate resins.

The reactivity of the resin is determined by the level of unsaturation in the resin; the higher the unsaturation the move reactive is the resin.

The flame retardent properties of the resin are also formulattion dependent. The optical properites i.e refractive index, clarity, and to some extent the mechanical properties of the resin are also formulation dependent.

PROCESS OF MANUFACTURE

The theoretical charge for a polyester reactions is one molar equivalent of glycol for each molar equivalent of acid. However it is common practice to use from 10-20% excess glycol to allow for glycol loss in the reflux condenser system and to bring the acid number doors to low value rapidly. A typical formulation is shown below.

Raw Material	Moles	Wt. lbs.
Propylene	1.1	83.7 (10% excess)
Maleic Anhydride	0.5	49.0
Phthalic Anhydride	0.5	74.0
		206.7
Losses (Estimated 10%)		20.7
Polyester Resin Yield		186.0
Styrene (30%)		79.7
Total Resin Solutions		265.7

The Raw materials are either weighed into the reaction kettle directly from their shipping container or in case of larger production operation from large storage tanks, bins, or hoppers to which materials have been previously charged.

The liquid ingredients (usually the glycol) are charged to the reactor first, with the agitator running the batch is heated to 175° to 210°F and the solid components are added (Maleic, phthalic etc.).

If the reaction involves a solvent reflux such as xylene, charged. a solvents reflux in removing water from the condensation reaction and serves to control the temperature of the reaction and maintain the same at the desired level.

A blanket, of inert gas should be introduced as the temperature is increased to prevent discoloration and cross-linking polymerisation through the unsaturated acid. This latter reaction is most likely to occur and where above 400oF. Once started it is almost impossible to stop and may proceed to get the entire batch.

The batch is gradually heated over a period of several hours to approximately 400oF. It is held at this temperature until, the acid number come down to the desired point. Cooking time depends upon the ingredients and can run upto 16 hrs. or even more. The condensation reaction that kept it under control occurs in exothermic and close observation.

SUPPLIERS OF PLANT AND MACHINERY

M/s. Ganson Private Limited,
677, Himalaya House,
23, Kasturba Gandhi Marg,
New Delhi - 110 001.

M/s. Wanson India Private Limited,
22, Mahatma Gandhi Marg,
Lajpat Nagar,
New Delhi - 110 024

PRESENT MANUFACTURERS/SUPPLIERS

M/s. Bakelite Hylam Limited,
Sanath Nagar,
Hyderabad - 8 (A.P).

M/s. Crystic Resin India Private Limited,
273-243,
Abdul Rehman Street,
Mumbai-400 003.

M/s. Industrial Resins and Polymers,
Road No.6-C,
New Estate,
Distt. Surat,
Udhana-394210.
Gujarat.

RAW MATERIALS

MALEIC ANHYDRIDE

M/s. Adarsh Chemicals and Fertilizers Limited,
P.B. No. 13, Udhana-394 210,
Distt. Surat, Gujarat.

M/s. Allied Aromatics Limited,
13, Camac Street,
Calcutta-700 016.

PHTHALIC ANHYDRIDE

M/s. Durgapur Chemicals Limited,
6, Little Russel Street,
Calcutta - 700 016.

M/s. Satyam Pharmaceuticals Private Limited,
Diamond House, 491-493,
Kalbadevi Road, Mumbai-400 002.

STYRENE

M/s. Hindustan Polymers,
Visakhapatnam.

M/s. Polychem Limited,
7, Jamshedji Tata Road,
Mumbai.

PROPYLENE GLYCOL

M/s. Central Commercial Agency (India),
27, Church Bunder,
Post Box No. 5090,
Mumbai-400 009.

BOILERS

M/s. Vikram Equipment Company,
E-63, Sector - IX,
Industrial Complex, Noida,
District Ghaziabad, (U.P.)
Phone : 892 36 43

M/s Urjex Industries,
S- 26, Industrial Estate,
Pratapur, Meerut - 250 102,
(U.P).

PLANT ECONOMICS

Rated Plant capacity = 260.00 KGS/day
POLYESTER RESIN

LAND & BUILDING COST Rs. 3,50,000.00
(Land 300 sq.mts)

PLANT & MACHINERY

1. Reaction Kettle
2. Condenser
3. Receiver
5. Styrene and Glycol Storage Tanks
6. High Pressure Boiler
7. Reflux Condenser
8. Decantor
9. Blending Kettle
10. Miscellaneous Equipment and Accessories
11. Generator

FIXED CAPITAL

1.	LAND & BUILDING	Rs.	3,50,000.00
2.	PLANT & MACHINERY	Rs.	6,28,000.00
3.	OTHER FIXED ASSETS	Rs.	2,80,000.00
	TOTAL	Rs.	12,58,000.00

RAW MATERIALS

1. Polypropylene glycol
2. Maleic Anhydride
3. Phthalic Anhydride
4. Styrene

TOTAL WORKING CAPITAL/MONTH

1.	RAW MATERIAL	Rs.	4,28,945.00
2.	SALARY & WAGES	Rs.	21,000.00
3.	UTILITIES & OVERHEADS	Rs.	46,600.00
	TOTAL	Rs.	4,96,545.00

TOTAL CAPITAL INVESTMENT

TOTAL FIXED CAPITAL	Rs.	12,58,000.00
TOTAL WORKING CAPITAL FOR 3 MONTHS	Rs.	14,89,635.00
TOTAL	Rs.	27,47,635.00

TURN OVER/ANNUM

By sale of 78,000 kg. of polyester resin	Rs.	85,80,000.00

PROFIT = RECEIPTS - COST OF PRODUCTION

= 85,80,000.00 - 67,44,869.70

= 18,35,130.30

PROFIT SALES RATIO = Profit / Sales x 100 = *21.39 %*

RATE OF RETURN = Operating profit / T.C.I x 100 = *66.79 %*

BREAK EVEN POINT (B.E.P) = 37.71 %

Manufacturers and Suppliers of Plant and Machinery

Reaction Vessels/Kettles

M/s. Anu Rashyan Udyog,
184, DSIDC Sheds,
Okhla Ind. Area-I,
New Delhi - 110 020.
Ph./Fax: - 6813624

M/s. Chemfab Engineering,
115/7, Maqsood Estate,
Marolnaka, Andheri Kurla Road,
Mumbai - 400 059.
Ph./Fax: - 8377514

M/s. Ruk-Mani Engg. & Fabricators,
1001/6, Phase-III,
G.I.D.C.,
Vapi - 396 195,
Gujarat.

M/s. Samarth Engg. Works,
At. & Post - Kon,
Kalyan Bhiwandi Road,
Kalyan - 421301.
Ph./Fax: - 415197/24292

M/s. Shiv Shakti Fabrications,
Mishra Compound,
Opp. Digvijay Compound,
Hindustan Naka, M.G. Road,
Kandivli (West), Mumbai - 400 067.

M/s. T.R. Sharma Engg. Works,
A-156, Hari Nagar,
Clock Tower,
New Delhi - 110 064.
Ph./Fax: - 5405328/5403729

M/s. M.D. Engineering Company,
117, MIE,
Bahadurgarh - 124 507,
Haryana.
Ph./Fax: 311431/011-8314546

M/s. Chemfab Engineering,
115/7, Maqsood Estate,
Marolnaka,
Andheri Kurla Road,
Mumbai - 400 059.
Ph./Fax: - 8377514

M/s. Flowink Industries (P) Ltd.
D-15, Comm. Complex,
Prashant Vihar,
Delhi - 110 085.
Ph.: 7267006/07
Fax: 011-7267007

M/s. Ruk-Mani Engg. & Fabricators
1001/6,
Phase-III,
G.I.D.C.,
Vapi - 396 195,
Gujarat.

M/s. Samarth Engineering Works,
At. & Post - Kon,
Kalyan Bhiwandi Road,
Kalyan - 421301.
Maharashtra State
Ph./Fax: - 415197/24292

Pressure Vessels

M/s. Chemfab Engineering,
115/7, Maqsood Estate,
Marol Naka,
Andheri Kurla Road,
Mumbai - 400 059.
Ph.: 8377514

M/s. Samarth Engg. Works,
At. & Post - Kon,
Kalyan Bhiwandi Road,
Kalyan - 421301.
Maharashtra State
Ph.: 415197/24292

Heat Exchangers

M/s. Chemfab Engineering,
115/7,
Maqsood Estate,
Marolnaka,
Andheri Kurla Road,
Mumbai - 400 059.
Ph.Fax: - 8377514

M/s. M.D. Engineering Company,
117, MIE,
Bahadurgarh - 124 507,
Haryana.
Ph./Fax: 311431/011-8314546

M/s. Ruk-Mani Engg. & Fabricators,
1001/6, Phase-III,
G.I.D.C.,
Vapi - 396 195.
Gujarat

M/s. Samarth Engg. Works,
At. & Post - Kon,
Kalyan Bhiwandi Road,
Kalyan - 421301.
Maharashtra State
Ph.Fax: - 415197/24292

Storage Tanks

M/s. Anu Rashyan Udyog,
184, DSIDC Sheds,
Okhla Ind. Area-I,
New Delhi - 110 020.
Ph./Fax: - 6813624

M/s. Chemfab Engineering,
115/7, Maqsood Estate,
Marolnaka,
Andheri Kurla Road,
Mumbai - 400 059.
Ph./Fax: - 8377514

M/s. M.D. Engineering Company,
117, MIE,
Bahadurgarh - 124 507,
Haryana.
Ph./Fax: 311431/011-8314546

M/s. Samarth Engineering Works,
At. & Post - Kon,
Kalyan Bhiwandi Road,
Kalyan - 421301.
Maharashtra State
Ph./Fax: - 415197/24292

M/s. Shiv Shakti Fabrications,
Mishra Compound,
Opp. Digvijay Compound,
Hindustan Naka,
M.G. Road, Kandivli (West),
Mumbai - 400 067.

Barrels

M/s. Vijay Industries
B-10, Mayapuri Ind. Area,
Phase-II,
New Delhi - 110 064
Phones/Fax: 5404624/5403857

Agitators & Stirrers

M/s. Chemfab Engineering,
115/7, Maqsood Estate,
Marolnaka,
Andheri Kurla Road,
Mumbai - 400 059
Ph.: 8377514

M/s. Ruk-Mani Enggs. & Fabricators
1001/6, Phase-III,
G.I.D.C.,
Vapi - 396 195
Gujarat

M/s. Samarth Engg. Works
At. & Post - Kon,
Kalyan Bhiwandi Road,
Kalyan - 421301
Maharashtra State
Ph.: 415197/24292

M/s. T.R. Sharma Engg. Works,
A-156, Hari Nagar, Clock Tower,
New Delhi - 110 064.
Ph.: 5405328/5403729

M/s. Vijay Industries
B-10,
Mayapuri Ind. Area,
Phase-II,
New Delhi - 110 064
Ph./Fax: 5404624/5403857

Boiler

M/s. Anu Rashyan Udyog
184, DSIDC Sheds,
Okhla Ind. Area-I,
New Delhi - 110 020
Ph./Fax: 6813624

M/s. Alfa Therm Limited
B-119,
Mayapuri Industrial Area,
Phase-I,
New Delhi - 110 064
Ph./Fax: 5132648, 5140102

M/s. Sita Boiler Company
195-B, LIbaspur Road
Samaipur,
Delhi - 110 042
Ph./Fax: 7294347/7291044

M/s. Shiv Shakti Fabrications
Mishra Compound,
Opp. Digvijay Compound,
Hindustan Naka, M.G. Road,
Kandivli (West),
Mumbai - 400 067

Dryer

M/s. Samarth Engineering Works
At. & Post - Kon,
Kalyan Bhiwandi Road,
Kalyan - 421301
Ph./Fax : 415197/24292

M/s. Shiv Shakti Fabrications
Mishra Compound,
Opp. Digvijay Compound,
Hindustan Naka, M.G. Road,
Kandivli (West),
Mumbai - 400 067

M/s. Vijay Industries
B-10,
Mayapuri Industrial Area,
Phase-II,
New Delhi - 110 064
Ph./Fax: 5404624/5403857

Autoclaves

M/s. M.D. Engineering Company
117,
MIE,
Bahadurgarh - 124 507
Haryana
Ph./Fax: 311431/011-8314546

M/s. Ruk-Mani Engineering and Fabricators
1001/6,
Phase-III,
G.I.D.C.,
Vapi - 396 195
Gujarat

M/s. Flowink Industries Pvt. Ltd.,
D-15,
Commercial Complex,
Prashant Vihar,
Delhi - 110 085
Ph.: 7267006/07
Fax: 011-7267007

Condensers

M/s. M.D. Engineering Company
117,
MIE,
Bahadurgarh - 124 507
Haryana
Ph.: 311431
Fax: 011-8314546

M/s. Ruk-Mani Engineering and Fabricators
1001/6,
Phase-III,
G.I.D.C.,
Vapi - 396 195
Gujarat

Blenders - Ribbon and Cone Type

M/s. Ruk-Mani Engg. & Fabricators
1001/6,
Phase-III,
G.I.D.C.,
Vapi - 396 195
Gujarat

S.S. & M.S. Sparkler and Sack Type Filter Presses

M/s. Ruk-Mani Engg. & Fabricators
1001/6,
Phase-III,
G.I.D.C.,
Vapi - 396 195
Gujarat

Transfer Pumps

M/s. Ruk-Mani Engg. & Fabricators
1001/6,
Phase-III,
G.I.D.C.,
Vapi - 396 195
Gujarat

Sand Mills

M/s. Ruk-Mani Engg. & Fabricators
1001/6,
Phase-III,
G.I.D.C.,
Vapi - 396 195
Gujarat

Double Speed Agitators

M/s. Ruk-Mani Engg. & Fabricators
1001/6,
Phase-III,
G.I.D.C.,
Vapi - 396 195
Gujarat

Paint & Chemical Plants

M/s. T.R. Sharma Engg. Works
A-156, Hari Nagar,
Clock Tower,
New Delhi - 110 064.
Ph./Fax: - 5405328
5403729

M/s. Sri Laxmi Engineering Works
Gali No.1, Main Chowk,
Samaipur,
Delhi - 110 042
Ph./Fax: - 7294981

M/s. Vogal Engineers
M-20, Gali No. 10,
Anand Parbat Indl. Area,
New Delhi - 110 005
Ph./Fax: - 5781800

M/s. Vibrotech Industries
24-B/6, Industrial Area,
Faridabad - 121 001
Ph./Fax: - 233251
233261

M/s. Tipco Engineering Works
Gali No.9, Nr. Khad Factory,
Samaipur,
Delhi - 110 042

Ball Mill

M/s. T.R. Sharma Engg. Works,
A-156,
Hari Nagar,
Clock Tower,
New Delhi - 110 064.
Ph./Fax: - 5405328
5403729

M/s. Sri Laxmi Engineering Works,
Gali No.1,
Main Chowk,
Samaipur,
Delhi - 110 042
Ph./Fax: - 7294981

Sugar

M/s. AVMS Enterprises,
25, Dena Industrial Estate,
Agra Road,
Majiwada,
Thane - 400 067
Ph./Fax: 5333955

M/s. Vishwakarma Industries,
D-13, Road No.14,
Industrial Area,
Bulandshahar Road,
Ghaziabad,
(U.P).
Ph./Fax: - 722651
731489

Fabrication (General)

M/s. Anu Rashyan Udyog,
184,
DSIDC Sheds,
Okhla Ind. Area-I,
New Delhi - 110 020
Ph.: 6813624

M/s. Chemech Engineering Works,
30, DSIDC,
Scheme - III,
Okhla Industrial Area - II,
New Delhi - 110 020

Oxygen Gas

M/s. M.V.S. Engineering Limited,
B - 232,
Okhla Indl. Area,
New Delhi - 110 020
Ph./Fax: - 6817916

Thermocouple

M/s. Eastern Automotive Machine Tools Private Ltd.
1243, M.I.E.,
Bahadurgarh -124 507
(Haryana)
Ph.: 8-233684

Vacuum Plant

M/s. Expovac Electronic & Engg.
382, Udyog Vihar,
Phase-II,
Gurgaon,
(Haryana)
Ph.: 8-34172

Mixer

M/s. M.D. Engineering Company
117, MIE,
Bahadurgarh - 124 507,
Haryana.
Phone : 311431
Fax : 011-8314546

Activated Carbon Machinery

M/s. Chemi Plant Engineers,
D-12,
Meerut Road,
Ghaziabad (U.P).
Ph./Fax: 712371
756908

Dust Collection System

M/s. Vibrotech Industries,
24-B/6,
Industrial Area,
Faridabad - 121 001.
Ph./Fax: 233251
233261

Powder Coating Plant

M/s. Vibrotech Industries,
24-B/6,
Industrial Area,
Faridabad - 121 001.
Ph./Fax: 233251
233261

Financial Institutions in India

Reserve Bank of India,
(The Central Banking Authority)
Central Office Building,
Shahid Bhagat Singh Road,
Mumbai - 400 001.
Phone : 2661602
Fax : 2662106

Export Credit Guarantee Corporation of India,
Express Towers, 10th Floor,
Nariman Point, Mumbai - 400 021.
Phone : 2845452/71/72/73
Fax : 2045253, 2023267

Export-Import Bank of India,
Centre One, 21st Floor,
World Trade Centre,
Cuffe Parade, Mumbai - 400 005.
Phone : 2185272, Fax : 2182572

General Insurance Corp. of India,
Suraksha, 170, J.T. Road,
Churchgate, Mumbai - 400 020.
Phone : 2833046
Fax : 2874129, 2046772
2833209, 2832656

Industrial Credit & Investment Corporation of India Limited,
ICICI Building,
163, Backbay Reclamation,
Churchgate, Mumbai - 400 020.
Phone : 2022535/94/115
Fax : 2046582

Inds. Reconstruction Bank of India,
19, N. Subash Chander Bose Rd.,
Calcutta - 700 001.
Phone: 2209941, Fax : 207182

Industrial Dev. Bank of India,
IDBI Tower, Cuffe Parade,
Mumbai - 400 005.
Phone : 2189111, 2189117
Fax : 2180411, 2181294

Industrial Finance Corporation of India,
Bank of Baroda Building,
16, Sansad Marg,
New Delhi - 110 001.
Phone : 3321013
Fax : 3320425

Life Insurance Corporation of India,
Yogakshema,
Jeevan Bima Marg,
Mumbai - 400 021.
Phone : 2022151, 2021383
Fax : 2028943, 2020274

National Bank for Agriculture and Rural Development,
Sterling Centre,
Dr. Annie Besant Road,
Worli, Mumbai - 400 018.
Phone : 4964396/97/98/99
Fax : 2851555

SCICI Limited,
141, Maker Tower F,
Cuffe Parade,
Mumbai - 400 005.
Phone : 2180800
Fax : 2181539
2181739

Small Industroal Development Bank of India,
Nariman Bhavan,
227, Vinay K. Shah Marg,
Nariman Point,
Mumbai - 400 021.
Phone : 2851274/80/82
Fax : 2044448

Unit Trust of India,
13, Sir Vithaldas Thackersey Marg,
New Marine Lines,
Mumbai - 400 020.
Phone : 2068468

All India Trade & Industry Organisations

All India Manufacturers Organisation,
4th Floor, Jeevan Sahakar,
Sir P.M. Road,
Fort,
Mumbai - 400 001.
Phone : 2661016/1272/4241
Fax: 2660838

Associated Chamber of Commerce and Industry of India,
Allahabad Bank Building,
17, Parliament Street,
New Delhi - 110 001.
Phone : 310704
Fax: 312193

Bombay Chamber of Commerce and Industry,
Mackinnon Mackenzie Building,
4, S.V. Marg,
Ballard Estate,
Mumbai - 400 001.
Phone : 2614681/2/3/4
Fax: 2621213

Builder's Association of India,
G-1/G-20,
Commere Centre,
7th Floor, J.D. Road,
Tardeo,
Mumbai - 400 034.
Phone : 4950507, 4927802
Fax: 4950507

Confederation of Indian Industry,
105, Kakad Chambers,
132, Dr. Annie Besant Road,
Worli,
Mumbai - 400 018.
Phone : 4931790/3332/4950861
Fax: 4939463/4945831

Federation of Indian Chambers of Commerce and Industry,
Federation House,
Tansen Marg,
New Delh - 110 001
Phone : 3319251/33/61
Fax: 3320714

Federation of Indian Export Organisations,
World Trade Centre One,
11th Floor,
Cuffe Parade,
Mumbai - 400 005.
Phone : 2185093
2183354
Fax: 2183875

Indian Merchants Chamber,
IMC Building,
Indian Merchants Chamber Marg,
Churchgate,
Mumbai - 400 020.
Phone : 2046633
Fax: 2048508

The Council of EU Chambers of Commerce in India,
Y.B. Chavan Centre,
General Jagannath Bhosale Marg,
Mumbai - 400 021
Phone : 2854563
2826064
Fax: 2854564

The Small Scale Acrylic Plastic Products Mfrs. Assoc. (SAPMA),
4/16, Sona Udyog Estate,
Andheri (East),
Mumbai - 400 069.
Phone : 8300359
8327268

LIST OF AVAILABLE "DETAILED PROJECT REPORTS"

1. AAC & ACSR ALUMINIUM CONDUCTORS
2. ABRASIVE EMERY
3. ABRASIVE PAPER
4. ABRASIVE
5. A.B.S. GARNUELS
6. ACETIC ACID
7. ACETIC ANHYDRIDE
8. ACETIC ACID FROM ETHANOL
9. ACETIC ACID FROM MOLASES
10. ACETATE DYES
11. ACETYLENE GAS
12. ACID SLURRY
13. ACRYLIC ADHESIVES
14. ACRYLIC SHEETS
15. ACRYLIC LATEX
16. ACRYLIC FIBRES
17. ACRYLIC YARN
18. ACRYLIC MIRROR (GOLDEN, PINK, BLACK & SILVER)
19. ACRYLIC & COTTON YARN SPINDLES
20. ACRYLIC EMULSION PAINTS
21. ACTIVATED CARBON FROM SAW DUST, RICE HUSK & COCONUT SHELL
22. ACTIVATED CARBON FROM RICE HUSK
23. ACTIVATED CARBON FROM WOOD
24. ACTIVATED CARBON FROM COCONUT SHELL
25. ACTIVATED BLEACHING EARTH
26. ACTIVATED FULLERS EARTH
27. ACTIVATED ALUMINA BALLS
28. ACTIVATED CALCIUM CARBONATE
29. ACETYLENE BLACK (CARBON BLACK)
30. ADHESIVE (DIFFERENT TYPES)
31. ADHESIVE (FEVICOL TYPE)
32. ADHESIVE (ALL TYPES)
33. ADHESIVE INDUSTRY (LAMINATED, FEVICOL, STICKER, DDL & OTHER TYPES OF ADHESIVES)
34. ADHESIVE FOR STICKER
35. ADHESIVE MAKING FOR JOINING HDPE PIPES/JOINTS
36. ADHESIVE BASED ON POLYURETHANE
37. ADHESIVE FOR TWO/ THREE WHEELER CLUTCH PLATES
38. ADHESIVE FOR CORRUGA-TION (DRY POWDER)
39. ADHESIVE TAPES FOR HOSPITAL USED
40. ADHESIVE FOR RUBBER TO RUBBER, THREAD RUBBER TUBE PUNC-TURE & LATEX RUBBER BASED
41. ADHESIVE POWDER FOR ELECTRIC LAMPS
42. ADHESIVE FOR CORRUGA-TION DRY POWDER/PASTE
43. ADHESIVE TAPES (PRESSURE SENSITIVE)
44. ADHESIVE (FOR PHOTO ALBUM)

Pay Rs. 3975/- for any Two Detailed Project Reports

The offer is valid upto 30 Days.

45. ADVERTISING AGENCY
46. AEROSOL SPRAY
47. AFTERSHAVE LOTION
48. AGRICULTURAL IMPLEMENT
49. AGRICULTURAL & GARDENING HOSE PIPE
50. AGRICULTURAL & GARDENING HOSE PIPE
51. AGARBATTIES (INSENCE STICK)
52. AIR BUBBLE PACKAGING
53. AIR CONDITIONERS (WINDOW TYPE)
54. AIR FRESHNERS (ROOM)
55. AIR FRESHNER (ODONIL TYPE)
56. AIR CONDITIONERS (CAR & ROOM) SERVICE
57. AIR CONDITIONING (CENTRALIZED)
58. AIR TAXI (12 SEATERS) [ON RENTAL BASIS OF TWO AIR CRAFTS]
59. AIR FRESHNERS & AIR PURI- FIERS (BLOCK RING TYPE)
60. AIR FILTERS (FOR SCOOTERS, CARS & EXCAVATORS ETC.)
61. AIR COOLER
62. ALUMINIUM ROLLING MILL & ALUMINIUM UTENSILS BASED ON ALUMINIUM SCRAP
63. ALKYD RESIN
64. ALTERNATORS
65. ALKALINE CELLS
66. ALUMINIUM ELECTROLYTIC CAPACITORS
67. ALUM (FERRIC)
68. ALUMINIUM COLLAPSIBLE TUBES
69. ALCOHOL BY RICE STRAW
70. ALUMINIUM & ALUMINIUM ALLOYS From Aluminium Scraps to Make Utensils (Induction Furnace)
71. ALUMINIUM SLUGS (For Collapsible Tube Containers)
72. ALUM (NON FERRIC)
73. ALUMINIUM BEVERAGES CANS
74. ALUMINIUM UTENSILS, SCHOOL BOXES FOR BOOK CARRYING
75. ALUMINIUM CANS FOR CAPACITORS
76. ALUMINIUM/STAINLESS STEEL PRESSURE COOKER & WATER FILTER
77. ALUMINIUM SILICATE
78. ALUMINIUM UTENSIL
79. ALUMINIUM EXTRUSION
80. ALL PURPOSE ADHESIVES
81. ALUMINIUM CHANNELS, BEEDINGS & PIPE
82. ALLOY STEEL PLANT
83. ALKYLATED PHENOL
84. ALLOY STEEL PLANT
85. ALKYLATED PHENOL
86. ALUMINIUM RE-ROLLING
87. ALUMINIUM SHEET, CIRCLES/UTENSILS
88. ALUMINIUM BOTTLES (Cold Extrusion of Aluminium)
89. ALCOHOL FROM POTATOES (From Non Molasses Based)
90. ALUMINIUM ALLOY CONDUCTORS
91. ALUMINIUM POWDER (ATOMIZED)
92. ALUMINIUM DOOR, WINDOW AND FITTINGS
93. ALUMINIUM/COPPER CABLE LUGS
94. ALCOHOL BY GRAINS
95. ALUMINIUM KNOBS (for Domestic Electric Appliances)
96. ALUMINIUM CIRCLE
97. ALUMINIUM ROLLING MILL (SHEET & CIRCLES)
98. ALUMINIUM ROLLING MILL & ALUMINIUM UTENSILS BASED ON ALUMINIUM SCRAPS
99. ALUMINIUM HYDROXIDE
100. ALUM FOR WATER TREATMENT
101. ALUMINIUM PRINTING PLATES FOR OFFSET PRINTING MACHINE
102. ALCOHOL INDUSTRIES BASED ON TAPIOCA STARCH

Price Rs. 2500/- for each "Detailed Project Report" Payable in advance through Draft/Cash/M.O. in favour of "ENGINEERS INDIA RESEARCH INSTITUTE". Or Ask by V.P.P. PH.: 291 8117, 291 6431, 292 0361 Fax: 91-11-291 6431 (24 Hrs.)

219. BANANA POWDER
220. BANQUET HALL
221. BAND SAW BLADES
222. BANANA PUREE
223. BARBED WIRE
224. BARIUM CARBONATE
225. BARIUM COMPOUND
226. BARIYAN & PAPPAD
227. BASMATI RICE TRADING
228. BATTERY PLATE
229. BATTERY CONTAINER
230. BAYGON SPRAY
231. BESAN PLANT
232. BED SHEET, BED COVERS, FURNISHING, ETC.
233. BEER PLANT
234. BEES WAX REFINING & BLEACHING
235. BEES WAX
236. BENEFICATION OF CHROMITE ORE PROCESSING CHARGE CHROME
237. BENZENE
238. BENZENE HEXA CHLORIDE
239. BENZYL BENZOATE
240. BENZYL PEROXIDE
241. BETA NAPHTHOLS
242. BI-METAL BUSHES
243. BI-CHROMATES OF SODIUM POTASSIUM & AMMONIUM
244. BINDIA & SINDUR
245. BITUMINIZED COMPOUND FOR WATER PROOFING
246. BITUMINOUS ROAD EMULSION
247. BI-CYCLE MANUFACTURE AND ITS PARTS
248. BI CYCLE PARTS
249. BIO COAL FROM AGRO WASTE
250. BITUMEN
251. BLANKETS
252. BLACK & WHITE T.V. PICTURE TUBE
253. BLEACHING DYEING, PRINTING/ FINISHING OF CLOTH
254. BLEACHING POWDER
255. BLEACHING &REFINING OF BEES WAX
256. BLEACHING & MORDANT DYEING OF YARN
257. BLACK/WHITE TV PICTURE TUBE
258. BLACK PEPPER
259. BLISTER FILM PVC
260. BLOCK BOARD
261. BLOCK MAKING
262. BLOOD BAGS
263. BLOW MOULDED PLASTIC CONTAINER
264. BLACK & GALVANIZED STEEL CONDUIT PIPES
265. BLEACHING LIQUOR (CALCIUM HYPO CHLORITE LIQUOR)
266. BLOWING AGENT
267. BLUE DETERGENT POWDER
268. BOILER DE-SCALING COMPOUNDS
269. BOOT/SHOE POLISH
270. BORIC ACID
271. BONE MILL
272. B.O.P.P. FILMS
273. BOPP TAPES
274. BORAX
275. BOARD MILL BASED ON RICE STRAW

276. BONE CRUSHING
277. BOLTS (MILD STEEL)
278. BOTTLING PLANT
279. B.P HARD COKE
280. BRAKE LININGS
281. BRAKE OIL, COOLANT & PACKING OF LUBE OIL & GREASE
282. BRAKE OIL
283. BRASS/COPPER SHEET CIRCLES & UTENSILS
284. BRA & PANTY (HOSIERY)
285. BREAD PLANT
286. BRICK FROM FLY ASH
287. BRASS HOLDERS
288. BRASS & COPPER TUBES
289. BRANDY
290. BRIQUETTED FUEL FROM AGRO WASTE
291. BRASS UTENSILS
292. BRASS SHEET ROLLING
293. BRASS PIPES
294. BRASS WARES
295. BROILER CHICKEN
296. BRASS STAIRCASE & WROUGHT IRON, RODS, RAILING, GATE & GRILL
297. BULK DRUGS
298. BUTTON FROM HOOVES & HORNS
299. BUILDING HARDWARE OF ALUMINIUM
300. BUTT HINGES OF BRASS SHEET
301. BUFFING & POLISHING COMPOUNDS
302. BUS TRANSPORT COMPANY
303. BUBBLE GUM & CHEWING GUM
304. .BUFFALO MEAT PROCESSING
305. BUTTONS (PLASTIC) FROM POLYESTER SHEETS & RODS
306. BUSINESS CENTRE (JOB WORK)
307. BUS AND TRUCK BODY BUILDING
308. CABLE JELLY COMPOUND
309. CASSETTE RECORDER/ PLAYER (STEREO)
310. CAMPHOR
311. CATTLE & POULTRY FEED
312. CARBON DIOXIDE
313. CARBON BRUSHES
314. CARBON ZINC CELL
315. CARBON-ACTIVATED
316. CARBON- ONE TIME
317. CARBON - HIGH FERRO
318. CARBON BLACK
319. CARBON BLACK FROM NATURAL GAS
320. CARBON ELECTRODE
321. CARBON BLACK FROM NATURAL GAS
322. CARBON POTENTIO METERS
323. CARBON MONO-OXIDE FOR WATER GAS
324. CARBON SEAL
325. CARBON POWDER
326. CARBON PAPER
327. CARBON PLATES - GRAPHITE
328. CARBON/METAL FILM RESISTORS
329. CARBON - (CINE-ARC)
330. CARD BOARD SLATE
331. CAPACITORS
332. CALCIUM CARBIDE
333. CALCIUM SILICATE BLOCKS
334. CARBONATED BEVERAGES
335. CAR BURGLAR ALARM
336. CAUSTIC SODA
337. CALCIUM CARBONATES
338. CAR AIR FRESHNER
339. CAR SHAMPOO
340. CASTOR OIL
341. CATTLE FEED
342. CATTLE & POULTRY FEEDS
343. CAST STEEL PANS FOR MELTING FURNACE
344. CAST IRON PIPES & FITTINGS (VERTICAL) FOR DOUBLE FLANGED PIPES
345. CALCINING OF MANGANESE & DEAD BURNT MANGANESE
346. CALCIUM CARBONATE BASED ON STEAM COAL
347 CASING UNIT OF SAUSAGE FOOD (100% EOU)
348. CARPET WOOL YARN SPINNING
349. CANNING OF MANGO PULP & MANGO SLICES
350. CAFFEINE BY TEA WASTE
351. CALCINED PETROLEUM COKE
352. CALCIUM CARBONATE, MAGNESIUM CARBONATE & METAL FROM DOLOMITE
353. CALCIUM CASEINATE & SODIUM CASEINATE

484. CLAY PLATES FOR ELECTRIC HEATERS
485. CLUTCH PLATE FOR 4 WHEELERS
486. CLUTCH PLATE FOR 3 WHEELER
487. CLEANING POWDER (VIM)
488. CLUTCH FACING & BRAKE LINING
489. CLEAR TRANSPARENT LACQUER FOR COATING ON BRASS BANGLES TO MAKE IT WEATHER RESISTANT
490. CLINICAL THERMOMETER
491. C.N.S.L. BASED RESIN IN LIQUID & Powder Form
492. COPPER WIRE DRAWING & ENAMELING
493. CORDLESS PHONE
494. CONCENTRATION OF MANGANESE ORE
495. COPPER & BRASS TUBES
496. CORRUGATED SHEET BOARD & BOXES
497. COPPER BOTTOM STAINLESS STEEL UTENSILS
498. COOLING COILS FOR AIR CONDITIONERS
499. COLOUR LAB (QSS-PHOTO)
500. COMPUTER CONTINUOUS STATIONERY
501. COMPUTER ASSEMBLY
502. COMPUTER MONITOR
503. COMPUTER RIBBON
504. COMPUTER RIBBON REFILLING & REINKING
505. COMPUTER MONITOR TUBE & T.V. PICTURE TUBE (B/W)
506. COMPUTER SOFTWARE (100% EOU)
507. COMPUTER FORMS AND SECURITY PRINTING PRESS
508. COMPUTER FORM (COMPUTER STATIONERY)
509. COMPUTER JOB WORK
510. COMPUTER ATTENDANCE REGISTER
511. COMPUTER PRINTER
512. COMPUTER KEYBOARD
513. COMPUTER EDUCATION INSTITUTE
514. COMPUTER (MINI/ PERSONAL)
515. COMPUTER-LAPTOP
516. COMPUTER PERIPHERALS
517. COMPUTER STATIONERY AND IMPORTED HARDWARE PARTS
518. COOLANT ENGINE
519. COLLEGE
520. COLD DRINKS
521. COLD PROCESSED TYRE RETREADING
522. COLD STORAGE
523. COLD STORAGE & ICE
524. COLD ROLLING MILL
525. COLD PROCESSED TREAD RUBBER
526. COLD CREAMS
527. COLD ROLLING OF STEEL STRIPS
528. COLD ROLLED PRESSED STEEL DOORS, WINDOW FRAMES
529. COTTON ADHESIVE TAPES & PLASTER OF PARIS BANDAGES For Hospital
530. COLOUR & B/W TV
531. COLOUR TELEVISION
532. COSTUME JEWELLERY
533. COTTON SEED OIL
534. COTTON YARN
535. CONDUIT IRON PIPES (C.I.PIPES)
536. CONDENSED MILK SWEETENED
537. COIR FOAM (RUBBERIZED COIR) CUSHION & MAT ETC.
538. CONCRETE HOLLOW BRICK/ BLOCKS
539. CONDENSED MILK
540. COCONUT OIL
541. COFFEE PLANTATION
542. COBALT OCTOATE
543. COIR PITH
544. COPPER NITRATE
545. CONCENTRATE OF TOMATO (TOMATO PASTE)

546. CONFERENCE BAG, FOLDERS ETC. (PLASTIC)
547. CORN FLAKES
548. COATING ON PLASTICS
549. COPPER OXY-CHLORIDES
550. COPPER PHTHALOCYNINE BLUE & GREEN
551. COATED PAPER & BOARD
552. CONVERTER
553. COPPER CLAD LAMINATES FOR PCB'S (PAPER & FABRIC BASED)
554. COPPER RODS FROM SCRAPS
555. COLLECTION OF MILK & PACKAGING IN POLYTHENE POUCHES (MILK CHILLING)
556. COURIER SERVICES
557. CONFECTIONERY
558. CONFECTIONERY INDUSTRY-SEMI AUTOMATIC PLANT (TOFFEE & CANDY MANUFACTURING)
559. COAL BRIQUETTING FROM COAL
560. COAL BRIQUETTES FROM AGRO WASTE
561. COUNTRY LIQUOR
562. COPPER STRIPS COILS
563. CONCAST STEEL BAR
564. COATING & PRINTING OF LAMINATED PAPER POUCH
565. COATING & LAMINATION ON PAPER (HOT MELT FILM LAMINATION METHOD)
566. COUNTRY LIQUOR FROM MOLASSES
567. COSMETIC UNIT
568. COMPOSITE CONTAINER
569. COPPER BERYLLIUM ALLOY SPRINGS
570. COLOUR MASTER BATCH FOR VARIOUS PLASTICS
571. COMPACT DISC PLAYER
572. COMPACT DISC (CD)
573. COTTON FINISHING
574. CONSTANT VOLTAGE TRANSFORMER (C.V.T.)
575. CORROSION CONTROLLING CHEMICAL (PIPE LINE)
576. COPPER FOIL
577. COPPER & BRASS INGOTS
578. COMPRESSOR (HERMETIC) FOR AIR CONDITIONER
579. COATING ON PLASTICS & GLASS
580. COATING OF CLEAR TRANSPARENT LACQUER ON BRASS BANGLES TO MAKE IT WEATHER RESISTANT
581. COCONUT PLANTATION
582. COCONUT PRODUCTS & BYE PRODUCTS PROCESSING COMPLEX (WETFRESH) 100% EOU
583. CONVEYER BELTS
584. COPPER SULPHATE
585. COIR INDUSTRY
586. COSMETIC (HERBAL & SYNTHETIC)
587. COTTON & ACRYLIC YARN SPINDLES
588. CO-EXTRUSION MULTI-LAYER FILM
589. COLOURED FLAME CANDLE
590. COMMUTATOR FOR ELECTRIC MOTOR
591. COTTON BUDS/SWABS
592. COATING ON METALLIZED POLYE-STER FILM/ METALLIZED PAPER/ ALUMINIUM FOILS
593. COOLER BODY & TRUNK (FABRICATION UNIT)
594. COSMETIC, DETERGENT POWDER & PERFUMERY COMPOUND
595. COLOUR MASTER BATCHES FOR VARIOUS PLASTICS
596. COUNTRY LIQUOR
597. COBALT OCTOATE

598. CONDENSER FOR MOTOR
599. COAL GRINDING
600. COCOA POWDER
601. COTTON ROLLS
602. COSTUME/IMITATION/ ARTIFICIAL JEWELLERY (CHAINS & BANGLES)
603. CONCENTRATE OF ROSE, JASMINE & LILLY EXTRACT
604. COPPER WINDING FOR SUBMERSIBLE PUMP & MOTOR
605. COMPACT FLUORESCENT TUBES
606. CONE FOR SOFTY ICE CREAM
607. CORRUGATION OF PLAIN GALVANIZED SHEET
608. CORN FLAKES
609. COTTON GINNING & PRESSING
610. COMPUTER PERIPHERALS
611. COMPUTER HARDWARE
612. COMPACT DISC PLAYER (AUDIO/VIDEO)
613. CO_2 WELDING WIRE
614. COPPER POWDER
615. COPPER EXTRACTION FROM PCB WASTES
616. CRYSTAL TABLEWARE
617. CRUCIBLE BY FIRE CLAY
618. CRACKING OF KERNELS (DESHELLING/DECORTICATING)
619. CRICKET BAT/BALL
620. CROCKERY WARES
621. CRAYON WAX
622. CRITICAL AUTO BODY SHEET METAL PARTS
623. CREPE BANDAGES
624. CUBICAL ELECTRICAL PANEL BOARD (SWITCH BOARD)
625. CUSHION COMPOUND, THREAD & VULCANIZING SOLUTION, FORMULATION AND MANUFACTURE
626. CUTLERY & SILVER JEWELLERY (GOLD PLATED)
627. CUTLERY (STAINLESS STEEL)
628. CURRY POWDER
629. CUTTING OIL
630. CYCLE & RIKSHAW FRAMES
631. CYANIDE ZINC BRIGHTENER
632. CYCLE TYRE & TUBES
633. CYLINDER LINERS FOR AUTOMOBILES
634. CYCLE HANDLE BAR GRIPS
635. CYCLE SPOKES
636. DAIRY FARM & PRODUCTS
637. DAIRY FARM AND DAIRY (MILK) PRODUCTS (PASTEURISED MILK, BUTTER, CAKE & PANEER)
638. DAIRY PRODUCTS
639. DAIRY PRODUCTS & MILK PACKAGING IN POUCHES
640. DALL/PULSE MILL
641. DAIRY FARM & MILK PDTS.
642. DAIRY PLANT
643. DETERGENT POWDER
644. DETERGENT CAKE & POWDER
648. DECORATIVE LAMINATED SHEET (SUNMICA)
649. DESK TOP PUBLISHING(DTP)
650. DEHYDRATED ONIONS & ONION POWDER
651. DEHYDRATION OF FRUITS & VEGETABLES
652. DEXTROSE SALINE
653. DEXTROSE FROM POTATO
654. DEHYDRATED GARLIC FLAKES
655. DEXTRIN & STARCH BASED ADHESIVE
656. DEXTRIN
657. DEXTROSE 5%
658. DEXTROSE (ANHYDROUS) FROM STARCH
659. DESICCATED COCONUT POWDER

660. DEXTROSE POWDER FROM STARCH
661. DEAD BURNT DOLOMITE
662. DETERGENT CAKE
663. DEXTROSE SALINE (I.V. FLUID) IN PLASTIC BOTTLES
664. DETERGENT WASHING POWDER (ARIEL TYPE)
665. DEHYDRATED CASTOR OIL
666. DENIM JEANS & JACKETS
667. DENIM CLOTH (INTEGRATED UNIT WITH BLEACHING, DYEING & PRINTING)
668. DETTOL TYPE ANTISEPTIC LOTION
669. DEPARTMENTAL STORE
670. DEHYDRATION OF VEGETABLES
671. DENIM CLOTH
672. DEHYDRATION AND CANNING OF FRUITS & VEGETABLES
673. DEHYDRATION OF FRUITS, VEGETABLES & NON-VEGETABLE PRODUCTS
674. DE-HULLING OF JAUN FOR BEER INDUSTRY
675. D.G. SET
676. DHOOP BATTI STICK
677. DISPOSABLE PLASTIC SYRINGES (STERILIZED)
678. DISPOSABLE PLASTIC CUPS, GLASSES, ETC.
679. DISTILLED WATER AMPOULES
680. DI-OCTYL PHTHALATE(DOP)
681. DISTRIBUTION TRANSFORMER
682. DIRECT COTTON DYE (NO COST ESTIMATION)
683. DIARY EQUIPMENT
684. DIAZO COATING LUMINESCENT PIGMENT
685. DISTILLED WATER
686. DISPOSABLE CIGARETTE GAS LIGHTER
687. DISPOSABLE NEEDLES
688. DIE MAKING FOR SHEET METAL WORKING
689. DIAMOND TOOLS FOR CUTTING / DRILLING & POLISHING
690. DIRECT BLACK DYE
691. DISH ANTENNA
692. DI-CALCIUM PHOSPHATE FROM ANIMAL BONES
693. DI-CALCIUM PHOSPHATE FROM ROCK PHOSPHATE
694. DIGITAL ELECTRONIC WATCHES
695. DISTILLATION OF ROSIN AND TURPENTINE
696. DIAMOND IMPREGNATED SEGMENTS (METAL BONDED) FOR MARBLE SAWING
697. DI-NITRO CHLORO BENZENE (D.N.C.B.)
698. DI-ETHYL PHTHALATE (DEP)
699. DISH ANTENNA & SATELLITE EQUIPMENTS.
700. DIAMOND CUTTING & EXPORT
701. DI-ETHYL OXALATE
702. DISPOSABLE BABY DIAPER
703. DIAGANOSTIC CENTRE
704. DIESEL GENERATOR SETS
705. 4,4-DIAMINO STILBENE 2,2 - DISULPHONIC ACID
706. DOOR BELL
707. DOOR LOCKS/PAD LOCKS
708. DODECYCLE BENZENE SULPHONATE
709. DOUGH MOULDING COMPOUND
710. DRY ICE
711. DRY DISTEMPER & LIME COLOURS
712. DRY GINGER
713. DRY CELL
714. DRYING OF RED CHILLIES, HALDI, DHANIA, PEAS, AND GREEN PEAS
715. DROSS LEAD SCRAP, LEAD POWDER
716. DRY CELLS & STORAGE BATTERIES

717. DRUM CLOSURES
718. DRIP IRRIGATION
719. DRY FRUIT ROASTING & PACKING
720. D.T.P. & OFFSET PRESS
721. D.T.P. CUM TABLE OFFSET
722. DUPLICATING INK
723. DUPLICATING INK (BLACK) FOR GESTENER DUPLICATOR
724. DUPLICATING STENCIL PAPER
725. DUPLEX/FILE BOARD
726. DYE STUFFS
727. DYE INTERMEDIATE
728. DYE FIXING AGENTS
729. DYEING OF HANK YARN FOR POWER LOOM
730. EAF BASED STEEL
731. EARTH LEAKAGE CIRCUIT BREAKERS (ELCB)
732. EASTER GUM (NOCOSTING)
733. E.C.G/E.E.G. PAPER
734. EDIBLE & NON EDIBLE OIL
735. EDTA AND ITS SALT
736. EDIBLE OIL (MUSTARD OIL)
737. EGG POWDER
738. EGG POWDER (100% EOU - AUTOMATIC IMPORTED PLANT)
739. EGG TRAY
740. EHT TRANSFORMER
741. ELECTRICAL GLS LAMP
742. ELECTRIC FANS
743. ELECTRONIC SERVICE CENTRE
744. ELECTRONICCHOKE
745. ELECTRICAL APPLIANCES
746. ELECTRONIC FLASHER FOR AUTOMOBILES
747. ELECTRONIC TOYS
748. ELECTRONIC GAS LIGHTER (MULTI SPARK)
749. ELECTRONIC TIMER
750. ELECTRONIC ENERGY METER
751. ELECTRIC IRON
752. ELECTRICAL INSULATION TAPES (USING BOPP FILM)
753. ELECTRONIC BALLAST (CHOKE)
754. ELECTRICAL LAMP (GLS)
755. ELECTRONIC QUARTZ CLOCK/WALL CLOCK
756. ELECTRICAL STAMPING
757. ELECTRONIC INDICATOR
758. ELECTRONIC TELEPHONES
759. ELECTRO MAGNETICRELAY
760. ELECTROPLATING ON GOLD AND THEIR CHEMICAL TREATMENT IN GOLDEN COLOUR & SILVER THREAD
761. ELECTROPLATING SCHEME PLANT
762. ELECTROPLATING OF SILVER & SILVER
763. ELECTRICAL INSULATION TAPE (USING BOPP FILM)
764. ELECTRICAL LAMP (INCANDESCENT LAMP)
765. ELECTRICAL REPAIR
766. ELECTRICAL HORN FOR AUTOMOBILE
767. ELECTROPLATING BRIGHTNER
768. ELECTROLYTIC CAPACITOR (MOTOR START)
769. ELECTRIC HEATER CLAY PLATES
770. ELECTRIC LAMP ADHESIVE POWDER
771. ELECTRONIC FAN REGULATOR
772. ELECTRICAL ACCESSORIES (SWITCH, SOCKET, PLUG,)
773. ELECTRO CARDIOGRAM MACHINE (ECG MACHINE)
774. ELECTRIC PORTABLE TOOL
775. ELECTRO POLISHING OF STEEL
776. ELECTROPLATING CHEMICALS
777. ELECTRIC MIXER
778. ELECTRIC CABLES (POWER AND CONTROL CABLES, MINING CABLES, FRLS CABLES, INSTRUMENTATION CABLES, SCREENED CABLES, SUBMERSIBLE PUMP CABLE ETC.)

779. ELECTRONIC SECURITY SYSTEMS
780. ELECTRONIC T.V. TUNER
781. ELECTRONIC TEST & MEASURING INSTRUMENT
782. ELECTRONIC TELEPHONES
783. ELECTRONIC TIMER (PROCESSED CONTROL)
784. ELECTRO REFINING OF ZINC
785. ELECTRONIC FLASH GUN
786. ELECTRONIC MAIL (E-MAIL)
787. ELECTRICAL AND ELECTRONIC PANEL METER (ANALOGUE, DIGITAL, VOLTMETER ETC.)
788. ELECTRICAL MOTOR STARTER
789. ELECTRONIC FIRE ALARM
790. ELECTRIC SWITCHES, PLUGS, SOCKETS & OTHER ACCESSORIES
791. ELECTRIC WATER HEATER
792. ELECTRIC MOTOR WINDING (FOR FAN, MIXIES ETC.)
793. ELASTIC & RIGID TAPES
794. ELECTROPLATING BRIGHTNER FOR NICKEL
795. ELECTRICAL FIXTURES (CHOKES & STARTER, PATTIES LIGHTENING FIXTURES ETC.)
796. ELECTROPLATING UNIT
797. ELASTIC THREADS & TWINE
798. ELECTRIC GENERATORS
799. ELECTRIC MOTOR
800. EMERGENCY LIGHT
801. EMBOSSING POWDER OR RESIN COMPOUND
802. EMERY POWDER
803. EMPTY AMPOULES
804. EMULSIFIER FOR PESTICIDE
805. EMPTY GELATIN CAPSULES
806. EMERY PAPER CLOTH
807. EMULSIFIER FOR CUTTING OIL
808. EMULSION PAINTS
809. EMPIRE SLEEVINGS
810. ENAMELING OF COPPER WIRE
811. ENGINEERING WORK SHOP
812. ENAMEL WARE
813. ENDOSULFAN
814. ENGINE VALVE
815. EPABX/EPAX SYSTEM
816. EPOXY RESINS & METAL FILLING COMPOUND
817. EPOXY RESIN BASED PRIMER (PUTTY)
818. EPOXY TRANSFORMER (CURRENT & POTENTIAL)
819. EPOXY RESIN
820. ERW STEEL CONDUIT PIPE
821. E.R.W. PIPES
822. ERW TUBES
823. ESSENTIAL OILS
824. ESSENCE & SOFT DRINK CONCENTRATE
825. ETHYL ALCOHOL FROM MOLASSES
826. ETHYL ACETO ACETATE FROM ALCOHOL
827. ETHYL HEXANOL FROM ETHYL ALCOHOL
828. ETHYLENE GLYCOL MONO STEARATE ETHYLENE GLYCOL DI-STEARATE
829. ETHYL ACETATE
830. ETHYL ACETATE
831. ETCHING OF BRASS
832. ETCHING PROCESS
833. EUCALYPTUS OIL
834. EUCALYPTUS TREE PLANTATION
835. EXERCISE NOTE BOOK & REGISTER
836. EXPANDED POLYSTYRENE MOULDING
837. EXTRACTION OF OIL (CARDAMOM, JEERA ETC.)
838. EXTRACTION OF GLUE POWDER
839. EXPANDED POLYSTYRENE EXTRUSION PROFILE USED FOR MATCH BOX MAKING

934. FRACTIONAL DISTILLATION OF D.M.O
935. FRACTIONAL DISTILLATION OF ESSENTIAL OIL & MEDICINAL PLANT EXTRACTS
936. FRUIT JUICES, SQUASHES, KETCHUP ETC.
937. FRUIT JUICE MAKING AND PACKING IN PLASTIC CONTAINERS (POUCHES)
938. FROZEN FRUITS & VEGETABLES
939. FRUIT DRINKS IN TETRA PACKS (FROOTI TYPE)
940. FRUIT JUICE MAKING & PACKING
941. FRP PRODUCTS
942. FRICTION DUST (LIQUID & POWDER) FROM CNSL
943. FRIED & ROASTED GROUNDNU, GRAM, PEA, ETC. IN POUCHES
944. FRUIT PULP & JUICE CONCENTRATE(i.e. MANGO AND PINEAPPLE PULP & CONCENTRATE)
945. FRENCH POLISH
946. FRUIT JUICES BOTTLING
947. FRUITS & VEGETABLE DRYING BY FREEZE DRYING METHOD
948. FRUIT JUICES, PICKLE PROCESSING & CANNING
949. FRUIT FLAVOURS (WHISKEY, VODKA, GRAPE, BUTTER SCOTCH & RUM)
950. FROZEN FINGER CHIP
951. FURNISHING FABRICS ON POWER LOOM
952. FURFURAL FROM RICE HUL
953. FUEL OIL
954. FUEL BRIQUETTES FROM AGRO WASTE
955. FUEL BRIQUETTES FROM JUTE CADDIES (BIO COAL FROM AGRO WASTE)
956. FURNACE OIL
957. GARLIC FLAKES
958. GAS PIPE (LPG)
959. GARLIC POWDER
960. GALVANIZED ERW PIPES
961. GAS LIGHTER
962. GALION THREAD
963. GAS FILLING OF LPG CYLINDER (LPG GAS BOTTLING PLANT)
964. GALVANIZING PLANT
965. GARLIC OIL & POWDER
966. GAS MANTLES
967. GAS DETECTOR FOR L.P.G.
968. GATE, GRILL, WROUGHT IRON & BRASS STAIRCASE, RODS & RAILING
969. GASKET SHEET
970. GENERATOR SET (PORTABLE)
971. GEMS & JEWELRY
972. GEMS MANUFACTURE
973. GEM CLIPS, PAPER PINS & STAPLE
974. GELATIN & OSSEIN FROM BONE
975. GEOMETRY BOX (MATHEMATICAL INSTRUMENTS)
976. GELATIN
977. GENERATOR (MUSICAL SOUND)
978. GENERATOR (D.G. SET)
979. GELATIN CAPSULES (HARD)
980. GRINDING UNIT (CEMENT)
981. G.I. WIRES
982. GINGER POWDER
983. GINGER OIL, SANDAL WOOD OIL, NAGARMUTHA OIL
984. G.I. PIPES
985. G.I. PIPE FITTINGS
986. GLAZED CERAMIC TILES
987. GLASS BOTTLE BY SCRAPS
988. GLS LAMPS & FLUORESCENT TUBE
989. GLASS SILVERING(MIROR)

990. GLACIAL ACETIC ACID
991. GLASS SHEET (AUTOMATIC PLANT)
992. GLASS WARE
993. GLASS TUBES- Report - Rs.2500/-
994. GLOW SIGNS
995. GLASS BOTTLES
996. GLS LAMPS/BULBS
997. GLASS WOOL
998. GLUE FROM LEATHER WASTE
999. GLASS SHEET FOR WINDOW PANES
1000. GLUE EXTRACTION & GLUE WHITE POWDER
1001. GLUCOSE & GLUCOSE SALINE
1002. GLASS MARBLES
1003. GLUE & GELATIN
1004. GLYCERIN PURIFICATION
1005. GLYCERIN EXTRACTION PLANT FROM COCONUT OIL
1006. GLASS FLOORING TILES
1007. GLASS SYRINGES
1008. GLUE POWDER FOR TECHNICAL GLUE FLAKES
1009. GOSSY POL (POLY PHENOL)FROM COTTON SEED OIL- COST Rs.2500/-
1010. GOAT FARMING
1011. GOAT SLAUGHTERING & BREEDING FARM
1012. GOLD EXTRACTION USING CYANIDE SOLUTION & ACID
1013. GOBAR GAS (BIO GAS)
1014. GOLDEN COLOUR SHADE
1015. GOLD ELECTROPLATING
1016. GOLD PLATING ON GLASS
1017. GOAT & SHEEP FARMING
1018. GOLF COURSE
1019. GOLD, ROLLED GOLD & SILVER PLATING
1020. GOLD JEWELLERY
1021. GOLD ELECTROPLATING OR METALLIC JEWELLERY ARTICLE INCLUDING METALLIC WATCH STRAPS
1022. GOLD & SILVER PLATING ON PVC & NYLON
1023. GOLD SALT
1024. GOLD PLATED SILVER JEWELLERY
1025. GOLD PLATED SILVER JEWELLERY AND CUTLERY
1026. GOLD COLOUR (POWER) FOR MORE BRIGHTNESS PROCESS AND FORMULATION FOR OBTAINING MORE BRIGHTNESS AND YELLOW COLOUR FOR PRECIPITATED GOLD POWDER
1027. GOLD COLOUR ELECTROPLATING ON CHEAPER ORNAMENTS WITHOUT USING GOLD
1028. GOLD CYANIDE POWDER
1029. GRAPE DEHYDRATION
1030. GRAPE WINE
1031. GRINDING OF SPICES (TURMERIC, RED CHILLIES, MASALA)
1032. GRANITE SLAB / TILE
1033. GRAPHITE POWDER FROM GRAPHITE ORE
1034. GRANITE MONUMENT
1035. GRANITE CUTTING & POLISHING UNIT
1036. GREEN HOUSE, PLANT MICRO PROPAGATION
1037. GRANULES (PLASTIC) FROM WASTE
1038. GRANULES (PLASTIC) FROM RESIN
1039. GROUND NUT OIL MILL
1040. GROUND NUT OIL REFINING
1041. GREASES MANUFACTURE
1042. GRANITE & MARBLE TILES
1043. GREETING CARD BY OFFSET PRINTING PRESS
1044. GRAPHITE CARBON PLATES

Price Rs. 2500/- for each "Detailed Project Report" Payable in advance through Draft/Cash/M.O. in favour of "ENGINEERS INDIA RESEARCH INSTITUTE". Or Ask by V.P.P.. PH.: 291 8117, 291 6431, 292 0361 Fax: 91-11-291 6431 (24 Hrs.)

1045. GRAPHIC DEVELOPER FOR GRAPHIC ART FILM AND GUM SOLUTION FOR PRINTING
1046. GHEE, BUTTER & PANEER
1047. GREASES FROM CASTOR OIL
1048. GRINDING WHEELS
1049. GRINDING MEDIA BALLS
1050. GRANITE CRUSHING
1051. GRAM DALS & FLOUR MILLS
1052. GRAM DALL/PULSE MILL
1053. GREEN PEAS PROCESSING & CANNING
1054. GRAPHITE ORE BENIFICATION UNIT
1055. GRADED & M.I. CASTING
1056. GRADES OF GUAR GUM
1057. GRIPE WATER
1058. GRANULATED MIXED FERTILIZER
1059. GRAVURE PRINTING CYLINDER
1060. GUM FROM TAMARIND SEED POWDER
1061. GUAR GUM
1062. GUAR GUM POWDER
1063. GUNNY BAGS
1064. GUM FOR PASTING LABELS/OFFICE PASTE (GUM)
1065. GUAR GUM POWDER (FOOD GRADE)
1066. HAZMOLA TYPE AYURVEDIC TABLET
1067. HAWAI CHAPPAL (RUBBER)
1068. HARD RUBBER BATTERY CONTAINER
1069. HATCHERY FARMING (BROILER)
1070. HAND BLOCK PRINTING
1071. HAND TOOLS
1072. HAIR SHAMPOOS
1073. HAIR DYE IN CREAM FORM
1074. HAMMERS
1075. HAIR FIXER
1076. HALOGEN LAMPS
1077. HAIR DYE POWDER
1078. HARD CHROMIUM & NICKEL CHROMIUM PLATING
1079. HANDKERCHIEF
1080. HANDICRAFTS
1081. HARD GREASE
1082. HAIR DYE IN HAIR OIL FORM
1083. HARD & SOFT FERRITES
1084. HARD GELATIN CAPSULES (EMPTY)
1085. HANK YARN DYEING FOR POWER LOOM
1086. HAMMER TONE PAINTS
1087. HARD COKE
1088. HARD CHROMIUM PLATING
1089. HAND MADE PAPER
1090. HAND LOOM PRODUCTS-KHES, BEDSHEET, BED COVERS, FURNISHING
1091. HARD BOARD FROM RICE HUSK
1092. HARD BAORD FROM BAGASSE
1093. HAWAN SAMAGRI
1094. HACK SAW BLADE
1095. HYDRATED LIME
1096. HDPE/LDPE MANUFACTURING FROM ETHYL ALCOHOL
1097. HOLIDAY RESORTS
1098. HOSPITALS
1099. HOSPITAL (Rs. 100 Cr. PROJECT)
1100. HOSPITAL/NURSING HOME
1101. HOLLOW CONCRETE BLOCK/ Brick
1102. HDPE FILM / SHEET
1103. HOTEL (3 STAR)
1104. HOTEL (5 STAR)
1105. HOTEL (NO STAR)
1106. HOT ROLLING MILL

1107. HOSE PIPE (RUBBER)
1108. HING (ASAFOETIDA)
1109. HOT DIP GALVANIZING
1110. HYDROGEN PEROXIDE
1111. HDPE/LDPE PIPES
1112. HIGH VOLTAGE WIRE
1113. HOSIERY INDUSTRY (FOR MEN)
1114. HOSIERY INDUSTRY (for WOMEN -BRA & PANTY)
1115. HOSPITAL RUBBER GOODS & SHEETS
1116. HDPE/PP WOVEN SACKS (BAGS)
1117. HDPE PIPE & FITTING
1118. HDPE & LDPE PIPE FITTING
1119. HDPE TARPAULINS
1120. HDPE BOX STRAPPINGS
1121. HDPE/LDPE PIPES & FITTINGS
1122. HDPE PIPE
1123. HERBAL KUM -KUM ROLI
1124. HEAT TRANSFER LABEL FOR RUBBER
1125. HEXAMINE FROM FORMALDEHYDE
1126. HEAT TRANSFER LABEL by SCREEN PROCESS
1127. HEAT TREATMENT OF LEAF SPRING
1128. HELICAL SPRING (COIL SPRINGS)
1129. HELMET
1130. HEALTH CENTRE
1131. HERBAL MEDICATED CIGARETTES
1132. HERBAL COSMETIC
1133. HERBAL TOOTH PASTE & TOOTH POWDER
1134. HESSIAN BAGS (LAMINATED) WITH PRINTING
1135. HESSIAN CLOTH
1136. HEPTAL DEHYDE
1137. HERBAL SHAMPOO/CREAM
1138. HEALTH CLUB CUM BEAUTY PARLOUR WITH HAIR SALOON & SONA BATH
1139. HELMET FOR COAL MINES
1140. HEAT CHAMBER PAINTING
1141. HINGES (PianoType)
1142. HINGES (M.S.)
1143. HIGH ALUMINA CERAMICS
1144. HIGH RUPTURING CAPACITY (HRC) FUSES
1145. HIGH TENSILE FASTENERS
1146. H.M BAGS
1147. HOMOEOPATHIC MEDICINES
1148. HOSIERY & TAILORS LABELS
1149. HOT DIP GALVAINZING
1150. HOSIERY PRODUCTS LIKE CHILDREN KNITWEAR, T-SHIRTS & ACRYLIC FIBRE
1151. HOMOEO & BIO MEDICINES WITH MOTHER TINCTURE
1152. HOT ROLLED (HR) COILS
1153. HOSIERY MERCERIZING
1154. HOSIERY CLOTH (COTTON) PROCESSING-BLEACHING, DYEING & FINISHING OF CLOTH
1155. HOIST & CRANES (MATERIAL HANDLING EQUIPMENTS)
1156. HOOKS & CLIPS (METAL)
1157. HOT MIX PLANT
1158. H - ACID
1159. H.T. & M.V. INDUSTRIAL CUBICAL SWITCH BOARDS
1160. HUME PIPES
1161. HURRICANE LANTERN/ STOVE
1162. HYDROGENATION OF CASTOR OILS

1163. HYDROCHLORIC ACID (HCL)
1164. HYDROGEN PEROXIDE BY AUTO OXIDATION PROCESS
1165. HYDRAULIC BRAKE CYLINDER
1166. HYDROFLUORIC ACID
1167. HYDRAULIC DOOR CLOSER
1168. HYBRID SEED
1169. HYDRATED CALCIUM SILICATE BRICKS
1170. HYPODERMIC NEEDLES FOR DISPOSABLE SYRINGE
1171. HYDRAULIC LIFTING DEVICES (FOR AUTOMOBILE SERVICING & REPAIR)
1172. HYDROGENATED CASTOR OIL
1173. HYDROGEN GAS PLANT (HYDROGEN & OXYGEN)
1174. IBUPROFEN
1175. ICE MAKING PLANT
1176. ICE CUBE PLANT
1177. ICE CREAM OF DIFFERENT FLAVOURS
1178. ICE CREAM STABILIZERS
1179. ICE CREAM & ICE CANDY
1180. ICE CREAM
1181. ICE CREAM CUPS OF PLASTIC
1182. ICE & COLD STORAGE
1183. IDLER ROLLERS FOR CONVEYERS (PLAIN & RUBBER COVERED)
1184. IF/RF COILS
1185. IGNITION CONDENSERS
1186. IGNITION CONDENSER
1187. IMMERSION HEATER
1188. IMITATION JEWELLERY
1189. INDUCTION FURNACE (M.S.
1190. STAINLESS STEEL PATTA
1191. INJECTION WATER & SALINE
1192. INSULATING VARNISH
1193. INJECTION MOULDED PLASTIC ARTICLES
1194. INDUSTRIAL REFRIGERATION
1195. INJECTION & BLOW MOULDED PLASTIC Products
1196. INJECTION MOULDED HOUSE HOLD ITEMS
1197. INSECTICIDES FROM NEEM OIL, LEAVES & NEEM SEEDS
1198. INJECTION MOULDED PLASTIC COMPONENTS
1199. INSTANT FOODS (IDLI MIX, SAMBAR MIX, VADA MIX, GULAB JAMUN, TOMATO SOUP MIX ETC.)
1200. INDUCTION FURNACE BASED C.I. CASTING
1201. INDUCTION HARDENING OF MACHINE COMPOUNDS
1202. INFORMATION MOVING DISPLAY
1203. INJECTION MOULDED PLASTIC COMPONENTS FOR ELECTRICAL/ ELECTRONICS INDL.
1204. INSULATING VARNISH (POLY VINYL BUTYRAL BASED FFC GRADE)
1205. INDUSTRIAL OXYGEN GAS
1206. INTRAVENOUS (I.V.) SET
1207. INDIAN PICKLE
1208. INDIAN MADE FOREIGN LIQUOR (IMFL)
1209. INDUCTION FURNACE

1210. INSULATING VARNISH(DryType)
1211. INTERNAL COMBUSTION ENGINE (for Agricu-ltural Equipments)
1212. INTEGRATED COMPLEX OF EASTERS & ALLIED PRODUCTS (DOP, DBP, ETHYL ACET-ATE, BUTYL ACET-ATE, WIRE ENAM-EL, JELLY CABLE COM-POUNDS)
1213. INSULATING VARNISH & WIRE ENAMEL
1214. INDUSTRIAL KNIFE
1215. INDIGO BLUE
1216. INVESTMENT CASTINGS
1217. INVESTMENT CAS-TINGS OF BRASS
1218. INVERTER
1219. INDUSTRIAL HARD OIL USED IN SOAP MAKING
1220. INDUSTRIAL GLOVES
1221. INVERTER & CONVERTER
1222. INSTANT ICE CREAM MIX
1223. INTEGRATED CIRCUITS
1224. INDUSTRIAL ALCOHOL FROM MOLASSES
1225. INVESTMENT CASTINGS FOR SS & HIGHER ALLOYS
1226. INDUSTRIAL ALCOHOL FROM ETHYLENE
1227. INSTANT TEA & COFFEE
1228. INJECTABLE FOR PHARMACEUTICALS
1229. INSTANT SOUP
1230. INSTANT NOODLES
1231. INSULATING LAGGING OF BOILERS & STEAM TUBES
1232. INTIMATE SCENT, CHEMICALS ETC. FROM ALL TYPES OF FLOWERS
1233. IONES FROM LEMON GRASS OIL
1234. IODIZED SALT
1235. IODIZED SALT (MOISTURELESS-FREE FLOWING)
1236. IRON POWDER FROM MILL SCALE SCRAP ARISING from Iron & Steel Rerolling Mill
1237. IRON TAWA
1238. IRON & STEEL WIRE & NETTING
1239. IRON OXIDE PIGMENT
1240. IRON (WROUGHT) & BRASS STAIRCASE, RODS, RAILING, GATE & GRILL
1241. ISO PROPANOL (ISO PROPYL ALCOHOL)
1242. ISOPRENE & NEOPRENE BASED RUBBER ADHESIVE
1243. I.V. CANNULA
1244. I.V. FLUID
1245. I.V. SET
1246. I.V. PLASTIC BOTTLES
1247. JAM & JELLY
1248. JAM, CHUTNEY, PICKLE & SQUASHES

1249. J-ACID
1250. JASMINE & LILY FLOWER OIL
1251. JACQUARD FABRICS
1252. JAUN DEHULLING FOR BEER INDUSTRY
1253. JEANS & JACKETS (DENIM)
1254. JEAN DYEING & FIXING BY INDIGO BLUE (JIGGER DYE & DIP DYE)
1256. JELLY FILLED CABLES
1257. JELLY & JAM
1258. JEWELLERY (Gold)
1259. JOB WORK UNIT (FOUNDRY & MACHINING)
1260. JUTE TAR FELT
1261. JUTE BAGS
1262. JUTE BATCHING OIL
1263. JUTE WASTE PRODUCTS
1264. JUTE PROCESSING TWIN & GUNNY BAGS
1265. JUTE TWIN INCLUDING COTTON & COIR
1266. JUTE BAGS FROM RAW JUTE
1267. JUTE, COIR, GRASS, ROPE SUTLI MAKING
1268. JUICES (Fruit)
1269. KATECHU (Kattha)
1270. KALI MEHNDI (HAIR DYE)
1271. KATTHA & CUTCH
1272. KATTHA
1273. KANTHAL/NICHRO-ME FURNACE HEATING WIRE
1274. KERNAL (CASHEW NUT KERNAL EXTRACT)
1275. KHANDSARI SUGAR
1276. KIMAM MANUFACTURE
1277. KITCHEN SINK (S.S)
1278. KNITTING FABRICS
1179. KNITTED CLOTH
1280. KRAFT PAPER (FROM WASTE PAPER)
1281. KRAFT PAPER & MILL BOARD
1282. KRAFT PAPER FROM WASTE CARTON BOXES
1283. KRAFT PAPER & SPECIAL PAPER
1284. LAMINATED OF PAPER WARE (CARDS) WITH GLOSSY PP (POLYESTER FILM)
1285. LAUNDRY & DRY CLEANER
1286. LACTIC ACID
1287. LACTIC ACID FROM WHITE SUGAR (BY FERMENTATION PROCESS)
1288. LATEX RUBBER THREAD
1289. LAMINATED SAFETY GLASS
1290. LAMINATED SAFETY & TOUGHENED GLASS-
1291. LAMINATED PARTICLE BOARD & HARD BOARD
1292. LATEX RUBBER ADHESIVE
1293. LAUNDRY & WASHING SOAP
1294. LAUNDRY SOAP
1295. LAMINATED HESSIAN BAG
1296. LAMINATED SPRAY BRASS ARTICLES/BADGES
1297. LAMP CAPS
1298. LAMINATED JUTE BAGS
1299. LABORATORY CHEMICAL UNIT
1300. LATEX RUBBER CONDOM
1301. LATHER SHAVING CREAM
1302. LAPTOP COMPUTERS
1303. LAMP FILAMENT
1304. LATEX FOAM PRODUCTS
1305. LADDU
1306. LACTOSE & BYE PRODUCT PROCESSING FROM MILK
1307. LAMINATION OF CO-EXTRUSION, THREE LAYERS-FILM WITH LAMINATION & PRINTING
1308. LAMINATION OF CO-EXTRUSION MULTI LAYER FILM IN ROLL FORM
1309. LAUNDRY FOR '5' STAR HOTEL
1310. LDPE/HDPE FROM ETHYL ALCOHOL
1311. LDPE/HDPE PLANT
1312 LDPE/HDPE PIPES
1313. LEATHER GARMENTS
1314. LEMON GRASS OIL BASED IONES

Readily available 15000 Detailed Project Reports

@ Rs. 2500/- each

(or Rs. 3975/- for any two)

1315. LEAD CRYSTAL
1316. LEATHER GOODS
1317. LEATHER TANNING & COLOURING
1318. LEATHER SHOE & CHAPPAL
1319. LEATHER BINDER (RESIN BASED)
1320. LEVELING & DISPERSING AGENT
1321. LEATHER STRAPS FOR WRIST WATCHES
1322. LEATHER SHOES
1323. LEATHER BOARD
1324. LECITHIN (SOYA BASED)
1325. LEATHER TANNING
1326. LEATHER GOODS
1327. LETTER PRESS PRINTING
1328. LEATHER AUXILIARIES & CHEMICAL
1329. LEATHER TANNING & LEATHER GARMENTS
1330. LEATHER DYES
1331. LEASING BUSINESS
1332. LEASING & HIRE PURCHASE
1333. LEAD STEARATE
1334. LEMON GRASS OIL
1335. LEAD REFINING USING LEAD DROSS, LEAD SCRAP, LEAD POWDER
1336. LEAD NITRATE
1337. LEATHER GARMENTS, SHOES & CHAPPALS
1338. LEATHER WASHERS
1339. LEAD MONOXIDE
1340. LEATHER SUIT-CASES, BRIEF CASES & TRAVELING BAGS
1341. LEAD EXTRACTION FROM SCRAP BATTRIES
1342. LEAD BATTERY PLATES & BATTERY ASSEMBLY
1343. LEAD PENCILS
1344. LEAD SMELTING
1345. LEAD OXIDE (A) LEAD MONOXIDE (B) REA LEAD (LEAD TETROXIDE) (C) GREY LEAD OXIDE
1346. LEAD EXTRACTION (SECONDARY) FROM SCRAPS (A) BATTERY PLATE (B) PIPES (C) SHEET
1347. LIQUID BINDI & SINDUR
1348. LIQUID GLUCOSE & ITS BYE PRODUCTS FROM MAIZE
1349. LIQUID SOAP
1350. LIQUID DETERGENTS
1351. LIQUID SHOE POLISH PUFF
1352. LITHOPONE
1353. LIQUID GLUCOSE FROM POTATOES
1354. LIQUID OXYGEN BOTTLING
1355 LIGHTNING ARRESTER AND ISOLATOR
1356. LIGHT LIQUID PARAFFIN
1357. LILLY FLOWER & JASMINE
1358. LIQUID SOAP BY PINE OIL
1359. LINK CHAIN
1360. LITMUS PAPER
1361. LIGHT EMITING DIODE (LED)
1362. LIME STONE, DOLOMITE CHIPS & POWDER
1363. LIME STONE CRUSHING, GRINDING AND PULVERISING (FOR MFG. CHIPS & POWDER)
1364. LIQUID DETERGENTS (NON IONIC)
1365. LIME COLOUR/CEMENT COLOUR/SYNTHETIC RED IRON OXIDE USED FOR FLOORING
1366. LIMIT SWITCHES & METAL PLUG SOCKETS
1367. LIQUID DETERGENT
1368. LIPSTICKS
1369. LINSEED OIL
1370. LICHEN (JHYAU) (CHARILA)
1371. LIQUID GLUCOSE
1372. LIST OF 100% EOU/EOU UNIT
1373. LINING MATERIAL FOR FLUID FLOWING PIPE (LIQUID PETROLEUM)
1374. LOW PRESSURE CELLULOSE LIQUID
1375. LOUDSPEAKER
1376. LOOM OIL
1377. LOW TENSILE TRANSFORMERS (L.T) upto 400 KVA

Price Rs. 2500/- for each "Detailed Project Report" Payable in advance through Draft/Cash/M.O. in favour of "ENGINEERS INDIA RESEARCH INSTITUTE". Or Ask by V.P.P. PH.: 291 8117, 291 6431, 292 0361 Fax: 91-11-291 6431 (24 Hrs.)

1378. LPG STOVE
1379. LPG CYLINDER TESTING CENTER
1380. LPG CYLINDER
1381. LPG GAS REGULATOR
1382. LPG GAS BOTTLING PLANT
1383. LPG GAS STOVE
1384. LPG GAS PIPE
1385. LPG GAS DETECTOR
1386. L.T TRANSFORMER REPAIRING (400 KVA)
1387. LUBE OIL FROM CNSL TO REDUCE FRICTION
1388. LUBE OIL & GREASES
1389. LUBE OIL RECLAMATION
1390. LUBE OIL BLENDING
1391. LUBRICATING OIL & GREASES (BLENDING OF LUBRICATING OILS) & MANUFACTURE OF GREASE
1392. LUBRICANT VISCOSITY INDEX IMPROVERS
1393. LUBRICANT (WIRE DRAWING)
1394. MACARONI & VERMICELLI
1395. MANUFACTURE OF T-SHIRTS WITH KNITTING FABRICS
1396. MANGO PEEL BASED PECTIN
1397. MASALA/SPICES
1398. MATCH BOX MAKING UNIT
1399. MARBLE & GRANITE TILES
1400. MANGANESE ORE CONCENTRATION
1401. MAGNESIUM CARBONATE, MAGNESIUM METAL, CALCIUM CARBONATE FROM DOLOMITE
1402. MAGNESIUM SILICATE (TALC)
1403. MAIZE/CORN STARCH
1404. MALTED MILK FOOD
1405. MARINE CONTAINERS
1406. MANILA ROPES
1407. MALACHITE GREEN
1408. MANGO PULP & MANGO SLICES CANNING
1409. MAIZE STARCH
1410. MAGNESIUM HYDROXIDE POWDER
1411. MAGNESIUM SULPHATE
1412 MAGNESIUM TRI-SILICATE
1413. MAIZE/CORN OIL
1414. MALEIC ANHYDRIDE
1415. MALTING PLANT
1416. MARKING INK FOR FIBER TIP PENS
1417. MACARONI
1418. MANGALORE TILES & BRICKS
1419. MAN POWER EXPORT
1420. MACHINE SCREWS & SELF TAPPING SCREWS
1421. MANGO POWDER
1422. MANGO JUICE
1423. MANGO KERNEL POWDER
1424. MAGNET
1425. MAGNESIUM CARBONATE & BI-CARBONATE
1426. MAGAZINE
1427. MATCH SPLINTERS & INNER BOX MAKING PLANT FROM POPLAR WOOD
1428. MATERIAL HANDLING EQUIPMENTS (HOISTS & CRANES)
1429. MANUFACTURING OF PHARMACEUTICALS-TABLETS, CAPSULES ETC.
1430. MANGO PROCESSING & CANNING (MANGO PULP)

1431. MANGO PRODUCTS, MANGO JUICE, PICKLES, CHUTNEY ETC.
1432. METAL CUTTING DIE DESIGN
1433. MEASURING TAPES (STEEL, METALLIC & PLASTIC)
1434. MENTHOL CRYSTAL & OTHER CHEMICALS
1435. METHANE GAS
1436. METAL SPECTACLE FRAME
1437. MELAMINE CRYSTALS
1438. METTOL FROM HYDRO QUINENE & METHYL AMINE
1439. MEDICAL X-RAY FILM, SLITTING & REPACKING
1440. MEDICAL PLANT EXTRACT
1441. METAL FINISHING
1442. MENTHOL & D.M.O.
1443. MELAMINE CROCKERY
1444. METHYL METHA CRYLATE
1445. MELAMINE FORMALDE-HYDE POWDER
1446. METAL HARDENING
1447. METAL FITTINGS FOR LEATHER GOODS & GARMENTS
1448. METAL CONTAINER
1449. MECHANICAL TOY
1450. MENTHOLCRYSTAL
1451. METAL BONDED DIAMOND IMPREGNATED SEGMENT FOR MARBLE SAWING
1452. METHYLATED SURGICAL SPIRIT
1453. METALLIZED POLYPRO-PYLENE FILM
1454. METAL NAPHTHANATE
1455. METALLIC GASKET (SPIRAL WOUND)
1456. METAL PRE TREATMENT CHEMICALS
1457. MENTHA OIL
1458. METALLIC ACID
1459. MERCURIC OXIDE
1460. METHYL METHACRY-LATE MONOMER & VARIOUS CHEMICAL ADDITIVES FOR PLASTIC BANGLES
1461. METAL POLISH SOAP
1462. METAL HOOKS & CLIP
1463. METALLIC STEARATES
1464. METHYLINE GLUE
1465. METHYL SALICYLATE
1466. MEAT PROCESSING (BUFFALO)
1467. METAL POLISHING BAR
1468. METHYL ETHYL KETONE
1469. M.G. KRAFT PAPER FROM WASTE PAPER
1470. MICRO SCALE STEEL PLANT
1471. MICROWAVE OVEN
1472. MINI CEMENT PLANT (BY ROTARY KILN PROCESS-800 TPD)
1473. MILK PRESERVATION & MARKETING TO WHOLESAL-ERS (IN POUCH)
1474. MILK/DAIRY PRODUCTS
1475. MINI RE-ROLLING MILL
1476. MINI PAPER PLANT FORM JUTE STICK & WHEAT HUSK/ RICE HUSK
1477. MILK/DAIRY PRODUCTS
1478. MILK CHOCOLATE
1479. MINI STEEL PLANT BY INDUCTION FURNACE
1480. MINI CEMENT PLANT
1481. MICA PAPER FOR ELECTRICAL INSULATION
1482. MINI SUGAR PLANT
1483. MICRO CRYSTALLINE WAX
1484. MINIATURE CIRCUIT BREAKER (MCB)
1485. MINI FLOUR MILL (ROLLER)
1486. MINI FLOUR MILL (PULVERISED)
1487. MINI PAPER PLANT (KRAFT PAPER)
1488. MINI PAPER PLANT FROM SISAL WOOD

1489. MITHAI/NAMKEEN
1490. MICRO CRYSTALLINE WAX FROM SLUDGE OF PETRO CHEMICAL REFFINERY
1491. MINIATURE WATCH BATTERY
1492. MICRO NUTRIENT MIXTURE (SOLID)
1493. MISHRI PEARL SUGAR CANDY
1494. MINI PAPER PLANT FROM EUCALYPTUS WOOD
1495. MILL & KRAFT PAPER FROM WASTE CARTON BOXES
1496. MINI PAPER PLANT (WHITE WRITING & PRINTING)
1497. MINERAL WATER IN POUCHES
1498. MINERAL WATER IN POUCHES & PLASTIC BOTTLES
1499. MIRIT SANJEEVNI SURA
1500. MINI STEEL PLANT
1501. MILK PRESERVATION & MARKETING (MILK CHILLING PLANT)
1502. MICRO NUTRIENTS MIXTURES
1503. MICRO WAVE TUBES USED IN MICRO WAVE OVEN
1504. MILK POWDER
1505. MILD STEEL BOLT
1506. MILD STEEL NUTS
1507. MINI (PERSONAL) COMPUTER
1508. MINIATURE TRANSFORMER
1509. MINI PAPER PLANT USING BAGASSE
1510. MILK POWDER, GHEE & SPICES
1511. MICRO PAPER
1512. MIRROR (GOLDEN, SILVER AND PINK)
1513. MICROVEE & ABSOLUTE FILTER
1514. MICRO MOTORS
1515. MIXERS/GRINDERS (MIXIE)
1516. MILK POWDER & GHEE
1517. MICRO CELLULAR SHEET FOR SHOE SOLE
1518. MILK TOFFEE
1519. MILK CHILLING PLANT & PACKING IN POUCHES
1520. MODERN COSMETIC INDUSTRY
1521. MOSQUITO COILS & MATS
1522. MOULDED CASE CIRCUIT BREAKER (MCCB)
1523. MOTHER BOARD
1524. MONOCHROME MONITOR FOR COMPUTER
1525. MOULDED LUGGAGE
1526. MOULDED LUGGAGE (V.I.P. TYPE)
1527. MOULDED LUGGAGE (CHEAP QUALITY)
1528. MOSQUITO REPELLENT MAT
1529. MOTHER TINCTURE & BIO-CHEMIC MEDICINES
1530. MOTEL/SMALL HOTEL
1531. MOSQUITO COILS
1532. MODERN RICE MILL
1533. MOSAIC TILES
1534. MOTOR START ELECTROLYTIC CAPACITORS
1535. MOSQUITO MAT RECHARGER

-: Note :-

Pay Rs. 3500/- only for Data Backup of each Detailed Project Report alongwith the Printout.

1536. MONO CHLORO ACETIC ACID
1537. MOBILE CATERING VAN
1538. MODERN VEHICLE WORKSHOP
1539. MODERN BREAD AND BAKERY UNIT
1540. MONOCHROTOPHOS (TECHNICAL)
1541. MOSQUITO REPELLENT OIL
1542. MOTEL/SMALL HOTEL, BANQUET HALL WITH RESTAURANT
1543. MOSQUITO COILS USING EUCALYPTUS LEAVES
1544. MODERN ADVERTISING AGENCY WITH DTP & FILM STUDIO
1545. M.S. INGOTS (INDUCTION FURNACE)
1546. M.S. WIRE DRAWING PLANT & ANNEALING
1547. M.S. HINGES
1548. M.S. INGOTS & H.R. STEEL STRUCTURES
1549. M.S. WELDING ELECTRODES
1550. M.S. DRUM & FABRICATION OF STORAGE TANK
1551. MUSTARD OIL (EDIBLE OIL)
1552. MULTI PURPOSE SPRAY DRIER
1553. MUSICAL DOOR BELL
1554. MUSHROOM CULTIVATION
1555. MUSHROOM CULTIVATION & PROCESSING WITH CANNING
1556. MULTI LAYER PRINTED CIRCUIT BOARD (PCB)
1557. MULTI PURPOSE COLD STORAGE FOR MEDICINES, FRUITS & VEGETABLES
1558. MULTIPLE RELAY FOR LOW VOLTAGE APPLICATION
1559. MUSHROOM(EOU) CULTIVATION & PROCESSING UNIT (DEHYDRATION & PICKLING OF OYSTER & PADDY STRAW MUSHROOM)
1560. MUTTON TALLOW FOR INDUSTRIAL USE
1561. MUFFLERS & SILENCERS FOR TWO WHEELERS
1562. MUFFLER & SILENCER PIPES FOR FOUR WHEELER
1563. MUSHROOM & PROCESSED FOOD
1564. MUSICAL SOUND GENERATOR
1565. MULTI LAYER FILM
1566. MULTI STOREY COMMERCIAL COMPLEX ALONGWITH RESIDENTIAL & DELUXE FLATS FOR FOREIGN TOURISTS & REVOLVING RESTAURANT
1567. MUSTARD OIL EXTRACTION & REFINING
1568. MURABBA
1569. MULTI LAYER CO-EXTRUSION, THREE LAYERS-FILM WITH LAMINATION PRINTING
1570. NAPHTHALENE BALLS
1571. NAMKEEN & SWEETS
1572. NAIL ENAMEL (NAIL POLISH)
1573. NAMKEEN INDUSTRY
1574. NAPHTHALENE BALLS
1575. NAPHTHA BASED THINNER
1576. NAIL CUTTER WITH FILER & MANICURE
1577. N-ACETYL, L-TYROSINE
1578. N.C. PUTTY
1579. N.C. THINNER USED IN AUTO PARTS
1580. N.C. SENDING SEALERS
1581. NEWS PRINT PAPER FROM RICE STRAW/BAGASSE
1582. NEWS PAPER
1583. NEOPRENE BASED ADHESIVES
1584. NEON SIGN
1585. NEON BULB
1586. NEEM OIL FROM SEEDS
1587. NEON LAMP INDICATORS
1588. NEON INDICATOR
1589. NEEM SEEDS INSECTICIDES
1590. NEEDLE ROLLERS FOR BEARING
1591. NEROL LAUNDRY SOAP
1592. NEWS PAPER FOR CHILDREN (DAILY)-EVENING NEWS PAPER

Price Rs. 2500/- for each "Detailed Project Report" Payable in advance through Draft/Cash/M.O. in favour of "ENGINEERS INDIA RESEARCH INSTITUTE". Or Ask by V.P.P. PH.: 291 8117, 291 6431, 292 0361 Fax: 91-11-291 6431 (24 Hrs.)

1593. NITRO CELLULOSE (LACQUER)
1594. NICHROME WIRE
1595. NICHROME/KANTHAL FURNACE HEATING WIRE
1596. NICKEL PLATING BRIGHTNER (PRIMARY OR CARRIER BRIGHTNER AND SECONDARY)
1597. NICKEL SALT
1598. NICKEL/CADMIUM BATTERY
1599. NICKEL PLATING
1600. NICKEL PLATING BRIGTNER
1601. NICKEL LINED SCREENS
1602. NICKEL SULPHATE
1603. NICKEL CATALYST
1604. NICKEL CATALYST FOR HYDROGENETION OF VEGETABLE OIL
1605. NICKEL ELECTROPLATING SALTS (ONLY MARKET SURVEY)
1606. NICKEL CHROMIUM PLATING & HARD CHROMIUM
1607. NICKEL RECLAMATION FROM SPENT CATALYST OF VANASPATI INDUSTRY
1608. NITROGEN & OXYGEN UNIT
1609. NILGIRI OIL
1610. NICOTINIC ACID
1611. NIRMA TYPE DETERGENT POWDER
1612. NITRO CELLULOSE
1613. NITRO MUSK
1614. NICOTINE SULPHATE FROM TOBACCO WASTE
1615. NON-STICK KITCHEN WARES (TEFLON COATED UTENSILS)
1616. NON-FERROUS SCRAP MELTING ROD CASTING & WIRE DRAWING
1617. NON-IONIC SURFACTANTS WETTING AGENTS
1618. NOODLES
1619. NON-BASMATI RICE FROM PADDY
1620. NON-IONIC LIQUID DETERGENT
1621. NON-ALCOHOLIC FLAVOUR
1622. NON-CARBONATED SOFT DRINK
1623. NON-FERROUS METAL ALLOY
1624. NON-FERROUS FORGING
1625. NON-EDIBLE & EDIBLE OIL MILL
1626. NOTE BOOK, REGISTER & FILES
1627. NON-WOVEN CARPETS (WADDED WITH POLYESTER FIBER)
1628. NUMBER COMBINATION AUTO LOCKS FOR LUGGAGES
1629. NUT, BOLTS, RIVETS/ WASHER
1630. NURSING HOME
1631. NURSERY SCHO-OL (PRE-NURSERY & NURSERY)
1632. NYLON YARN CRIMPING DOUBL-ING, BLEACHING, DYEING ETC.
1633. NYLON POLYESTER & P.P. ROPE MAKING
1634. NYLON ZIP FASTENERS
1635. NYLON SOCKS
1636. OCTYL ALCOHOL
1637. OFFSET PRINTING PRESS
1638. OFFSET SECURITY PRINTING PRESS
1639. OFFSET COLOUR & TREADLE TYPE PRINTING PRESS
1640. OFFSET PRINTING INK
1641. OIL (COTTON SEED)
1642. OIL (MUSTARD)
1643. OIL (GROUND NUT)
1644. OIL MILL
1645. OIL SEALS
1646. OIL (CASTOR)

1647. OIL (RICE BRAN)
1648. OIL (ESSENTIAL)
1649. OIL BOND DISTEMPER PAINT
1650. OLEORESIN OF SPICES
1651. OLEORESIN FROM CHILLY
1652. ONE TIME CARBON PAPER
1653. ONION POWDER
1654. ONION & POTATO POWDER
1655. OPTICAL GLASS GRINDING
1656. OPTICAL FIBER CABLE
1657. OPTICAL WHITENER
1658. OPEN END SPINNING PLANT
1659. OPTICAL WHITENER
1660. ORTHO BORIC ACID
1661. ORGANIC SOLVENT PURIFICATION PLANT
1662. ORTHO TOLUENE SOLVENT
1663. ORGANIC MANURE
1664. OSSEIN & GELATIN
1665. OSSEIN FROM ANIMAL BONES
1666. OXYGEN GAS
1667. OXALIC ACID
1668. OXALIC ACID FROM WASTE VEGETABLES
1669. OXYGEN & NITROGEN PLANT
1670. OXALIC ACID FROM SAW DUST
1671. OXIDISED WAX
1672. OYSTER MUSHROOMS (CULTIVATION & PROCESSING UNIT)
1673. PAINT INDUSTRY
1674. PACKAGING OF NAMKEEN, BHUJIA, DALMOTH ETC. IN FLEXIBLE POUCHES
1675. PARAFFIN WAX FROM SLACK WAX
1676. PAINT BRUSHES
1677. PAPER BAGS
1678. PALM OIL
1679. PARACETAMOL
1680. PAPPAD PLANT
1681. PAN MASALA IN POUCHES & TIN PACKS
1682. PAPER FROM BAMBOO
1683. PAPER FROM WASTE PAPER (KRAFT PAPER)
1684. PAPER FROM WASTE PAPER (WRITING & PRINTING PAPER)
1685. PAPER FROM BAGASSE
1686. PAPER FROM RICE STRAW
1687. PAPER CONES & TUBES
1688. PAPER & PULP
1689. PAPER FROM EUCALYPTUS
1690. PAPER ENVELOPS
1691. PAPER FROM RICE HUSK & WHEAT HUSK
1692. PAPER FROM PAPYRUS GRASS
1693. PAPER (HAND MADE PAPER)
1694. PAPER CUPS
1695. PAPER PLANT FROM TREE BARK & EUCALYPTUS WOOD
1696. PAPER BASED PHENOLIC SHEET (FOR ELECTRICAL APPLIANCES)
1697. PAPER WASTE RECYCLING
1698. PAPER & PAPER BOARD
1699. PAPER PRODUCTS
1700. PAPAIN
1701. PAPAIN FROM PAPAYA
1702. PAPAYA CULTIVATION
1703. PAPAYA & TOMATO CULTIVATION
1704. PAPAYA CULTIVATION & PAPAIN MANUFACTURE
1705. PARTICLE BOARD
1706. PAPER COATED ALUMINIUM & COPPER WIRES
1707. PANEL, FLUSH DOOR, WINDOWS, OFFICE FURNITURE & HOUSE HOLD FURNITURE
1708. PANEER
1709. PAPER PLATES
1710. PAINT & VARNISH
1711. PARACETAMOL BY PNCB
1712 PARAAMINO BENZOIC ACID

1713. PAINT INDUSTRY (LIME COLOUR, DRY DISTEMPER, OIL BOUND DISTEMPER, ENAMEL PAINT, RED OXIDE PRIMER/RESIN, MICA BASED PAINT)
1714. PAN MASALA & POUCH MAKING PLANT
1715. PARA CHLORO NITRO BENZENE
1716. PASTEURIZATION OF MILK (FLAVOURED MILK)
1717. PARTICLE BOARD FROM RICE HUSK
1718. PAN MASALA, TOBACCO, ZARDA & KIMAM
1719. PAINT-BITUMINOUS BASED CORROSION RESISTANT
1720. PAINT REMOVERS
1721. PALM OIL CRUSHING UNIT
1722. PAPER VARNISH
1723. PAPER FROM AKRA
1724. PARTICLE BOARD WOOD CHIPS
1725. PARTICLE BOARD & BLOCK BOARD WITH SENDING & LAMINATION OF PARTICLE BOARD
1726. PAPER CONES FOR LOUDSPEAKER
1727. PATCHES (TUBE REPAIR MATERIAL)
1728. PAINT INDUSTRY (PRIMER)
1729. PAPER PLANT (KRAFT & WHITE WRITING & PRINTING PAPER)
1730. PAPAIN FROM PAPAYA (PAPAYA LATEX)
1731. PCB SHEETS
1732. PCC ELECTRIC POLES
1733. PCC/RCC PIPES
1734. PEPSI COLA IN POLY TUBES
1735. PETROMAX CONTAINER
1736. PERFUMERY COMPOUND
1737. PERFUMERY COMPOUND, COSMETICS ETC.
1738. PERFUMED PHENYL (PINE OIL DISINFECTANT)
1739. PERFUMERY COMPOUNDS (AROMATIC)
1740. PERFUME (SPRAY)
1741. PERFUMERY COMPOUND (SYNTHETIC AGARBATTI)
1742. PERFUMES (SCENT) FROM LEMON GRASS OIL AND JASMINE OIL
1743. PET BOTTLE/CONTAINERS
1744. PERSONAL COMPUTER
1745. PECTIN BY RAW PAPAYA
1746. PECTIN FROM APPLE POMACE
1747. PECTIN FROM CITRUS, LEMON & ORANGES
1748. PECTIN BY MANGO PEELS
1749. PECTIN FROM ORANGE/ LIME PEELS
1750. PERFUME FOR SOAP, DETERGENT & AGARBATTI (YARA YARA)
1751. PERFUME & SCENTS
1752. PERFUMED PHENYL (THICK)
1753. PETROLEUM COKE
1754. PESTICIDE FORMULATIONS
1755. PETROLEUM JELLY
1756. PESTICIDES (MELATHION, MANCOZEV, COPPER OXY-CHLORIDE, WATTABLE SULPHUR, ZINC PHOSPHIDE)

1757. PEANUT COATING (SPICES, HONEY, CHEESE, CHOCOLATE, SALT)
1758. PENCIL (LEAD)
1759. PELLETIZER PLANT (FOR CATTLE FEED, POULTRY FEED, SHEEP FEED, PIG & OTHER FEED)
1760. PETHA PACKAGING
1761. PEPPERMINT OIL
1762. PHARMACEUTICAL
1763. ALCOHOL FROM NON-MOLASSES BASED
1764. POWER LOOM
1765. POWDER COATING (CHAMBER TYPE)
1766. POUCH FILLING for SAUNF, SUPARI & ELAICHI ETC.
1767. PUBLISHING & PRINTING UNIT
1768. POTATO STARCH
1769. POLYTHENE BAGS & AUTOMATIC PRINTING
1770. PVC FABRIC YARN ON POWER LOOM (TERRYCOT)
1771. PVC CONDUIT PIPE
1772. PVC PIPE & FITTINGS
1773. PHARMACEUTICAL UNITS (TABLETS, CAPSULES, SYRUPS, LOTION, OINTMENT, POWDER INJECTABLE, EYE DROPS & EYE OINTMENT ETC.)
1774. PHENACETIN
1775. PHTHALOCYNINE BLUE & GREEN
1776. PHOTO POLYMER COATING FOR PLATE & BLOCK MAKING
1777. PHOTO GRAVURE & FLEXO GRAPHIC PRINTING INK FOR PLASTIC FILM PRINTING
1778. PHOSPHORIC ACID FOR POLLUTION CONTROL
1779. PHOTO ALBUM ADHESIVES
1780. PHENOLIC RESIN
1781. PHENOLIC FORMALDEHYDE RESIN (PF RESIN)
1782. PHOTOGRAPHIC DEVELOPERS & FIXERS
1783. PHENYL ACETIC ACID
1784. PHOTO DEVELOPER & FIXER
1785. PHENOL
1786 PHOTO ETCHING OF STAINLESS STEEL PLATES
1787. PHOTO TYPE SETTING
1788. PHENYL (BROWN & WHITE)
1789. PHENYL (BLACK) IN LIQUID FORM
1790. PHOSPHORIC ACID FROM ROCK PHOSPHATE
1791. PHOTO COLOUR LAB (QSS)
1792. PHOTO EMULSION FOR ROTARY SCREEN PRINTING
1793. PHOSPHORIC ACID (Purification) FROM CRUDE
1794. PILFER PROOF CAPS & CROWN CAPS
1795. PILFER PROOF CAPS (P.P. CAPS)
1796. PIG IRON
1797. PICKLES, MURABBAS, SAUCES ETC. (VEGETARIAN & NONVEG. PICKLES)
1798. P.I.D. CONTROLLER
1799. PIGMENTS (DYE PIGMENTS)
1800. PISTON ASSEMBLY (ALUMINIUM ALLOY)

1801. PISTON ASSEMBLY (ALUMINIUM ALLOY)
1802. PIGGERY/MEAT/CHICKEN PROCESSING
1803. PINEAPPLE JUICE & CANING
1804. PINE APPLE SLICE CANNING
1805. PIGMENT DYE & DYE INTERMEDIATES
1806. PICKLE & SAUCES
1807. PIGMENT BINDER FOR TEXTILE PRINTING
1808. PIGGERY FARM
1809. PICKLES
1810. PICTURE VARNISH
1811. PLASTIC MOULDED T.V CABINETS
1812. PLASTIC INJECTION MOULDED AUTO COMPONENTS
1813. PLASTIC PRODUCT-AUDIO, VIDEO CASSETTE SHELL)
1814. PLASTIC BUCKETS & DOLI
1815. PLASTIC DRINKING STRAW
1816. PLASTIC FILM CAPACITOR
1817. PLAIN PAPER COPIER
1818. PLASTIC GRANULES (HDPE, LDPE, PP) FROM PLASTIC SCRAPS/WASTE
1819. PLATINUM LABORATORY APPARATUS
1820. PLASTIC SPRAY LAMINATED BRASS ARTICLES/BADGES
1821. PLASTIC TOOTH PICK
1822. PLASTIC I.V. BOTTLES
1823. PLASTIC FILM & SHEETS WITH PRINTING (FLEXO & ROTO) LDPE/HDPE/PP/HM/ PVC
1824. PLASTIC CORRUGATED SHEET & BOXES
1825. PLASTIC BUTTONS FROM POLYESTER SHEET & RODS
1826. PLASTIC ADVERTISEMENT BALLOONS
1827. PLASTIC CONTAINER (BLOW MOULDED)
1828. PLASTIC INJECTION MOULDING PROJECTS
1829. PLASTIC SHEET FROM PLASTIC SCRAPS
1830. PLASTIC CANES
1831. PLASTIC SYRINGE (DISPOSABLE)
1832. PLASTER OF PARIS BANDAGES
1833. PLASTER OF PARIS
1834. PLASTER OF PARIS BANDAGES & COTTON ADHESIVE TAPE
1835. PLASTIC BUTTONS
1836. PLASTIC CONFERENCE BAGS, FOLDERS ETC.
1837. PLASTIC MOULDED FURNITURE
1838. PLASTIC WASTE REPROCESSING
1839. PLASTIC SUTLI
1840. PLANT PROTECTION EQUIPMENTS

EIRI

Areas of Expertise

IDENTIFICATION OR PRODUCT

CONDUCTING MARKET SURVEY

PREPARATION OF PROJECT PROFILES & FEASIBILITY STUDIES

PREPARATION OF TECHNOECONOMIC FEASIBILITY STUDIES

PREPARATION OF FINANCING SCHEME & LOAN APPLICATION

GUIDANCE OF PROCEDURES FOR GOVERNMENT CLEARANCE

TURNKEY SERVICES

TECHNOLOGY TRANSFER

1841. PLASTIC COLLAPSIBLE TUBES
1842. PLASTIC TANKS (WATER STORAGE SINTEX TYPE TANKS)
1843. PLASTIC MOULDED TOYS
1844. PLASTIC WARES
1845. PLASTIC SPRAY LAMINATED ARTICLES
1846. PLASTIC MOULDED ARTICLES
1847. PLY WOOD & PLY BOARD
1848. PLY WOOD
1849. PLY WOOD BOARD
1850. PLY WOOD & PLY BOARD (PHENOL BONDED, BOILING WATER PROOF, TERMITE, RESISTANCE, LAMINATED & COMMERCIAL PLY WOOD & PLY BOARD)
1851. PLASTIC STRIPPABLE COATING MATERIAL
1852. PLASTER OF PARIS (CALCIUM SULPHATE)
1853. POLYSTYRENE MOULDING (EXPANDED)
1854. POTATO POWDER
1855. POLYESTER RESIN
1856. POULTRY & CATTLE FEED
1857. POULTRY FEED
1858. POLYESTER YARN
1859. POUCH PACKING FOR MILK
1860. POWER PLANT
1861. PORK PROCESSING & FARMING
1862. POUCHES FOR OIL & GHEE PACKING
1863. POLYPROPYLENE BOX STRAPPING
1864. POWER SUPPLY (LINER&SWITCHMODE)
1865. POWER TRANSFORMER
1866. POLYURETHANE FOAM FLEXIBLE & RIGID
1867. POTATO CHIPS/WAFERS
1868. POWER SUPPLY (SWITCH MODE)
1869. POTATO GRANULE
1870. PROCESSED FRUITS
1871. POLYPROPYLENE/HDPE BOX STRAPPING
1872. POULTRY & BROILER FARMING
1873. POULTRY & HATCHERY FARMING
1874. POULTRY FARM
1875. POTABLE ALCOHOL FROM GRAINS & ROTTEN FRUITS
1876. POTASSIUM SILICATE
1877. POLY VINYL ALCOHOL
1878. POLY BUTENS FROM CAREFFINATES
1879. POLYESTER HOSIERY LABELS & PATCHES
1880. POLYURETHANE FOAM (P.U. FOAM)
1881. POLYPROPYLENE SPINNING FILAMENT YARN

Price Rs. 2500/- for each ``Detailed Project Report'' Payable in advance through Draft/Cash/M.O. in favour of ``ENGINEERS INDIA RESEARCH INSTITUTE". Or Ask by V.P.P. PH.: 291 8117, 291 6431, 292 0361 Fax: 91-11-291 6431 (24 Hrs.)

1882. PORTABLE TELEVISION
1883. POLYSTER YARN FROM WASTE
1884. POLYSTER BEADING
1865. POUCH MAKING & GRAVURE PRINTING
1886. POWDER COATING
1887. POLY VINYL ACETATE
1888. POLYTHENE PRINTING BAG (P.P & H.M. FLEXIBLE FOUR COLOURS ROTO GRAVURE PRINT)
1889. POWER TRANSFORMERS UPTO 600 KVA
1890. POLYTHENE BAGS & TUBES
1891. POLYESTER RESIN FOR WIRE ENAMEL
1892. PORTABLE GENERATOR SET
1893. POTASSIUM NITRATE
1894. POTASSIUM PERMANGA-NATE (IN SOLUTION FORM)
1895. POWER COATING PAINT (EPOXY, ACRYLIC & POLYESTER BASIS)
1896. POTATO & ONION POWDER
1897. POTATO CHIPS WITH IMPORTED MACHINERY
1898. POLYURETHANE RIGID FROM MOULDING
1899. POLYURETHANE SOLE
1900. POLYURETHANE FOAM & ITS PRODUCTS
1901. POUCH PACKING FOR MILK
1902. POWER PLANT
1903. PORKPROCESSING & FARMING
1904. POTASSIUM IODIDE
1905. POTATO POWDER AUTOMATIC IMPORTED PLANT
1906. POTABLE LIQUOR
1907. POLYESTER YARN
1908. POLISH (WAX)
1909. POLISH (CAR)
1910. POTASSIUM DI-CHRO-MATE/BI-CHROMATE
1911. POWER INVERTER
1912. POLYPROPYLENE & MULTIFILAMENT SPINNING YARN
1913. POLYESTER MICRO FIBER
1914. POWER PLANT (HYDRO BASED)
1915. POLYETHENE POUCHES FOR GHEE, BUTTER, OIL, MILK ETC.
1916. POLYTHENE BOTTLES FOR MINERAL WATER, I.V. FLUIDS ETC.
1917. POPLAR PLANTATION
1918. PRINTED TIN CONTAINERS
1919. PRINTING INKS
1920. PRINTING INKS (FLEXO GRAPHIC)
1921. PRINTED CIRCUIT BOARD (PCB)
1922. PROCESSING OF FRUIT & VEGETABLE
1923. PRUSSIAN BLUE
1924. PRINTING PLATE FOR OFFSET PRINTING MACHINE
1925. PROCESSED FOOD (READYMADE)
1926 PRECIPITATED CALCIUM CARBONATE
1927. PROCESSED CHEESE
1928. PRE STRESSED CONCRETE RAILWAY SLEEPER

1929. PRINTING PRESS (LETTER PRESS)
1930. PRINTING PRESS (OFFSET)
1931. PRESSURE DIE CASTING ALUMINIUM
1932. PROTEIN & PROTEIN BASED PRODUCTS
1933. PRECIOUS METAL PLATING & MANUFACTURE OF THEIR SALTS
1934. PRESSURE COOK-ER & ALUMINIUM UTENSILS
1935. PRESSURE COOKER (ALUMINIUM/STAINLESS STEEL) & WATER FILTER
1936. PRESSURE SENSITIVE ADHESIVE TAPES
1937. PRESSURE SENSITIVE ADHESIVE FOR BOPP TAPES (ACRYLIC BASED)
1938. PRECIPITATED CALCIUM CARBONATE FROM BYE-PRODUCTS LIME SLURRY & CARBON DIOXIDE
1939. PRINTING INK (ROTO GRAVURE & FLEXO GRAPHIC)
1940. PRINTING INK (OFFSET)
1941. PROCESSED FOOD & MARINE PRODUCTS
1942. PRINTING INDUSTRY (DTP & OFFSET)
1943. PRESSURE COOKER
1944. PRESSURE COOKER (ALUMINIUM & STAINLESS STEEL)
1945. PRECIPITATED SILICA
1946. PRODUCTS BASED ON INDUSTRIAL WASTE (COVERING TEN PROJECT PROFILES)
1947. PROCESSED FOOD & SPICES
1948. PROCESSED CONTROL TIMER (Electronic Timer)
1949. PRAWN FISH FARMING
1950. P.U. (POLYURETHANE) RIGID FOAM
1951. PUMIC WHITE ABRASIVE CAKE/STICK
1952. PULVERIZED FLOUR MILL
1953. PULSE MILL (DAL MILL)
1954. PULP FROM WOOD, BAMBOO OR GRASS
1955. PULP FROM BAMBOO & WOOD
1956. PUTTY (METAL CASEMENT PUTTY)-ASIAN PAINT TYPE
1957. PUTTY & WATER PROOFING PLANT
1958. PURIFICATION OF CASEIN
1959. PVC INSULATION TAPES
1960. PVC WIRES & CABLES
1961. PVC WIRES/TWIN FLAT CABLE
1962. PVC PIPES & FITTINGS
1963. PVC GRANULES/ COMPOUNDS BY CHEMICAL PROCESS
1964. PVC GRANULES FROM PVC SCRAPS (POLLUTION CONTROL)
1965. PVC GRANULES/ COMPOUNDS BY PLASTIC WASTE
1966. PVC RIGID PIPE
1967. PVC INSULATED CABLES
1968. PVC PROFILES (DOOR & WINDOW)
1969. PVC FOOTWEAR

1970. PVC SOLES FOR LEATHER SHOE UPPERS
1971. PVC STABILIZERS
1972. PVC/XLPE (ARMOURED) CABLES
1973. PVC WIRE & CABLES/PIPES & FITTINGS
1974. PVC CASING CAPING MATERIAL FOR ELECTRICAL FITTING
1975. PVC/PLASTIC/SOFT/RIGID/FILM SHEETS
1976. PVC LEATHER CLOTH
1977. PVC CABLES
1978. PVC FLOOR TILES
1979. PVC ELECTRICAL INSULATION TAPE WITH PRINTING (STEEL GRIP TYPE)
1980. PVC COATING ON LEATHER SHEETS
1981. PVC BATTERY SEPARATOR
1982. PVC PIPES & FITTINGS (RIGID PIPE, FLEXIBLE PIPE, CONDUIT PIPE, ELBOW FITTING, T-JOINTS ETC.)
1983. PVC RULLER
1984. PVC SOLVENT CEMENT
1985. PVC SUCTION HOSES
1986. PVC FLEXIBLE PIPES
1987. PVA BASED ADHESIVES
1988. PVC ON G.I. WIRE
1989. PVC ROOFING SHEET
1990. PVC FILM
1991. QSS COLOUR PHOTO LAB
1992. QUICK LIME
1993. RAILWAY SLEEPERS (PRE STRESSED CONCRETE)
1994. RAISING COMPOUNDS OR EMBOSSING POWDER
1995. RABBIT FARMING
1996. RAINBOW COLOUR ON PVC FILM & SHEET
1997. RAINBOW COLOUR ON METALS
1998. RAZOR BLADE
1999. RCC SPUN PIPES
2000. REACTIVE DYES
2001. READY MADE PROCESSED FOOD
2002. RECTIFIED SPIRIT FROM MOLASSES & MAHUA FLOWER
2003. REROLLING OF SARIYA (TOR)
2004. RESTAURANT
2005. REFINED OILS (COTTON SEEDS, GROUNDNUT, SUNFLOWER ETC.)
2006. RESIN BASED LEATHER BINDER
2007. REROLLING OF STEEL
2008. RECOVERY OF LEAD FROM DISPOSED LEAD ACID BATTERY
2009. REFRIGERATOR & MINI REFRIGERATOR
2010. RESIN CORED SOFT SOLDERING WIRE
2011. RECLAMATION OF TRANSFORMER OIL
2012. RED IRON OXIDE
2013. RE-ROLLING MILL (ALUMINIUM) & UTENSILS
2014. REFINED SUNFLOWER SEED OIL
2015. RESIDENTIAL APARTMENT
2016. RESIDENTIAL & DELUXE FLATS
2017. RECLAMATION OF USED ENGINE OIL
2018. RECLAMATION OF WAX SLUDGES FOR MANUFACTURING OF MICROCRYSTALINE WAX
2019. READY MADE GARMENTS

EIRI
You can ask for
Detailed
Feasibility Reports
in any of your required
product which may be of any
scale Cost Rs. 5000/-

2020. READY MADE GARMENTS AND HOSIERY
2021. REFINING OF GROUNDNUT OIL
2022. RECONDITIONING OF EMPTY CEMENT JUTE BAG
2023. RED OXIDE PRIMER
2024. REFINING OF CASTOR OIL
2025. RECHARGEABLE TORCHES
2026. READY MADE GARMENTS MERCHANDISE PLANT
2027. RECOVERY OF SILVER NITRATE FROM PHOTO GRAPHIC WASTE FIXERS
2028. REMOTE CONTROL SYSTEMS (FOR STARTING DOOR, OPEN & CLOSE HEADLIGHT ON & OFF FOR CAR)
2029. RECOVERY OF SILVER FROM WASTE FIXTURE BLEACH OBTAINED FROM PHOTO COLOUR LAB BY SULPHIDE PROCESS
2030. RECYCLING OF WASTE CELLULOSE ACETATE INTO CELLULOSE ACETATE SHEETS
2031. RED OXIDE PIGMENTS FROM IRON PICKLING PLANT WASTE
2032. REFRACTORIES
2033. REFINED OIL & GROUNDNUT OIL
2034. REROLLING OF STEEL CUTTING
2035. RED MUD PVC PIPES & FITTINGS
2036. REXINE CLOTH & ALIKE PRODUCTS
2037. RECONDITIONING OF T.V PICTURE TUBE
2038. RECONDITIONING OF FLUORESCENT TUBE
2039. RECTIFIED SPIRIT FOR POTABLE ALCOHOL, INDUSTRIAL ALCOHOL & MEDICAL ALCOHOL
2040. RE-REFINING OF USED LUBRICANT
2041. RECTIFIED SPIRIT FROM RICEPADDY STRAW
2042. RED OXIDE PRIMER (ANTI CORROSIVE)
2043. READY MADE GARMENTS (100% EOU)-STITCHING, WASHING, DYEING, PRINTING & FINISHING ETC.)
2044. REFINED VEGETABLE OILS
2045. REROLLING OF STEEL SECTIONS
2046. REFINING OF MUSTARD OILS
2047. REPACKING OF MEDICINES
2048. READY MADE SALWAR SUITS
2049. RED OXIDE PIGMENTS
2050. RECLAMATION OF HYDRAULIC OIL
2051. RED MIRROR BY ELECTROLESS DIPPING METHOD
2052. REACTIVE DYE M5B DYE
2053. RIGID PVC PIPES & FITTINGS (RIGID PIPES, PIPE FITTINGS LIKE ELBOW FITTINGS, T-JOINTS ETC.)
2054. RE-WINDING OF BURNT ELECTRIC MOTOR
2055. RECLAMATION OF NICKEL FROM SPENT CATALYST OF VANASPATI INDUSTRY
2056. RECLAMATION OF SPENT BLEACHING EARTH
2057. REFRIGERANT ALFA-R134
2058. RESISTORS (WIRE WOUND)
2059. RESIN CORED SOFT SOLDERING WIRE
2060. RESIN COATED SAND (SHELL MOULDING SAND)
2061. RED PHOSPHORUS
2062. RICE HUSK BASED CEMENT
2063. RICE&CORNFLAKE
2064. RICE MILL
2065. RICE FLAKES (CHUDA)
2066. RICE POLISHING AND PACKAGING IN POUCHES
2067. RIGID PVC PIPES
2068. RIGID PVC PIPES & FITTINGS
2069. RICE BRAN OIL
2070. RICE TRADING (BASMATI)
2071. RICE POLISHERS
2072. RIVETS
2073. ROLLING BEARING FORGING OF OUTER/INNER RINGS
2074. ROLLER FLOUR MILL

Price Rs. 2500/- for each "Detailed Project Report" Payable in advance through Draft/Cash/M.O. in favour of "ENGINEERS INDIA RESEARCH INSTITUTE". Or Ask by V.P.P. PH.: 291 8117, 291 6431, 292 0361 Fax: 91-11-291 6431 (24 Hrs.)

2075. ROLLING MILL
2076. ROLLING OF STAINLESS STEEL SHEET (PATTA)
2077. ROTARY PRINTING & DYEING ON COTTON/ SYNTHETIC TEXTILE
2078. ROOFING TILES (CEMENT)
2079. ROSIN & TERPENTINE DISTILLATION
2080. ROSE CRYSTALS
2081. ROSE PLANTATION & ROSE OIL EXTRACTION
2082. ROLLER FLOUR MILL & MUSTARD OIL MILL
2083. ROTO GRAVURE PRINTING
2084. ROASTED & FRIED DRY FRUITS, GROUNDNUTS/ PEANUTS WITH PACKAGING
2085. ROUND GLASS MARBLES
2086. ROASTED/SALTED/COATED CASHEWNUT, PEANUT, ALMOND (IMPORTEDAUTOMATIC)
2086A. RIGID & ELASTIC TAPES
2087. RUBBER BALLOONS (DECORATIVE, TOYS & INDUSTRIAL BALOONS)
2088. RUBBER HAWAI CHAPPALS
2089. RUBBER ADHESIVES
2090. RUBBER CHAPPALS & GENTSLEATHER SHOES
2091. RUBBERISED CORK SHEETS
2092. RUBBER SHEET & ALLIED HOSPITAL GOODS
2093. RUBBERIZED COIR FOAM
2094. RUBBER FOAM MATTRESS
2095. RUBBER SHEET FROM USED TYRE
2096. RUBBER SHEET FOR SHOE SOLE
2097. RUBBER LATEX FOAM PRODUCT
2098. RUBBER CONDOM
2099. RUBBER SOLUTION
2100. RUBBER AUTO PARTS
2101. RUBBER LINING
2102. RUBBER GOODS FROM WASTE RUBBER
2103. RUBBING COMPOUND FOR AUTOMOBILE
2104. RUBBER BANDS
2105. RUM FLAVOUR
2106. RUBBER TOYS
2107. RUBBER PLASTIC STAMP & PAD (AUTOMATIC)
2108. RUBBER HOT WATER BOTTLES
2109. RUBBER COTS & APRONS
2110. RUBBERIZED CLOTH
2111. RUST PREVENTIVE (PETROLEUM)
2112. RUBBER COMPOUND TOYS (USING PLASTER OF PARIS)
2113. RUBBER BUSHING
2114. RUBBER HOSEPIPES & RUBBER GLAZING
2115. RUBBER PLANTATION
2116. RUBBER MOULDING & LINING OF RUBBER SHEETING
2117. RUBBER ADHESIVE (All PURPOSE)-NEOPRENE & ISOPRENE BASED
2118. RUBBER ADHESIVE
2119. RUBBER ROLLERS
2120. RUBBER ROLLER FOR PRINTING MACHINE
2121. RUBBER ROLLER FOR RICE MILL
2122. RUBBER CONVEYOR BELT
2123. RUBBER HOSE PIPE
2124. RUBBER RECLAMING
2125. RUBBER CAPS FOR PHARMACEUTICAL USE
2126. RUBBER ROLLERS FOR TEXTILE MILLS & PAPER INDUSTRIES
2127. RUBBER ROLLER& EBONITE ROLLER
2128. RUBBER (LATEX) LINED JUTE MATS
2129. RUBBER PROCESS OIL
2130. RUBBER BELTING (FAN/V BELT)
2131. RUBBER (FIELD) CONVERTED TO THE 60% LATEX RUBBER
2132. RUBBER ERASERS . (SCHOOL RUBBER)
2133. RUBBER AUTO GASKET
2134. RUBBERISED CANVAS SHOES
2135. RUBBER (SYNTHETIC)
2136. RUBBER HOSES FOR AUTOMOBILE
2137. SAFETY GLASS
2138. SANITARY WARE & WALL TILE/FLOOR TILE
2139. SALINE & INJECTION WATER
2140. SANITARY NAPKIN
2141. SANITARY NAPKIN & DISPOSABLE BABY DIAPERS
2142. SAW MILLS
2143. SAFETY MATCHES (MATCH BOX)
2144. SAND PAPER (ABRASIVE PAPER)
2145. SALT GLAZED STONE WARE PIPES & FITTINGS
2146. SAND LIME BRICKS
2147. SAGOL
2148. SAUSAGED FOOD CASING (100%EOU)
2150. SAFETY PINS
2151. SALINE & INJECTION WATER
2152. SALTED GROUNDNUT
2153. SAGO SEED FROM POTATO & SWEET POTATO (SABOO DANA)
2154. SAFETY MATCH & FIREBOX
2155. SALT LICKS FOR CATTLES
2156. SANITARY NAPKINS (TAB ENDED-TUBE FILLED)
2157. SAFETY BELT
2158. SABOO DANA
2159. SCOOTER TYRE & TUBE
2160. SCREEN PRINTING INKS
2161. SCREEN PRINTING ON PAPER/CARDS
2162. SCREEN PRINTING
2163. SCREEN EMULSION
2164. SCREWS FOR AUDIO CASSETTE
2165. SCENT & PERFUME FOR AGARBATTI
2166. SCENTS/PERFUME
2267. SCENT BY LEMON GRASS OIL & JASMINE OIL
2168. SCENTED SUPARI
2169. SCENT (INTIMATED SCENT, CHEMICALS ETC.)

TERMS

Price Rs. 2500/-

(Rs. Two Thousand & Five Hundred only)

for each

Detailed Project Report

(Market Survey cum Detailed Techno Economic Feasibility Report)

or

US $ 250/-

each for overseas clientele, payable fully in advance through Draft/M.O./Cash in favour of

ENGINEERS INDIA RESEARCH INSTITUTE

New Delhi

or

Ask to send by V.P.P.

(All the mentioned reports herewith are fluently available)

Price Rs. 2500/- for each "Detailed Project Report" Payable in advance through Draft/Cash/M.O. in favour of "ENGINEERS INDIA RESEARCH INSTITUTE". Or Ask by V.P.P. PH.: 291 8117, 291.6431, 292 0361 Fax: 91-11-291 6431 (24 Hrs.)

2170. SCREEN PRINTING ON TEXTILES
2171. SCHOOL
2172. SCOOTER RIMS
2173. SECURITY SYSTEM
2174. SECONDARY LEAD EXTRACTION FROM SCRAPS (A) BATTERY PLATE (B) PIPES (C) SHEETS
2175. SNACK FOOD (CRAX TYPE-ROLL & BALL TYPE)
2176. SNUFF FACTORY
2177. SELF TAPPING STEEL SCREWS
2178. SEWING NEEDLES (FOR USED WITH DOMESTIC/ INDUSTRIAL SEWING MACHINE)
2179. SECURITY OFFSET PRINTING PRESS
2180. SEWING THREADS, REELS & BALLS
2181. SEMI CONDUCTORS FOR TRANSISTORS & DIODE
2182. SEMI CONDUCTOR DEVICES
2183. SESAME OIL FROM SESAME SEEDS
2184. SERVO CONTROLLED STABILIZERS (1-100 KVA)
2185. SEWING MACHINE (PARTS MACHINING & ASSEMBLY)
2186. SEMI AUTOMATIC BRICKS PLANT
2187. SEMI AUTOMATIC CONFECTIONERY PLANT
2188. SEAMLESS M.S. TUBES
2189. SEALING MATERIAL COMPATIBLE TO CERAMIC & NICHROME WIRE
2190. S.G. IRON & MALLEABLE IRON CASTING
2191. S.G. IRON & ALLOY STEEL CASTINGS
2192. SHEET GLASS
2193. SHAMPOOS
2194. SHOE POLISH PUFF
2195. SHOVELS
2196. SHOCK ABSORBERS
2197. SHAMPOOS FOR DOGS
2198. SHAMPOO & CREAM (COLD CREAM, ALL PURPOSE & VARNISHING CREAM)
2199. SHUTTLELESS LOOM
2200. SHAVING CREAM & SHAVING SOAP
2201. SHAWLS (POWER LOOM)
2202. SHOE UPPER
2203. SHOE POLISH (BOOT POLISH)
2204. SHEET METAL PRODUCTS (FERROUS/NON-FERROUS)
2205. SHIP CONTAINERS
2206. SHEEP & GOAT FARMING
2207. SHOE LACES
2208. SHOES, CANVAS AS WELL AS BOOT, RUBBER KNEES, JUNGLE BOOT COMBAT, RUBBER LINED
2209. SHAVING CREAM (LATHER)
2210. SHERBAT
2211. SHOTS & GRITS OF HIGH CARBON STEELS
2212. SHUTTLE COCKS FOR BADMINTON
2213. SHOE TACKS
2214. SHEHNAZ HUSSAIN'S INSTITUTE FOR SKIN, HEALTH & HAIR CARE (HEALTH CLUB CUM BEAUTY PARLOUR TRAINING INSTITUTE)
2215. SILK COCOON CULTIVATION (GROWING OF SILK COCOON FROM SILK WORM)
2216. SILICA GEL
2217. SINGLE SUPER PHOSPHATE (S.S.P)
2218. SILICON COMPOUND
2219. SILICON EMULSION (MOULD RELEASING AGENTS)
2220. SILK SCREEN PRINTING ON SAREES (BLOCK & SCREEN PROCESS)

2221. SILK WASTE PROCESSING & SPINNING
2222. SILK REELING UNIT
2223. SILICA SAND
2224. SILICON RELEASE PAPER
2225. SILVER NITRATE
2226. SILVER DIP (CLEANING SOLUTION)
2227. SIZING OF YARN
2228. SINTERED BUSHES
2229. SINTERED BUSHES (SELF LUBRICATED)
2230. SINTERED METAL PRODUCTS
2231. SHISHAM PLANTATION
2232. SILICON RUBBER NIPPLE/ TEAT
2233. SILENCERS FOR TWO/ THREE WHEELERS
2234. SINGLE CORE TWIN FLAT CABLE
2235. SILICON EMULSION
2236. SILVER EXTRACTION FROM WASTE HYPO SOLUTION BY CHEMICAL PROCESS
2237. SILVER EXTRACTION BY WASTE HYPO SOLUTION, X-RAY FILM
2238. SILVER JEWELLERY & CUTLERY (GOLD PLATED)
2239. SILVER & GOLD JEWELLERY
2240. SINGLE SUPER PHOSPHATE (S.S.P) & SULPHURIC ACID
2241. SILVER & GOLD PLATING ON PVC & NYLON
2242. SILICON
2243. SINDHUR
2244. SILVER DIP (CLEANING SOLUTION)
2245. SILVER PLATED UTENSILS
2246. SINTERED BEARINGS
2247. SILVER JEWELLERY
2248. SILVER BRAZING FOIL
2249. SILK FABRICS (POWER LOOM)
2250. SILICON FROM RICE HUSK
2251. SKIMMED MILK (LIQUID)
2252. SKIMMED MILK POWDER
2253. SKYLATED PHENOL
2254. SKY BAGS
2255. SKIMMED MILK POWDER & GHEE
2256. SMOKE LESS COAL
2257. SOFT DRINKS (NON CARBONATED)
2258. SODIUM DICHROMATE & SODIUM SULPHATE
2259. SOLVENT EXTRACTION & REFINING OF SOYA BEAN
2260. SORBITOL
2261. SODIUM TRI-POLY PHOSPHATE
2262. SODIUM THIO-SULPHATE FROM SODIUM SULPHATE
2263. SODIUM SULPHATE
2264. SOLID FUEL CAKE
2265. SODIUM HEXA META PHOSPHATE
2266. SODIUM SULPHIDE FROM AMMONIUM SULPHITE & SODIUM CHLORIDE
2267. SOFT DRINK CONCENTRAT (SACCHARINE BASED)
2268. SOAP COATED PAPER
2269. SODIUM BENZOATE
2270. SOLVENT EXTRACTION PLANT
2271. SOCKS KNITTING
2272. SODA ASH
2273. SODA LIME
2274. SOLAR CELL
2275. SOLAR COOKER
2276. SOLAR PHOTO VOLTAGE MODULES (SOLAR ELECTRICAL CELLS & PANEL)
2277. SOLAR PHOTO VOLTAIC SYSTEM
2278. SOLAR PUMP
2279. SOLAR ELECTRICAL CELLS & PANELS
2280. SOLAR PUMP
2281. SOLAR ENERGY WATER HEATER (GEYSER)
2282. SOLAR POWER EQUIPMENTS

2283. SOLAR MODULES
2284. SOYABEAN PRODUCTS
2285. SOYABEAN BARIYAN
2286. SOFT DRINKS CONCENTRATES & ESSENCES (ORANGE, COLA, LIME, PINE APPLE) FLAVOURS FOR BAKER & SODA WATER
2287. SOLVENT EXTRACTION PLANT FROM COCONUT CAKE
2288. SODIUM BICARBONATES
2290. SOLDERING PASTE
2291. SOYA MILK FROM SOYABEAN
2292. SOYA SAUCE (CHINESE)
2293. SOLDER WIRE (SOFT RESIN CORED)
2294. SOAP RIVETS (HOLLOW TYPE)
2295. SOYABEAN BARIYAN
2296. SOAP FROM SOAP STOCK (SOAP INDUSTRY)
2297. SOFTWARE (COMPUTER)
2298. SOYABEAN OIL
2299. SOLVENT & THINNERS
2300. SOFT DRINK (COLD DRINKS)
2301. SODIUM META SILICATE
2302. SODIUM ACETATE
2303. SODIUM SULPHITE FROM SODIUM DIOXIDE
2304. SODIUM THIO-SULPHATE BY SODIUM SULPHATE
2305. SODIUM SILICATE FROM SILICA SAND
2306. SODIUM SULPHATE (ANHYDROUS)
2307. SODIUM SILICATE FROM RICE HUSK/PADDY HUSK
2308. SODIUM DICHROMATE (BICHROMATE)
2310. SODIUM SULPHIDE
2311. SODIUM SULPHIDE BY BARIUM SULPHATE PROCESS
2312. SODIUM CAFFINATES & CALCIUM CAFFINATES
2313. SODIUM SULPHITE
2314. SODIUM NITRATE
2315. SODIUM NITRITE
2316. SODIUM LAURYL SULPHATE
2317. SODIUM ALUMINATE
2318. SODIUM HYDRO SULPHITE (ZINC REDUCTION PROCESS)
2319. SODIUM HYDRO CHLORITE (BLEACH LIQUOR)
2320. SODIUM NAPHTHOANATE
2321. SODIUM BI-SULPHITE
2322. SODIUM SULPHIDE FROM SALT CAKE
2323. SODIUM PETROLEUM SULPHONATE
2324. SODIUM PERBORATE (TETRA HYDRATE)
2325. SODIUM CYCLAMATE
2326. SODIUM ALGINATE
2327. SODIUM META SILICATE
2328. SODIUM CHROMATE
2329. SODIUM TRI-POLY PHOSPHATE
2330. SODIUM ALUMINIUM SULPHATE
2331. SODIUM FLUORIDE
2332. SODIUM HYPO-CHLORITE (BLEACH LIQUOR)
2333. SODIUM BENZOATE
2334. SODIUM PERBORATE (TETRAHYDRATE)
2335. SODIUM SALT (2,4-D)
2336. S.W.PIPES
2337. SOLVENT EXTRACTION & REFINING PLANT (COTTON SEED OIL
2338. SOFT DRINK ESSENCES
2339. SOFT & HARD FERRITES
2340. SOAP SHOP
2341. SOYA MILK & PANEER
2342. SPONGE RUBBER (LATEX FOAM RUBBER)
2343. SPECIAL STEEL (HIGH ALLOY)
2344. SPRAY DRIED DETERGENT POWDER
2345. SPRAY LAMINATED BRASS ARTICLES/BADGES (PLASTIC)
2346. SPARK PLUGS
2347. SPORT SHOES

Cost
Rs. 2500/-
for each
Detailed
Project Report

2348. SPORT SHOES (IMPORTED) AUTOMATIC PLANT-ACTION, LIBERTY TYPE
2349. SPONGE IRON
2350. SPECTACLE FRAMES (PLASTIC)
2351. SPIRAL WOUND METALLIC GASKET
2352. SPECTACLE FRAMES (METAL)
2353. SPICES (MASALA)
2354. SPRAY DRIER
2355. SPEAKER PARRY RING (FORMULAE)
2356. SPINNING OF VISCOSE STAPLE FIBER INTO YARN
2357. S.S. HINGES
2358. STEP DOWN TRANSFORMER
2359. STEEL DRUM & BARRELS
2360. STENCIL COATING SOLUTION
2361. STARCH & DEXTRIN BASED ADHESIVES
2362. STENCIL PAPER (DUPLICATING)
2363. SOAP JELLY
2364. SPIKENARD (JATAMANSI)
2365. SPRAY PERFUME
2366. SPINDLE OIL
2367. SPICE OILS OR OLEORESINS (EXTRACTION OF ESSENTIAL OILS- CARDAMOM, JEERA, AJWAIN, GINGER OIL & OTHER SPICES)
2368. STARCH (MAIZE/CORN)
2369. STAINLESS STEEL CASTINGS BY INDUCTION FURNACE
2370. STAINLESS STEEL SHEET ROLLING & MANUFACTURE OF STAINLESS STEEL UTENSILS
2371. STAINLESS STEEL PATTA
2372. STAMP PADS & PAD INKS
2373. STAPLES, GEM CLIPS & PAPER PINS
2374. STRAW BOARD & MILL BOARD
2375. STEEL PLANT (EAF-BASED)
2376. STANNOUS CHLORIDE
2377. STEEL ROLLING MILL
2378. STEEL/ALUMINIUM COAST FOR WINDING OF TEXTILE YARNS
2379. STITCHING WIRE
2380. STEEL WOOL
2381. STUFFING JOINT BOX OF PLASTIC
2382. STARCH & ALLIED PRODUCT FROM MAIZE
2383. STEAM IRON (LIGHT WEIGHTED)
2384. STEARIC ACID
2385. STRAW BOARD
2386. STEEL WIRE ROPES
2387. STEEL TUBE/ PIPE
2388. STEEL FOUNDRY
2389. STARCH, DEXTROSE, SORBITOL, VITAMIN - C, ETC. FROM MAIZE
2390. STEARATES MANUFACTURE
2391. STRIPPERS FOR ROTAORY PRINTING EMULTION
2392. STAINLESS STEEL UTENSILS (COPPER BOTTOM)
2393. STEEL BALL BEARINGS
2394. STEEL FURNITURE
2395. STEREO CASSETTE RECORDERS/PLAYERS
2396. STABLE BLEACHING POWDER
2397. STRAW BOARD & GREY BOARD
2398. STEEL CASTING FOR RAILWAYS
2399. STONE CRUSHER
2400. STAINLESS STEEL UTENSILS (COPPER ELECTROPLATED)

Price Rs. 2500/- for each ``Detailed Project Report'' Payable in advance through Draft/Cash/M.O. in favour of ``ENGINEERS INDIA RESEARCH INSTITUTE''. Or Ask by V.P.P. PH.: 291 8117, 291 6431, 292 0361 Fax: 91-11-291 6431 (24 Hrs.)

2401. STEEL FORGING (AUTOMOBILE PARTS)
2402. STEEL WIRE HEALDS
2403. STARCH FROM TAPIOCA
3323. STREET LIGHT FITTING
2404. STAMPING HOT FOILS
2405. STEEL REROLLING MILL (STEEL RODS & COILS FROM SCRAPS)
2406. STAINLESS STEEL TIFFIN BOX (LUNCH BOX)
2407. STEEL TAPES FOR CABLE ARMOURING
2408. STICKER MAKING-AUTOMATIC PLANT
2409. STEEL BALLS
2410. STEEL BALLS FOR BALL POINT PENS
2411. STICKER & LABELING PLANT
2412. STAIN REMOVERS
2413. SURAT JARI
2414. STARCH BOOK BINDING CLOTH
2415. STEEL STRIPS (COLD ROLLED)-ELECTRICAL SILICON WITH ORIE-NTED GRAINS FOR ELECTRICAL MACHINES & TRANSFORMERS
2416. STARCH BOOK BINDING CLOTH
2417. STEEL TANKS FOR DRINKING WATER (WATER STORAGE TANKS OF M.S)
2418. STEEL PLANT (25-T UHF ELECTRIC ARC FURNACE & HOT ROLLING)
2419. STEEL STRIPS (COLD ROLLED)-ELECTRICAL SILICON WITH ORIENTED GRAINS FOR ELECTRICAL MACHINES & TRANSFORMERS
2420. STEEL WIRE DRAWING & GALVANIZING
2421. STORAGE BATTERY
2422. STUFF TOYS
2423. STAINLESS STEEL VACUUM FLASK (UN-BREAKABLE)
2424. STARCH FROM WHEAT FLOUR
2425. STAINLESS STEEL KNIFE
2426. STEEL PIPES
2427. STAINLESS STEEL CUTLERY
2428. STEEL INGOTS (GAS FIRE FURNACE)
2429. STARCH & ALLIED PRODUCTS FROM BROKEN RICE, LIQUID GLUCOSE, DEXTROSE ANHYDROUS
2430. STEEL WIRE/ROD
2431. SUNFLOWER PLANTATION
2432. SUBMERGED ARC WELDED PIPES (SAW PIPE)
2433. SUNFLOWER OIL
2434. SUBMERSIBLE PUMP
2435. SULPHUR POWDER FROM SULPHUR CRYSTALS/LUMP
2436. SUGAR CANE WAX FROM PRESS MUD
2437. SURGICAL/ABSORBENT COTTON
2438. SURFACE FLOOR & CAR POLISHES
2439. SUPER ENAMELED COPPER WIRE (COPPER SCRAPS)
2440. SUGAR MANUFACTURING PLANT BY CARBONATION PROCESS
2441. SURGICAL EXAMINATION GLOVES (DISPOSABLE)
2442. SULPHUR CRYSTAL
2443. SUGAR CANE JUICE PRESERVATION
2444. SUNMICA
2445. SURAT ZARI (ZARI MANUFACTURE FOR SAREE)
2446. SURGICAL COTTON & BANDAGES
2447. SURGICAL COTTON AND SURGICAL ADHESIVE TAPES
2448. SULPHUR BLACK DYES

2449. SURGICAL GLOVES FROM LATEX
2450. SURGICAL BANDAGE, SANITARY NAPKINS & ALLIED PRODUCTS
2451. SURGICAL ADHESIVE TAPE ON CLOTH SURFACE
2452. SURGE SUPPRESSER
2453. SULPHUR RECOVERY FROM SLUDGE
2454. SUNFLOWER SEED OIL EXTRACTION
2455. SURGICAL BANDAGES
2456. SUPER ENAMELED COPPER WIRE
2457. SUGAR PLANT
2458. SULPHURIC ACID (H_2SO_4)
2459. SURA
2460. SUGAR CUBES
2461. SUPER ENAMELING FOR WINDING
2462. SURGICAL METHYLATED SPIRIT
2463. SUGAR COATED CASHEWNUT, ALMONDS.
2464. SWITCH MODE POWER SUPPLY (SMPS)
2465. SWEATER, MUFF-LER & KNITTING INDUSTRY
2466. SWITCH BOARD
2467. SWEET AROMA OF BETAL NUT
2468. SYNTHETIC IRON OXIDE (YELLOW)
2469. SYNTHETIC IRON OXIDE (RED)
2470. SYNTHETIC RED & YELLOW IRON OXIDE
2471. SYNTHETIC ASAFOETIDA(HING)
2472. 2-4-D SODIUM SALT
2474. SYNTHETIC ALMOND OIL
2475. SYNTHETIC TALLOW
2476. SYNTHETIC DETERGENT (BLUE POWDER)
2477. SYNTHETIC ADHE-SIVE FOR DECORATIVE LAMINATE BONDING
2478. SYNTHETIC PEARL COATING ON POLYSTY-RENE BEADS
2479. TARTARIC ACID
2480. TAPE DECK MECHANISM
2481. TAB ENDED PULP FILLED NAPKINS (Sanitary Napkin)
2482. TABLET & CAPSULE
2483. TABLET, CAPSULE, SYRUPS, LOTION & OINTMENT
2484. TAMARIND JUICE CONCENTRATE
2485. TARTARIC ACID FROM MALEIC-ANHYDRIDE
2486. TAR FROM PINE WOOD
2487. TABLE FAN
2488. TABLE WARE & CERAMIC TILES
2489. TALCUM POWDER (FACE & TOILET)
2490. TALC (MAGNESIUM SILICATE)
2491. TAPER ROLLER BEARINGS
2492. TAILORS CHOKES
2493. TANTALUM CAPACITOR
2494. TABLE OFFSET & D.T.P
2495. TANNIC ACID
2496. TABLE TENNIS BALL
2497. TALLOW PROCESSING FOR SOAP MANUFACTURING
2498. TABLET, CAPSULE, SYRUP & LOTION
2499. TEA PACKAGING & DISTRIBUTION JOB WORK
2500. TETRA PACK FOR MILK PACKAGING & OTHER LIQUIDS
2501. TENNIS BALL & CRICKET BALL
2502. TEA PLANTATION
2503. TEA INDUSTRY
2504. TEA & COFFEE PROCESS-ING AND PACKAGING
2505. TEAK & MUSHROOM PLANTATION

2506. TEAK PLANTATION
2507. TEFLON MANUFACTURING
2508. TEFLON COATED ELECTRIC CABLES
2509. TELEPHONE CABLES/CORD
2510. TERELENE PRODUCTS
2511. TENT & TARPAULINE
2512. TEFLON TAPES
2513. TEA PACKAGING
2514. TELEPHONE AMPLIFIER
2515. TEXTURISED POLYESTER YARN
2516. TENNIS BALL
2517. TEFLON COATED UTENSILS (NON-STICKS)
2518. TEXTILE GOLD STAMPING PASTE
2519. TEXTILE PRINTING PIGMENT BINDERS
2520. TELEVISION ANTENNA
2521. TELEVISION (COLOUR AND BLACK & WHITE)
2522. TELEVISION (PORTABLE)
2523. TEXTILE DYEING BLEACHING FINISHING & PRINTING
2524. TERRY TOWEL
2525. TEXTILE AUXILLIARIES & CHEMICALS
2526. TEFLON TAPES & CABLE
2527. TEFLON COATED UTENSILS (NON-STICK)
2528. TEXTILE PRINTING PASTE (GUM)
2529. TELEVISION
2530. TEA PACKAGING & DISTRIBUTION
2531. TERRY TOWELS/TERRY FABRICS WEAVING UNIT
2532. TELEVISION (B/W)
2533. TELEPHONE CABLE (JELLY FILLED)
2534. TEA BAGS
2535. TEA (INSTANT)
2536. THREE STAR HOTEL
2537. THERMOMETER (CLINICAL)
2538. THINNERS
2539. THERMOCOLE MOULDING
2540. THREAD, CUSHION COMPOUND AND VOLCANIZING SOLUTION FORMULATION & MANUFACTURE
2541. THERMO PLASTIC ELECTRICAL SWITCHES & FITTINGS
2542. THERMOCOLE PACKAGING
2543. THERMO COUPLE TIPS
2544. THERMOCOUPLES
2545. THERMOCOLE SHEET & MOULDED PRODUCTS
2546. THERMO PLASTIC POLYURETHANE
2547. THERMOCOLE
2548. THERMOFORMED PACKAGING (BLISTER & POUCH PACKING)
2549. THREE WHEELER ASSEMBLY
2550. THINNER/SOLVENTS & ITS ALLIED PRODUCT
2551. THERMOSTATE FOR REFRIGERATOR
2552. TIN PRINTING & ANODIZING ON ALUMINIUM
2553. TIN CONTAINER
2554. TILES (MOSAIC)
2555. TILES (GLAZED CERAMIC)
2556. TIE ROD ENDS
2557. TITANIUM OXIDE
2558. TITANIUM NITRIDING
2559. TISSUE CULTURE (100% EOU)
2560. TITANIUM DIOXIDE BY CHLORINE
2561. TISSUE & AIR MAIL PAPER
2562. TISSUE & TOILET PAPER ROLL & AIR MAIL PAPER
2563. TISSUE PAPER ESPECIALLY FACIAL PAPER, MOIST TOILETTERIES, CLEANSING TISSUE & RELATED PRODUCTS
2564. TIN PRINTING
2565. TIMBER/WOOD SEASONING
2566. TOMATO POWDER
2567. TOMATO CONCENTRATE
2568. TOYS (PLASTIC)
2569. TOYS (ELECTRONICS)
2570. TOMATO PULP
2571. TOMATO WAFFERS
2572. TOBACCO & ITS PRODUCTS
2573. TOILET PAPER
2574. TOXIC COMPOUNDS EFFECTS ON HUMAN BODY
2575. TOYS (STUFF)
2576. TOILET SOAPS
2577. TOOTH BRUSH
2578. TOOTH PASTE (GEL-COLGATE, CLOSE-UP TYPE)
2579. TOOTH PASTE & POWDER
2580. TOOTH PASTE
2581. TOOTH BRUSH, TOOTH PASTE & POWDER
2582. TOMATO PRODUCT IN POUCHES
2583. TOUGHNED GLASS FOR WRIST WATCH
2584. TORCH & TRI LIGHT UNITS INTEGRATED PLANT INCLUDING MINIATURE BULB & TUBES, ENGINEERING PLASTIC MOULD/DIES MANUFACTURE
2585. TOILET & HERBAL SOAP
2586. TOMATO & PAPAYA CULTIVATION
2587. TOILET PAPER & NAPKIN
2588. TOY BALLOONS, DECORATIVE BALLOONS
2589. TOFFEE (MILK)
2590. TOWEL, SOCKS & HOSIERY
2591. TOMATO PASTE
2592. TOMATO KETCHUP, JAMS, JELLY ETC.
2593. TOGGLE SWITCHES
2594. TONER INK
2595. TOILET SEATS & COVERS
2596. TOUGHENED GLASS & SILVER MIRROR GLASS
2597. TOBACCO TOOTH PASTE FROM TOBACCO DUST
2598. TOBACCO TOOTH PASTE FROM TOBACCO
2599. TRANSPARENT LACQUER (CLEAR) FOR COATING ON BRASS BANGLES TO MAKE IT WEATHER RESISTANT
2600. TREAD RUBBER (CAMEL BLACK)
2601. TRI-PHENYL PHOSPHITE
2602. TRI SODIUM PHOSPHATE
2603. TRICYCLE RIKS-HAW ASSEMBLY
2604. TRI-METHOPRIME
2605. TRI BASIC LEAD SULPHATE
2606. TRANSFORMER OIL RECLAMATION
2607. TRANSFORMER
2608. TRANSFORMER (DISTRIBUTION)
2609. TRANSFORMER OIL
2610. TRAVELLING AGENCY
2611. TRACING PAPER
2612. T-SHIRT & KNITTING FABRIC
2613 T.V. & AUDIO CABINETS & THEIR ASSEMBLING UNIT
2614. TURKEY RED OIL
2615. TUBULAR POLES, TRANSMISSION LINE, HARDWARE & MAIN SWITCH FOR ELECTRICAL TRANSMISSION
2616. TURPENTINE OIL
2617. TURPENTINE OIL FROM EXTRACTIONS OF DIPETROCORPUS TREE
2618. TUTI FRUITY FROM PAPAYA FRUITY
2619. TURMERIC POWDER (EDIBLE GRADE)
2620. TURMERIC OIL OLEORESIN FROM RAW TURMERIC
2621. TUBE VALVES
2622. TUBULAR POLES FOR ELECTRICAL TRANSMISSION
2623. TUNGSTEN FILAMENT
2624. TURPENTINE & ROSIN DISTILLATION
2625. T.V. PICTURE TUBE (B/W) & COMPUTER MONITOR TUBE
2626. T.V CUM VIDEO GAMES
2627. T.V. SIGNAL BOOSTERS
2628. TWISTED YARN (NYLON)
2629. TWO-T 2-STROKE OIL
2630. TWO WHEELERS REPAIR & SERVICE WORKSHOP
2631. TYRE RETREADING
2632. TYRE RETREADING BY COLD PROCESS
2633. TYRE RETREADING (HOT PROCESS)
2634. TYRE & TUBES FOR SCOOTER, MOTOR CYCLE, RIKSHAW, 2/3 WHEELERS
2635. TYRES, TUBES AND FLAP (MOPED TO TRUCK)
2636. 2-4-D SODIUM SALT
2637. U-CLAMPS, U-BOLTS & NUTS
2638. U.J. CROSS & KING PIN
2638. ULTRAMARINE BLUE
2639. UMBRELLA

2640. UNDECYLENIL ACID
2641. UNSATURATED POLYSTER RESINS
2642. UNINTERRUPTED POWER SUPPLY (UPS)
2643. UN ARMOURED, PVC INSULATED CABLES
2644. UTENSILS (SILVER PLATED)
2645. UTENSILS (ALUMINIUM)
2646. UTENSILS (BRASS)
2647. UREA FORMALDEHYDE POWDER
2648. UREA FORMALDEHYDE RESIN
2649. UREA
2650. UREA FERTILIZER PLANT
2651. UREA FORMALDEHYDE & MELAMINE FORMAL-DEHYDE MOULDING POWDER
2652. UTENSILS (STAINLESS STEEL)
2653. UTENSILS (TEFLON COATED)
2654. U.V. PAINT
2655. VACUUM METALIZING
2656. VANASPATI GHEE
2657. VALVE GUIDES
2658. VARNISH & PAINT UNIT
2659. VASELINE
2660. VARNISH THINNER (SOLVENT)
2661. VACUUM-METALLISING LACQUER
2662. VAT DYES
2663. VACUUM CLEANER
2664. V-BELTS
2665. VCP & VCR
2666. VENETIAN BLIND
2667. VELVET CLOTH BY FLOCKING PROCESS
2668. VEGETABLE OIL REFINING (BY PHYSICAL PROCESS)
2669. VEGETABLE OIL (EXTRAC-TION & REFINNING)
2670. VELCROW FASTENING TAPE (FASTNER HOOP LOOP TAPE & SYNTHETIC)
2671. VETENERY MEDICINES
2672. VERMICELLI
2673. VERMICELLI & MACARONI
2674. VIDEO & T.V. GAMES
2675. VIDEO & AUDIO CASSETES
2676. VIDEO CASSETES
2677. VIDEO STUDIO
2678. VIDEO & AUDIO MAGNETIC TAPES
2679. VINEGAR & MALT VINEGAR FOR INDUSTRIAL & DOMESTIC USE
2680. VIDEO CASSETE ASSEM-BLING & RECORDING
2681. VITAMIN-C FROM POTATO EXTRACT
2682. VISCOSE RAYON YARN FROM COTTON LINIERS
2683. VIDEO CAMERA
2684. VIDEO FILM STUDIO
2685. VIDEO CASSETTES (COMPLETE MANUFACTUR-ING & ASSEMBLING UNIT)
2686. VIDEO TAPE
2687. VIDEO FILM STUDIO TO MAKE FILMS ETC. IN VIDEO CASSETTES & FILM ROLLS
2688. VIDEO CASSETTES LIBRARY
2689. VISCOSE STAPLE FIBRE (RAYON STAPLE FIBER)
2690. VOLTAGE REGULATOR (FOR AUTOMOBILES)
2691. VOLTAGE STABILIZER
2692. VOLTAGE STABLIZER
2693. VODKA FROM WASTE GRAIN
2694. WAX CRAYON
2695. WAX FLOOR POLISH
2696. WASHING & LAUNDRY SOAP
2697. WALL TILES/FLOOR TILES/ SANITARY TILES
2698. WASHING MACHINE (AUTOMATIC ELECTRO COMPUTERISED)
2699. WAX (PARAFFIN)
2700. WAX (MICRO CRYSTALLINE)
2701. WATCH LEATHER STRAP
2702. WALL PAPER PRINTING
2703. WAX EMULSION
2704. WAX FOR PAPER
2705. WATER PROOF CEMENT COMPOUND
2706. WAX EMULSION
2707. WATER FILTER CANDLES
2708. WATER FILTER & PRESS-URE COOKER
2709. WASHING MACHINE & GEYSER
2710. WATER PROOFING BITUMINISED COMPOUND
2711. WAX FOR PAPER INDUSTRY
2712. WATCH CASE BUFFING
2713. WATER FOR INJECTION AMPOULES PLANT
2714. WATER PROOF MARKING INK
2715. WATTLE EXTRACT (TANNIN POWDER)
2716. WAX PAPERED MATHC STICK
2717. WATCH GLASS
2718. WAX & CHEMICAL COATED BRAIDED TINSEL WIRE
2719. WALL PAPER
2720. WASHING CAKE, DETERGENT CAKE & POWDER
2721. WATER PROOFING FORMULATIONS FOR PAPER CONES USED FOR SPEAKERS
2722. WATER PROOFING FOR COTTON CLOTH
2723. WATER METER
2724. WATER STORAGE TANK
2725. WATER PROOFING PAINT
2726. WATER (MINERAL)
2727. WATER METER
2728. WATER STORAGE TANK
2729. WATER PROOFING PAINT
2730. WATER (MINERAL)
2731. WASHING POWDER & WASHING SOAP
2732. WELDING FLUXES
2733. WELDING RODS (SPECIAL) & M.S. WELDING ELECTRODES
2734. WELDING BRASS ROD
2735. WETTING OIL
2736. WELDED WIRE MESH
2737. WEET AROMA OF BETAL NUT
2738. WELDING CABLE
2739. WEET AROMA OF BETAL NUT
2740. WELDING CABLE

2741. WELDING ELECTRODES
2742. WELDING WIRE ELECTRODES (CO2)
2743. WHITE CEMENT
2744. WHTIE OIL FROM KEROSENE OIL
2745. WHEAT PUFF
2746. WHEAT PORRIDGE (DALIA)

2747. WHEAT FLOUR MILL
2748. WHEEL RIMS
2749. WHITE PHENYL
2750. WHITE OIL
2751. WHISKY FROM COMMERCIAL ALCOHOL
2752 WIRE (MILD STEEL)
2753. WIRE & CABLE (PVC)
2754. WIRE (COPPER)
2755. WRITING & PRINTING PAPER
2756. WIRE DRAWING & ENAMEL
2757. WIRE MESH
2758. WIRE RODS (ALUMINIUM)
2759. WINE & BEER
2760. WINE
2761. WIRE DRAWING (ALUMINIUM)
2762. WIRE DRAWING (COPPER)
2763. WIRE DRAWING (MILD STEEL)
2764. WIRE WOUND RESISTORS
2765. WIRE DRAWING & ANNEALING
2766. WIRE DRAWING LUBRICANT
2767. WIRE NAIL
2768. WINDING WIRES, PVC INSULATED SUBMERSIBLE MOTOR
2769. WICK STOVE
2770. WIRE ROPE (STEEL)
2771. WIRE PRODUCTS
2772. WIRE ROPE SLING
2773. WIRE ROPE (STEEL)
2774. WIRE PRODUCTS
2775. WIRE ROPE SLING
2776. WIRE MESH & GAUGE
2777. WIND MILL
2778. WINE, BRANDY, WHISKY & CHAMPAGNE
2779. WINE (I M.F.L)
2780. WIRE NAILS & WIRE DRAWING
2781. WIND ENERGY POWER
2782. WOOD CHARCOAL & BYE PRODUCTS
2783. WOODEN BOXES
2784. WOOLLEN KNITWEAR
2785. WORSTED WOOLLEN YARN
2786. WOODEN ACCESSORIES FOR SEWING MACHINE
2787. WOOLLEN YARN
2788. WOOLLEN YARN SPINNING
2789. WOOLLEN YARN CARPET DYEING
2790. WOODEN DOOR & WINDOW
2791. WOOD WOOL INDUSTRY
2792. WOOD POLISH
2793. WOODEN DRUM FOR AA/ ACSR CONDUCTOR STORAGE
2794. WOOL BATCHING OIL
2795. WOOLLEN FELT
2796. WOOD SEASONING
2797. WOODEN FURNITURE
2798. WOOLLEN YARN SPINNING PLANT
2799. WOOLLEN SWEATERS
2800. WOVEN HOSIERY LABELS
2801. WOOLLEN CARPETS
2802. WOODEN CANE FURNITURE
2803. WOOD GASIFIER
2804. WRIST WATCH DIAL
2805. WRIST WATCHES
2806. WROUGHT IRON & BRASS STAIRCASE RODS
2807. XANTHATES
2808. XEROX PAPER
2809. XLPE CABLES
2810. X-RAY MACHINE
2811. X-RAY DEVELOPERS
2812. X-RAY FILM SLITTING & REPACKING (MEDICAL)
2813. X-RAY TUBES
2814. X-RAY FILMS
2815. YARN INDUSTRY
2816. YARN - COTTON
2817. YARN - WOOLLEN
2818. YARN DYEING (COTTON)
2819. YARA YARA
2820. YARN DYEING & TEXTURISING
2821. YARN DYEING (COTTON)
2822. YARN (PVC FABRIC)
2823. YARN (VISCOSE RAYON)
2824. YARN (POLYESTER YARN FROM WASTE)
2825. YARN DYEING (CARPET WOOLLEN)
2826. YARN (NYLON)
2827. YARN (TWISTED)
2828. YARN SPINDLES
2829. YARN - SIZING
2830. YARN - HANK
2831. YEAST INDUSTRY
2832. ZARDA & KIMAM
2833. ZARDA-BABA CHHAP
2834. ZARDA & PAN MASALA
2835. ZINC OXIDE
2836. ZINC SULPHATE
2837. ZINC CHLORIDE
2838. ZINC METAL
2839. ZINC BRIGHTNER
2840. ZINC COATING ON WIRE
2841. ZINC STEARATE

NEWLY

PREPARED

DETAILED PROJECT REPORTS

during publishing of this chemical book

(from Sl. No. 2842-2919)

2842. AUTOMOBILE WORKSHOP/ GARAGE & SERVICE CENTRE FOR TRUCK
2843. COTTON CLOTH
2844. PACKAGING FOR NAMKEENS, BHUJIA, DAL MOTH ETC. IN FLEXIBLE POUCHES
2845. ROTO GRAVURE PRINTING & POUCH MAKING
2846. P.V.C. COMPOUNDS (ELECTRICAL GRADE)
2847. STEEL WIRE/ROD (CONTINUOUSLY CAST)-5 M.M. DIAMETER
2848. SYNTHETIC ADHESIVE FOR DECORATIVE LAMINATES BONDING
2849. LPG VALVES & REGULATOR
2850. HERBAL HAIR OIL (AYURVEDIC) LIKE BANPHOOL OIL
2851. TELEPHONE (PUSH BUTTON & CORDLESS)
2852. PHOTO POLYMER COATING FOR PLATE BLOCK MAKING
2853. STOVING PAINT
2854. CLUTCH PLATES FOR 4 WHEELERS
2855. PRINTING FLEXO & PHOTO/ LDPE/HDPE/PP/HM/PVC (FLEXO GRAPHIC & ROTO GRAVURE PRINTING
2856. BALL POINT TIPS (NOZZLES)
2857. ACRYLIC CO-POLYMER EMULSION
2858. STEEL TRANSMISSION LINE TOWER & HOT ROLLING MILL TO PRODUCE STEEL SECTIONS
2859. ACETYLENE & OXYGEN GAS (INTEGRATED UNIT)
2860. ANTISEPTIC CREAM (BORO PLUS BRAND TYPE)
2861. PLASTIC INJECTION MOULDED T.V. CABINETS
2862. GATE GRILL & WINDOW FRAME
2863. FABRICATION OF HEAT EXCHANGER
2864. CARAMEL COLOUR (FOOD COLOUR)
2865. SANITARY NAPKINS (TAB ENDED-PULP FILED) AUTO MATIC IMPORTED PLANT
2866. PLASTIC BOTTLES & CAPS
2867. LAMINATED HDPE WOVEN SACKS
2868. MINERAL WATER (Rs.3 CRORE PROJECT)
2869. HAND MADE PAPER FROM WASTE PAPER
2870. CERAMIC COATED STEEL PIPE
2871. BLOW MOULDED PLASTIC CONTAINER (POLYETHYLENE BOTTLES FOR MINERAL WATER, I.V. FLUIDS ETC.
2872. ESTER GUMS (NO COST ESTIMATION PART
2873. TERPINEOL FROM TURPENTINE
2874. FIBRE CORRUGATED SHEET (FRP, AUTO SCOOTER ROOF/ CEILING)

Price Rs. 2500/- for each "Detailed Project Report" Payable in advance through Draft/Cash/M.O. in favour of "ENGINEERS INDIA RESEARCH INSTITUTE". Or Ask by V.P.P. PH.: 291 8117, 291 6431, 292 0361 Fax: 91-11-291 6431 (24 Hrs.)